THE
BIRMINGHAM POST
1857 : 1957

A CENTENARY RETROSPECT

by

H. R. G. WHATES

Published by

The Birmingham Post & Mail Limited

38 New Street, Birmingham

1957

Preface

by

THE CHAIRMAN OF THE BIRMINGHAM POST & MAIL LTD.

THE LORD ILIFFE, G.B.E.

A CENTURY HAS PASSED SINCE JOHN Frederick Feeney founded *The Birmingham Post* to serve a growing city which already in 1857 was the thriving centre of an expanding and prosperous community. During these hundred years the tradition Feeney established has guided those who have been responsible for the direction, managerial and editorial, of the journal which has increased in stature and influence in keeping with the important community which it is its duty to serve. The task of the *Post* has been twofold: to record, for the people of Birmingham and the Midlands, the movement of events on the international and national scene; and, more especially, to mirror the life of their own city and neighbourhood, indeed, to be 'their paper'.

The pages which follow tell something of the great social, industrial, commercial and civic developments which have profoundly influenced the life of Birmingham and the Midlands in the last hundred years. They tell something, also, of the part played by the *Post* and the influence it has exerted in this century of change. The book is the work of Mr. H. R. G. Whates, once on the London staff of the *Post* and later Editor of its sister paper, *The Birmingham Mail*. He has discharged a difficult task with a journalist's 'flair' and notable literary accomplishment.

Acknowledgements

MY THANKS ARE DUE IN THE first place to my colleagues, past and present, from all departments who have given ungrudging help in the compilation of this history. In particular I am indebted to Mr. T. W. Hutton, the former editor, whose contributions in Chapter 18, and to other chapters dealing with the period of his association with the editorial direction of *The Birmingham Post* from 1913 to 1950, have been indispensable.

Mr. Alan Pitt Robbins kindly placed at my disposal family papers relating to his distinguished father, Sir Alfred Robbins, 'Lobbyist in the Palace of Westminster and London Letter writer in the parish of St. Bride's', London Correspondent of *The Birmingham Post* from 1888 to 1924. It has been a peculiarly personal satisfaction to have been able to pay tribute to an eminent journalist who did so much to establish the traditions of the Lobby and, in so doing, to enhance the status of the profession. Apart from the Office and the files of the paper, the principal sources of material have been our invaluable City Reference Library, notable in the person of Miss D. M. Norris, and the Birmingham Library, Margaret Street, where Mr. Charles Parish and Miss O. M. Allday have most diligently and patiently helped in hunting up obscure references in the library's fascinating collection of old books and pamphlets on Birmingham and its citizens of past days.

I owe much to Mrs. R. Crabb (Miss Judy Marshall) for her fruitful cultivation of literary sources and methodical harvesting of the results. My daughter, Janet Whates, carried out careful and enterprising researches in the British Museum Newspaper Room, Colindale and elsewhere in London. She also read my manuscript, made some constructive criticisms and offered useful suggestions I have been glad to adopt. Professor Aspinall, of Reading University, has generously given me permission to make use of material from his important and entertaining work, *Politics and the Press*, 1780-1850; and Mr. Levi Fox has given leave to quote from Dugdale Society Occasional Papers, No. 8. *Press and Public in Early Nineteenth Century Birmingham*, by Professor Asa Briggs.

My thanks are due also to the following publishers and copyright holders for permission to quote from books mentioned in the text:

Longmans, Green & Co. Ltd.:
British History in the Nineteenth Century. G. M. Trevelyan

My Apprenticeship and *Our Partnership.*   Beatrice Webb

Hodder and Stoughton and the Executor:
Life of Robert, Marquis of Salisbury.
Lady Gwendoline Cecil

The Town Clerk, Birmingham:
History of Birmingham. Vol. II.   Asa Briggs

John Murray (Publishers) Ltd.:
Gladstone.   Philip Magnus

William Heinemann Ltd.: and Pearn, Pollinger & Higham Ltd.:
Portrait of Clare.   Francis Brett Young

Allen & Unwin Ltd.:
The Struggle for the Freedom of the Press.
William H. Wickwar

Macmillan & Co. Ltd.:
The Life of Joseph Chamberlain.
J. L. Garvin and Julian Amery

To correspondents in many parts of the country and overseas who have replied to enquiries and helped me to clear up doubtful points, my indebtedness is manifold; as it is, too, to several citizens of Birmingham who have borne with my questioning and contributed to the evocation of the atmosphere of times past.

A special word of thanks is due to Dr. Edward D. Mason for generously placing at my disposal his collection of cartoons from the *Dart* and other bygone Birmingham periodicals and allowing me to reproduce some specimens relating to the policies and personalities of the paper. Few things are so valuable in recalling the temper of times past than contemporary cartoons, especially critical and disrespectful cartoons of former worthies. That the practice of local and personal cartooning has died out is a misfortune that will be more keenly regretted in the future than it is to-day.

H. R. G. W.

Contents

Illustrations

They come for news; man's nature's greedy of it.

.   .   .   .

News of all sorts and sizes, I have studied hard

And from the general courants and gazettes,

Public and private, letters from all parts

Of Christendom, though they speak contraries,

Weigh'd and reduc'd them to such certainties

That I dare warrant 'em authentical

Under my hand and seal.

News from Plymouth
Sir William Davenant, 1635

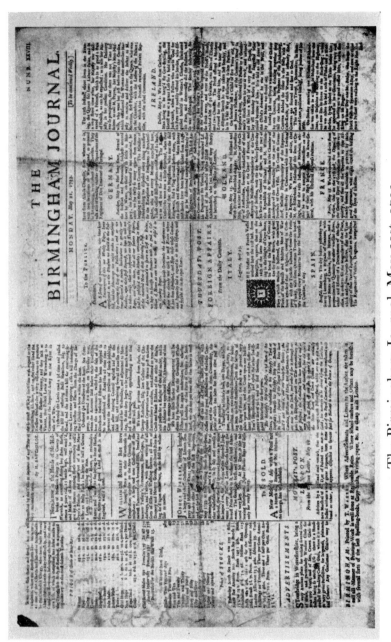

The Birmingham Journal, May 21st, 1733

The Swan Hotel, High Street

Introductory

TOWARDS THE END OF HIS LONG editorship, John Thackray Bunce was asked to say something of the history of *The Birmingham Post*. 'I don't know that we have any history,' he replied. 'We got the lead from the first and have kept it ever since. That is all.' This from a man who was at the centre of affairs during the formative years from 1862 to 1899 is almost incomprehensible. He had been the trusted adviser and close friend of the remarkable body of men who carried through the municipal revolution in the 'seventies and 'eighties and the confidant of Joseph Chamberlain, both then and later when Chamberlain moved on to the wider stage of national politics. Under him the paper had been an active and indispensable collaborator in great and exciting events. If ever a newspaper editor was entitled to feel that he had marched with destiny, it was Bunce of the *Post*. He did not lack a sense of history or of obligation to posterity. He initiated the series of volumes of the 'History of the Corporation of Birmingham' a detailed work of reference involving immense labour; and wrote histories of St. Martin's Church and the General Hospital that are irreplaceable, and still readable, records. As a citizen and a journalist he must have been aware of the place of his newspaper in the affairs of the second half of the nineteenth century and of the absorbing story that he alone could tell. Perhaps he meant to write a history of the paper, or, which would have been much the same, an autobiography, after he retired. He did not live long enough, however, to add anything more to his substantial list of books. Nor, apparently, did he leave any personal papers to enable someone else to remedy the defect. His unique knowledge of the period died with him.

No one else connected with the paper would have been likely to fill the void left by Bunce. Three members of the Feeney family,—the founder, John Frederick; his son, John; and John's nephew, Charles Hyde—controlled the destinies of the paper, either alone or with partners, from the beginnings until 1944. One of the strongest characteristics they had in common was an almost excessive aversion to personal publicity of any sort. This extended to their business as newspaper proprietors. They had a serious conception of their duty to the community and high ideals as to the conduct of a newspaper; but they felt under no obligation to talk or write about ideals or duties or to discuss in public what they regarded as their private business,—which, indeed, it was, as the ownership of the papers remained a private undertaking until they passed into the hands of the present proprietors. There must have been at some time business records and personal correspondence, but the idea of preserving them for the archives would have been foreign to the Feeney outlook. It is conceivable that, besides the feeling that their affairs were nobody else's business, the innate modesty of these reserved men would prevent them from realising that their detailed conduct of the newspapers would ever be of any interest to those who came after them.

Finally, Sir Charles Hyde had organised the collection and salvage of paper in the West Midlands during the First World War and when the need arose again in 1939, he threw himself into the work of salvage with great vigour and enthusiasm. Never the man to ask from others more than he would do himself, he set an example in his own office from which we have not yet recovered. Any business or family papers that may have survived from earlier days will have gone the way, during the war time salvage drives, of much other material that is now missed.

The other dominating personality in the history of the *Post*, Sir John Jaffray, went to the other extreme temperamentally. By contrast with the retiring Feeney's, he was the psychologists' ideal specimen of the extravert, the busy man of affairs always in the public eye and often on the public platform, an active politician and a director of companies, as time went on, far beyond the range of newspaper ownership. Whenever cartoonists or writers referred to *The Birmingham Post* it was always Jaffray who personified the paper. It was he who earned and received a baronetcy in the flood tide of Unionist success. Originally he was a writer by trade but he soon devolved editorial duties on Bunce and concentrated his energies on business management and public life. In one of the few passages in the files that can certainly be attributed to Jaffray, there is a significant phrase that shows his affinity with the Feeneys' outlook in regard to newspaper ownership. In a moving tribute to his dead partner, John Frederick Feeney, he remarks that, 'It is not well that the personal relations of a newspaper proprietory should be obtruded upon the public.' He adhered to this principle to the end of his active life and after his death his family passed out of the life of Birmingham. He has left nothing directly and originally bearing on the paper's history.

In trying to recover and reconstruct the past of *The Birmingham Post,* one is reminded of Lord Burnham's remark in doing a similar task for his famous paper. 'The *Daily Telegraph* may have broken records,' Lord Burnham writes, 'Certainly it kept none.' He had to work on only 'casual references in books by members of the staff, a few scrappy memoranda and letters, a fairly reliable memory, and the files of the newspaper itself.' There are no books written by members of *The Birmingham Post* staff that throw any light on the paper; letters and memoranda have gone the way of all scrap; living memories do not reach much beyond the paper's Jubilee in 1907. There are, indeed, the files, over 30,000 daily papers, but they tell very little about themselves. The personal and business

3

reticence of the proprietors, and the journalistic tradition of anonymity, combine in an objectivity more admirable in theory than helpful to a newspaper historian. However, a provincial newspaper, unlike a 'national' newspaper produced in London, is closely integrated with the life of the community it serves. It is woven into the tapestry of local history and its story is inseparable from the events it chronicles. Those who have served the paper are a part of the city's tradition; and, contrariwise, many of the leading men in many walks in life have made their impact on the paper and contributed something of their personalities, by way of writings and otherwise, to the paper's character. The city has always had a lively intellectual life that has burst into print at various times in a number of small, usually short-lived, periodicals. Theatrical notices and gossip, music and the arts, and, above all, chatter of a personal, and too often faintly scurrilous, nature provided the fare. The *Post*, its conductors and personalities, came in for a good share. These small periodicals, odd, amateurish, painfully humorous, sententious but often entertaining, help to build up a picture of contemporary society, and throw some light on the *Post* and the people who read it. The spring-time of these bright but ephemeral plants was in the 'seventies and 'eighties. Some lasted quite a while and are remembered with amusement and affection by older people to whom they were part of a golden youth. The *Dart* and the *Owl*, with their cartoons; the *Town Crier*, 'a respectable specimen of a local comic,' says *Showell's Dictionary*, with more than an implication that there were others undeserving of the compliment; and *Edgbastonia*, a distinctly 'classy' monthly, are just a few with a general appeal. Throughout our period, too, a number of morning, evening and weekly newspapers of a more professional sort made their entrances and exits and diversified the scene in the interests of various parties, groups and causes. There is material here for a sequel to Professor Briggs's Dugdale

4

Society study of the Birmingham press in the early nineteenth century; and the material is available in our excellent City Reference Library.

There are a number of books of reminiscences and some admirable biographies covering what may be described as the heroic age in Birmingham's history, of which Dr. Dale's Life of Dr. Crosskey and Wright Wilson's Life of George Dawson deserve special mention as evocative of the atmosphere and ideals of a creative period. The two-volume History of Birmingham sponsored by the City Council and written by Professors Conrad Gill and Asa Briggs is an essential piece of background reading. The late Canon J. H. B. Masterman wrote a valuable short history for The Story of the English Towns series published by the Society for Promoting Christian Knowledge. Finally, the official *Life of Joseph Chamberlain*, by the late J. L. Garvin and Mr. Julian Amery, M.P., provides a firm framework of events and characters for the greater part of the first hundred years of the *Post's* existence. Doubtless the Chamberlain Papers will throw further light on the relations between the statesman and the newspaper, for the *Life* is punctuated with frequent references to a correspondence between Chamberlain and Bunce over the years. But these important Papers, recently presented by the family to the University of Birmingham, will not be available for study until the new University Library is built and opened.

None of these external sources—apart from the History of the Corporation started by Bunce and carried on by other journalists associated with the *Post*—is the work of a member of the paper's staff and all glance at the paper, if at all, from the outside. Birmingham journalists, unlike many of their metropolitan fellows, have not been given to writing about themselves or each other. Two birds of passage, Sir John Hammerton in *Books and Myself* and H. J. Jennings in *Chestnuts and Small Beer* give glimpses of

5

the inside of the office in their day. Hammerton was editor of the *Weekly Post* for three years at the turn of the century and Jennings was the first editor of *The Birmingham Mail* when it was launched in 1870. The former was frankly on his way to London and the latter's principal interest in life was the theatre. In a barren land their contributions are refreshing but tantalisingly brief and sketchy.

That exhausts the list of sources, internal and external, to which this history is indebted and it is in no spirit of ingratitude that one could wish there had been more. Perhaps the publication of this inadequate and incomplete record may bring to light material that has escaped a necessarily hurried search. It will be most gratefully received, and there will be time to deal with it properly before a bicentenary sequel goes to press. Or, rather, there *should* be ample time,—the obsessive dream of the journalist whose existence is haunted by problems of space and time unknown to cosmic scientists.

The Birmingham Journal

WHEN THE NEWSPAPER STAMP Duty was abolished in 1855, it became possible to produce and sell a newspaper for a penny. Six years later the last of the quaintly-named 'taxes on knowledge ',—the Paper Duty —also was repealed and it became not only possible but decidedly profitable. From these years dates the renaissance of the free press and the foundation of most of the leading provincial dailies. They sprang up from, in the main, the established weeklies that had survived the fierce competition and bitter discouragements and persecution of the early decades of the 19th century. They made vigorous growth, for they were conducted by tried and experienced newspaper men who had learned their business the hard way. Printers, journalists, propagandists, agitators, they had managed to survive the lean years by a combination of qualities of which keen business acumen was perhaps the outstanding common factor, though not the principal driving force. Few started newspapers in the first half of the 19th century with the idea of making a fortune; and, indeed, few managed to make even a living out of it. But that small minority of weekly newspaper owners who survived to launch daily papers in the 1850's had proved that a genuinely free, democratic press was possible, an economic proposition standing on its own feet without dependence on subsidies from politicians or parties and without recourse to even more questionable methods of raising outside revenues.

Freedom was due to the growth of advertising, which began to be a useful source of revenue towards the end of the 18th century. That it took another fifty years or so to put the newspapers on a firm footing of independence was due entirely to the penal taxation that forced the price of a weekly paper during and after the Napoleonic Wars up to 7d. a copy. For the past hundred years the British press has rested economically on the inter-relationship between circulation and advertisements,—circulation depending on merit as judged by the impartial tribunal of public opinion and advertisers following the lead of circulation on the simple principle of placing their announcements where they will be seen by the largest number of the most likely buyers, and paying rates in proportion.

The birth of a free press dates from 1694, when the Licensing Act lapsed in the afterglow of the 'Glorious Revolution' of 1688. For the first time writers and printers could publish without obtaining leave from civil or ecclesiastical authorities. Weekly newspapers began to appear in the leading provincial cities,—the *Norwich Post* in 1701, the *Bristol Post-Boy* in 1702, the *Exeter Post-Man* in 1704, and many others in the following decade. The distribution of these early provincial weeklies is a reminder of the relative importance of the English towns and cities before the Industrial Revolution transformed the pattern. The contrast with the renaissance 150 years afterwards is striking. In 1855 the first provincial dailies appeared in Manchester, Liverpool, Sheffield and Edinburgh, with Birmingham, Glasgow and Newcastle-on-Tyne following two years later. The old rural England had been submerged, though not obliterated, for to this day it preserves a fine series of weekly newspapers in the county and market towns that most worthily uphold the traditional standards of journalism and of service to their communities.

The freedom granted in 1694, however, seems to have been given in a fit of absent-mindedness. It took some time for the principalities and powers to realise what they had done; but once the fact of a free press penetrated their consciousness, they soon began to set about attempting to control the press again,—an instinct that is never

8

far from the minds of those in authority in all ages. The instrument of control that occurs most readily to politicians in a parliamentary State is taxation. There is a story of Faraday, the great electrical scientist, trying to explain a piece of apparatus to Gladstone. A forlorn hope, as he soon saw, when Gladstone's soaring mind strayed from technical details to resounding high principles. 'But, after all,' enquired the statesman, 'what *good* is it?' To which the scientist, in a flash of cynicism, replied, 'Why, Sir, presently you will be able to tax it.' So the politicians of Queen Anne's day saw that the way to bring the new-born free press to heel was to tax it. In 1712, just as the provincial weeklies were getting under way, Parliament imposed the Stamp Act which put a levy of one penny per copy on a single-sheet newspaper or pamphlet. However, parliamentary draftsmanship, then as now, is an inexact science. The Act was so loosely worded that anything larger than a single sheet came under a merely nominal rate of duty of Three Shillings per edition. The printers of weekly newspapers simply increased the size of their publications and evaded the duty.

The paradoxical result of the original Stamp Act was, therefore, to enlarge the weekly newspaper and, as it so happened, to set the pattern of the newspaper much as we still know it today. For in the early 18th century,— and, indeed, until the advent of the electric telegraph— news was a scarce commodity. The printer who had to fill additional space to evade the worst of the Stamp Duty, turned to literary features to supplement his scanty ration of news; and the combination of news and features which is a commonplace of the newspaper, weekly or daily, became established inadvertently by a slovenly Act of Parliament. By 1725 the legislature woke up to its blunder and the loopholes in the Act were stopped. Newspapers were required to pay $\frac{1}{2}$d. tax per half-sheet, and the price of the one-and-a-half sheet

9

weeklies, which had been selling for a penny, was put up to 2½d. per copy. But the pattern once fixed, remained. The subsequent history of the Stamp Duty, the Advertisement Duty and the duty on paper, is the familiar story of steady increases, until the penal impositions of the war and post-war periods that, as already mentioned, put the selling price of a weekly up to 7d. a copy, and took newspapers out of the reach of the mass of working people. Taxation also made publication a commercially hazardous undertaking.

Nor was it only commercially hazardous, for this was the period of coercion and panic, when Habeas Corpus was suspended, public meetings, lectures and debating societies were prohibited and the laws of sedition and blasphemy were refurbished and used harshly and capriciously in a futile attempt to stamp out discussion in print of everything supposedly tinged with 'Jacobinism.' The struggle for the freedom of the press, so admirably recorded in the history with that title by W. H. Wickwar, claimed its martyrs and produced its fanatics and eccentrics. One way or another, however, the printing presses never ceased to provide an outlet for the gathering forces of the Age of Reforms. Not all were wholly admirable. 'If the current of public opinion is denied course through constitutional channels,' G. M. Trevelyan shrewdly observes, 'it will make its way out by the sewers.' Under George the Fourth the press plumbed the depths of scurrility and muck-raking; not without ample material to work upon from the highest circles in the land. After Peel, as Home Secretary, in 1822 abandoned as hopeless the policy of coercion, political and press prosecutions declined, and the tone of the newspapers improved. A recrudescence of the spirit of coercion under the Whig Government in 1830 was nipped in the bud by a jury that acquitted Cobbett. In the same year Thomas Attwood founded the Political Union in Birmingham to agitate for Parliamentary reform. This was the beginning of that alliance of the middle and working classes in Radical politics that dominated public life throughout the Victorian age. Birmingham took the lead and kept it in the movement owing to the remarkable social homogeneity of the city's life. There was none of that bitter cleavage between masters and men that characterised the great industrial centres in the North. The strength of Nonconformity, the common ideals most inadequately summed up in the notion of 'respectability,' the sense of worth and opportunity felt by all classes in a growing and fecund community of inventive craftsmen, welded Birmingham into a progressive unity that sharply and indignantly resented its political impotence. In the Age of Reform Birmingham was pulsating with vitality and restless energy and the spirit of the town found expression in its press.

In the 1830's Birmingham had two weekly newspapers, both of which survived to give birth to dailies when the time came. *Aris's Birmingham Gazette* had already an unbroken record of publication since 1741, when a London printer set up his press and publishing business in the Midland town. Its files are an invaluable source of local history and entertainment and it survived until November, 1956, when it was merged with *The Birmingham Post*. *The Birmingham Journal*, parent of *The Birmingham Post*, cannot claim such venerable ancestry, but in the period we are discussing—the Age of Reform—it was the most celebrated Birmingham paper in the fierce battles that raged around the Reform Bill of 1832 and later the Chartist movement of 1838-39. Its influence was not confined to Birmingham and the Midlands. Professor Asa Briggs recalls (Press and Public in early 19th century Birmingham. Dugdale Occasional Papers, No. 8), that in 1839 an official investigator found seventy-one weekly copies of *The Birmingham Journal* as far away as Dunfermline.

Before becoming a thorn in the flesh to authority in Birmingham and Scotland, however, the *Journal* had

had a chequered history and had passed through vicissitudes in various hands. There was, indeed, a *Birmingham Journal* before *Aris's Gazette* but it had a brief life only and very little is known about it. No files have been preserved and the only known copy, dated Monday, May 21, 1733, and numbered No. 37, hangs in this office, framed between sheets of glass. It appears to have started, therefore, on November 14, 1732, and was run by Thomas Warren, a friend of Dr. Samuel Johnson, a printer 'over against the Swan Passage in Birmingham' or 'at the Printing Office, against the Swan Tavern in Birmingham', a site in the High Street. No descent can be claimed from this early sheet. The year of its demise is unknown, but was probably before 1740.

The unbroken story of *The Birmingham Journal* starts in 1825, when William Hodgetts, a printer and bookseller, revived the title for a weekly paper issued in the Conservative interest. The circumstances are related by Edwards in his 'Personal Recollections of Birmingham' published in 1877. It was started by 'a few old fogies' who used to meet at 'Joe Linden's, The Minerva' in Peck Lane. Awful and unpardonable offence had been given by *The Times*, which had ridiculed some action by the Tory Party in Birmingham. A summons went out to frequenters of 'Joe Linden's' to attend an important meeting on a certain day. The offending article was read and 'a well-fed, prosperous-looking, fox-hunting iron merchant from Great Charles Street' moved that *The Times* had disgraced itself and insulted Birmingham and that it was the duty of every Birmingham man to stop its circulation in the town. The copy of the paper containing the offensive article was ceremonially burned and then the meeting went on to the more practical business of opening a subscription to start a new paper to represent the 'loyal' party in the town. On Monday, May 23, 1825, a notice appeared in the *Courier*, a London Tory paper. 'New Birmingham Paper', it ran. 'On

Saturday, the 4th of June, at twelve o'clock (and on every succeeding Saturday, at the same hour), will be published a Weekly Paper, to be called *The Birmingham Journal*, and circulated the same Evening at a distance of twenty-five miles round Birmingham, and in most of the principal towns in the Kingdom early the following day. Printed and published for the Proprietors by William Hodgetts, No. 16 Spiceal Street, to whom, or to the Editor, all communications (free of postage), must be addressed."

Two years later, Hodgetts, who had subscribed Fifty Pounds to the original fund, paid out the other partners and became sole proprietor. In 1830 he enlarged the paper and brought Johnathan Crowther from Manchester to be editor and to carry the paper over from Toryism to Radicalism, when its influence and circulation began rapidly to increase. The first and Tory editor was a Professor Bakewell, of whom one only has the unflattering comment of a rival that he was 'a very good reporter but one of the most milk-and-watery scribes the world ever saw'. In 1830, under Crowther, the circulation was 1,812 copies for the issue of Saturday, 29th May. The average sales in 1829-30 were about a thousand copies a week. These figures are not so derisory as they may seem to a modern reader accustomed to think of popular newspaper circulations in millions. On a basis of 20 people reading each copy,—a conservative estimate for those times—more than one in four of the inhabitants of Birmingham, by Professor Asa Briggs' reckoning, were readers of the *Journal* of 29th May, 1830. The estimated sale of newspapers and periodicals of all kinds in Birmingham in the year 1831 was 7,000 a week. Four hundred copies a week was a high circulation around 1830. In 1827, the *Birmingham Independent*, on its way to extinction, appealed for a guaranteed 250 subscribers to enable it to maintain publication. It failed to get them. If it had, it could have carried on even at this low level.

In 1832 Hodgetts sold the *Journal* to Joseph Parkes, a noted Unitarian and Utilitarian Radical, for £2,000. Next year he made another venture with a new paper, the *Birmingham Advertiser*, without enduring success. 'Ultimately,' says Joseph Hill in 'The Bookmakers of Old Birmingham' published in 1907, 'he carried on a quiet business in Cannon Street'. There is much virtue, to be sure, in that adjective 'quiet', after the hurly-burly of newspaper enterprise in the Birmingham of the 1830's.

The new proprietors,—associated with Parkes were Scholefield and Redfern in Radical politics and in the control, if not actual ownership, of the paper—were actuated by political and propagandist motives. Men have acquired newspapers for a variety of reasons. In the beginning the usual motive was the business instinct of a local printer wishing to keep his plant at work by supplying an unpretentious sheet of local information. It served an essentially useful purpose as a means of communication within a restricted community. Another motive, deriving from antiquity, was, of course, the wish to influence the minds and actions of one's fellow-men, to advocate causes, spread ideas abroad and exercise a measure of power over the course of events. Parallel with this went the fundamental human story-telling instinct, perhaps the most disinterested and satisfying aspect of journalism. From the start, therefore, the broad divisions of newspaper enterprise were present and as the size and complexity of newspaper production increased they tended to take shape as distinct departments. Ownership and business management; the editorial conduct of story-telling and what, for want of a better word, one must call propaganda; and the technical business of printing, the 'Works' side, are the basic, indispensable features. They have been present in a great variety of combinations of control. The early printers started to employ writers; men with a message and the urge to write looked for printers who would

14

take the by no means negligible risks of publishing their writings; control would fluctuate according to the business abilities of individuals; the owners might be printers in the first place or writers with a flair for commercial enterprise. Editor-proprietors are still a distinguished feature of weekly newspaper ownership.

Towards the end of the 18th century, when advertising emerged as an important item of newspaper revenue, the newspaper proprietor who was neither a printer nor a journalist came on the scene. He,—or more often they, for it was commonly a partnership of two or three men who raised the money to buy or start a paper—had usually graduated as a craftsman in the trades of printing or journalism. But when he became a proprietor he tended to drop the practice of his craft and to concentrate his energies on management. There were, of course, many fine gradations and the proprietor who could write a leading article and set it up in type was a well-known and much respected figure in the newspaper world. He may still exist today in theory, if not in practice, in some smaller newspaper offices; and he stands as a symbol of the intimate harmony that should exist in the conduct of a newspaper. Human nature being what it is, and the complexity of the business having grown as it has, that harmony is a matter of compromise and the reconciliation of divergent interests and the fascinating interplay of character. Under modern conditions of limited liability, too, ownership, as represented by shareholders, and management are not identical. The newspaper industry, as the press seems to prefer to call itself nowadays, has taken the full impact of the Managerial Revolution and, to be frank, has thriven on it.

This digression into the developing structure of newspaper enterprise has a bearing on *The Birmingham Journal* of the 1830's and, indeed, on the whole subject of this book. It should make the point that it is not always, or often, possible to deduce from the past who,

15

at any given moment, was the moving spirit, the dominating personality, on a newspaper that gave the paper its character and shaped its policy. Human beings, Lytton Strachey wrote, are too important to be treated as mere symptoms of the past. There is no temptation to fall into this error in writing about a newspaper, for its past, present and future are all composed of the characters, foibles and limitations of fallible human beings. Vast technical and mechanical developments have occurred in newspaper production in the past hundred years, but ultimately they are all reduced to the projection of individual personalities through the medium of print. So the story of *The Birmingham Post*, as of any other living organism, is first and foremost the story of the men who have made it.

The story of *The Birmingham Journal* comes to life with its acquisition by Joseph Parkes in 1832, though the new proprietor himself seems to have had little to do with the actual conduct of the paper. His contribution was the removal of the office from Hodgett's printing establishment in Spiceal Street to the site in New Street occupied to this day and, rather more important, the appointment of a remarkable man as editor. R. K. Douglas, who took the chair in New Street in 1833, was a national figure in the reform movement. He began the tradition of active identification with progressive politics that was carried on by the controlling personalities of *The Birmingham Post* until the disruption of the Liberal Radical movement. He was a powerful writer who, so a hostile critic put it, 'concocted Radical leaders in bad taste and questionable English',—a foolish gibe, as anyone can see for himself who cares to read the files. A more accessible example of his style is the famous National Petition of 1838, 'magnificently written, with its biblical cadences and its eloquent simplicity,' to quote Professor Briggs. The drawing up of this manifesto of the Chartist movement was the summit of Douglas's public career. He was

16

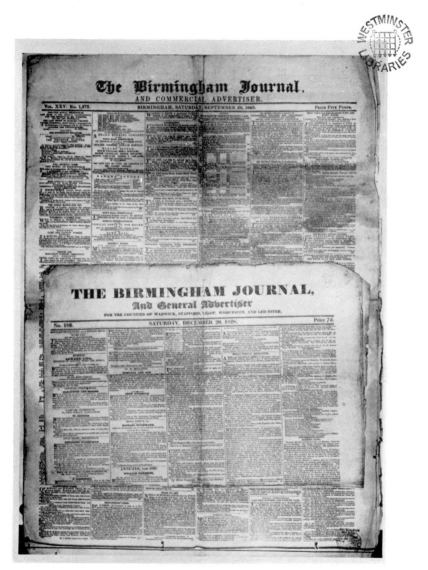

Growth of the Journal

Thomas Attwood, M.P.

secretary of the Birmingham Political Union, revived in 1837, when the hopes engendered by the great 1832 Reform Act had been disappointed and the trade boom of 1832-36 had collapsed. Distress and unemployment were increasing in the industrial cities. Attwood, one of the first two Members of Parliament for Birmingham, newly-enfranchised by the Reform Act, thought he knew the remedy. He was a banker, a currency crank and rather a bore. His ideas were confused and contradictory and were never more than a personal idiosyncracy, but they were the basis of the resuscitated Union programme and were vigorously promulgated in *The Birmingham Journal*.

When the Birmingham Political Union merged with the nation-wide Chartist movement, Attwood's currency ideas were swamped by the extreme, and more lucid, political programme. They belonged, also, to the moderate, middle-class wing, the 'moral force' men, and they foundered once for all when the 'physical force' element under O'Connor captured the Convention in 1839. Douglas, who had been the first chairman of the Convention, and the other two Birmingham delegates, Salt and Hadley, resigned from the Convention and the Chartist movement was set on the wretched round of dissension, recklessness and incompetent leadership that led to a dismal and ignominious end.

At the height of the campaign the *Journal's* circulation in 1837, according to the Stamp Office returns, was 2,115 copies weekly. Freeling's 'Grand Junction Railway Companion, 1838' describes the *Journal* as being, 'Thoroughly Radical: the organ of the Political Union. The articles are generally terse and vigorous.' Another source quotes a circulation of 2,500 weekly in 1838. These were substantial figures for the time and bear out the claim that the *Journal* was the most influential paper in Birmingham, and nationally important in the reform movement. It stood, however, for moderation and

17

constitutional methods and, in the temper of the times, could never hope to rival the relatively huge circulation of Fergus O'Connor's notorious *Northern Star*, that openly advocated violence and drove Chartism to its ruin. Douglas had never wavered. As long ago as 1836 the *Journal* had attacked O'Connor directly, declaring that, whatever his party said and professed, their real purpose was illegality, disorder and civil war. Such virtue did not receive its just reward. What with the political disruption and the continuing industrial depression, the *Journal's* circulation languished after 1839. Writing thirty years later, on the flood tide of commercial prosperity, John Jaffray said its circulation had fallen 'to a few hundred copies a week'. With the confidence born of success, he wrote of the *Journal* that, 'while nothing could exceed the vigour of its politics, and the intellectual ability of its conductors, the business element was wholly lacking.'

In 1844, John Frederick Feeney went to London, saw Mr. Joseph Parkes, and arranged to purchase the *Journal*, which thereupon passed into the hands of the family that continued to control it and its newspaper successors and offshoots for the next hundred years.

3
Taxes on Knowledge

IN THE GENERAL STATE OF ALARM
that followed the French Revolution, the Napoleonic
Wars and the post-war turmoil at home, public men
made no secret of the fact that the heavy taxation of
newspapers was meant to kill the Radical press and to
limit the circulation of newspapers generally to the
propertied upper and middle classes. Edmund Burke had
described the press as the grand instrument for the sub-
version of order, morals, religion and human society
itself. The press was credited by other excited and
frightened patriots with a main share in instigating the
French Revolution and with responsibility for the nerve-
shattering naval mutinies at the Nore and Spithead in
1797. That the press was 'a tremendous engine in the
hands of mischievous men' was a widely-held opinion
among the ruling classes. Taxation was regarded as one
way of keeping ownership of newspapers in responsible
hands, who would be amenable to, if not dependant on,
official patronage and subsidy; and of keeping newspapers out of the hands of the lower orders. For the great
offence of the press in the eyes of politicians in the
unreformed Parliament was that it increased the number
of people who exercised some sort of judgment on public
affairs. Throughout the country the newspapers enabled
people to read Parliamentary debates and to discover
that one set of Parliamentarians was denouncing the
folly and wickedness of another set who formed the
government. There was, indeed, a good measure of truth
in this view and it appealed alike to Tories and Whigs,
who in turn expected to form the Government. Public
opinion, as it began to shape, had no other means of
expressing itself or of imbibing nourishment. Public
meetings and political platform oratory scarcely existed;

attempts to educate the people were regarded as sub-
versive, particularly after the passing of the 'Six Acts'
following the 'Peterloo massacre' in 1819. The press was
the only outlet for criticism, discontent and discussion
of reform.

Besides heavy taxation and repressive laws, the embryo
free press laboured under many disabilities. Until 1814,
all newspapers were produced on hand presses, with a
maximum output of about 250 copies an hour. In that
year *The Times* first introduced steam-driven printing
presses, which could run off copies at 1,100 an hour.
Communications were backward, though road improve-
ments were comparatively rapid in the first three decades
of the century and the railways practically solved the
problem soon after. But the great handicap was taxation
and, despite a reduction of the Stamp Duty in 1836 to
one penny per copy, it remained so until the abolition
in 1855.

The press survived, however, because of the powerful
public demand and the ingenuity of publishers, book-
sellers, agitators and newsvendors in evading the worst
effects of the duties. There was some flat defiance of the
law in the shape of unstamped newspapers which the
authorities found hard to check, though they tried with
a lot of brutality against poor and ignorant newsvendors.
There was, too, Cobbett's device of issuing a cheap
edition of his *Political Register* to sell at twopence, against
the one shilling and a halfpenny for the stamped edition.
He made use of a perfectly legal provision by producing
it as a tax-free pamphlet; but this was stopped by the
'Six Acts'.

The really effective means of evading the prohibitive
duty, however, was the development of group reading,
whereby every copy of a newspaper was made to serve
anything up to thirty or more people. This also overcame
in large measure the handicap of public illiteracy. In
1835 Brougham reckoned that no free country had so few

newspapers per head of population as Britain; he said that the United States of America had thirty times as many. An enquiry in 1839 showed that ten out of eleven people in the country were totally uneducated. But if the working man could neither afford to buy a newspaper nor read one, he could subscribe a fraction of the cost and listen to a reading as one of a group. It was a common practice for many years for a workshop to buy a newspaper to be read aloud by a literate member while the rest listened to him in solemn silence and with unflagging attention. The reading was followed by comment, discussion and explanation and everyone learned something. A public opinion was in process of formation and the newspapers were winning a mass readership.

When Thomas Attwood founded the Birmingham Political Union to promote the cause of Parliamentary Reform, he started the practice of having newspapers read at large public meetings. People met in Union Street, the Bull Ring and other Birmingham thoroughfares during their dinner hour and in the evenings to hear the news of the day. The practice continued during the Chartist agitation in the late 'thirties. Quiet, orderly meetings they must have been, without benefit of microphones, and a good training in elocution and voice production for those who later would blossom on public platforms to address their fellow-men. It would be interesting to examine the evidence, too, of the influence of public readings on the literary style of writers for the newspapers. Can they be held responsible for the orotund and prolix style of leader-writing developed in the newspapers to such extremes in later years? What effect did they have on public speaking when the platform eventually came into its own as the nation's forum? Though necessarily quiet and orderly, however, these street gatherings to read the newspapers were frowned on by authority, at that time especially apprehensive of assemblages and always ready to disapprove of the pleasures of the people.

On July 4th, 1839, so William Lovett, the Chartist leader recalls in his *Life and Struggles*, a crowd of at least 800 people gathered in the Bull Ring and 'paid very polite attention to a person reading a newspaper'. The new-fangled police from London, perhaps strange to Birmingham habits, attacked the crowd with truncheons and broke the meeting up. That is Lovett's version, however, given at his trial, and the police may have had other causes than a newspaper reading to anticipate trouble from an ebullient Birmingham crowd.

Another expedient about this time was the public reading room where, for a subscription of one guinea a year, people could read a large selection of newspapers, pamphlets and often books. It was symptomatic of the difficulties of law enforcement in those days that reading rooms openly took unstamped, and therefore illegal, newspapers for their customers. Every large town and most small towns had subscription reading rooms.

In July, 1825, the proprietors of the Birmingham News Room erected 'a handsome building for their use' on the corner of Bennetts Hill and the newly-opened Waterloo Street. It really was a handsome building, designed by Messrs. Rickman and Hutchinson in the classical style, with Ionic columns, and later was found worthy of occupation by a bank, the Birmingham Banking Company, an institution that has always set store by impressive architecture. Inside was one large room opening through folding doors into smaller rooms. On the first floor was a refectory and, surprisingly, a billiards room. A suite of rooms was added later to house copies of the public records and reference books. The reading room proper contained the leading London, Provincial and foreign newspapers; shipping, commercial and law intelligence; and files of local newspapers and the more important papers such as *The Times* and the *London Gazette*. The News Room was open daily, including, for a few hours, Sundays. In the intellectual desert that

22

was Birmingham in the early 19th century the News Room was an oasis of light and leading and, from the Tory point of view, a hotbed of middle-class mischief. A common practice was to sell the papers from reading rooms at half price the day before the next number was due, thus starting them on another round of circulation. These reading rooms, often associated with a bookseller's shop, were primarily respectable, middle-class establishments, even though they did defy the law by taking unstamped papers. A wider public was catered for by coffee houses that took in newspapers for their customers; and the widest circulation of all was provided by the ale-houses that brought papers to the smallest and most remote villages as well as into the crowded working class districts of the swarming industrial towns. Ale-house and coffee-house reading extended greatly after the reduction of the stamp duty in 1836; for although the price of a paper remained too high for the individual working man, it was within the capacity of public houses and coffee rooms wishing to provide an added attraction.

Finally, there was the very extensive practice of hiring newspapers to groups of readers, usually for a charge of one penny. Curiously enough it was illegal, though that did not seem to make much difference. It simply provided another pretext for sporadic outbreaks of the persecution of newsvendors by magistrates and others with a grudge. When Pitt's government increased the Stamp Duty and the advertisement duty in 1789, some (but not all) newspaper proprietors, anxious about sales, asked for a *quid pro quo* in the shape of a ban on hiring and Parliament rather unthinkingly agreed. The practice, however, which had been going on for over twelve years and was a substantial source of revenue to many poor people, was too well established to be stopped by a mere threat of a fine of £5, unaccompanied by any effective system of enforcement. Nor could the public see anything wrong or immoral in hiring, so the unjust law

23

was simply ignored. Even the newspaper proprietors who had asked for the ban seem to have lost interest in it when they found their sales flourishing through the working of all the other expedients. Newspapers themselves often urged readers to lend their copies to poorer neighbours and provincial newspapers carried advertisements offering to lend copies of *The Times*. A frequent practice among newsvendors was to hire out papers during the day and post them to country customers in the evening at half-price.

In one way and another, therefore, the newspapers, in spite of heavy taxation, circulated throughout the length and breadth of the land and penetrated into every stratum of society. The very fact that those in authority tried to stop newspapers getting into the hands of the lower orders was an incentive to reformers to seek ways and means of stimulating newspaper reading. The press was the first, and almost the only, instrument of progress until the Anti-Corn Law League, under Cobden and Bright, in the 1840's fashioned the new instrument of agitation and public enlightenment by means of public meetings. The press created public opinion and made it articulate. As early as 1831, that ardent Radical, Brougham, raised a question that is still occasionally a subject of argument. Do newspapers create public opinion or merely reflect it? The answer is that the press does both, according to the particular circumstances of the moment and the vigour and ability of particular editors. Brougham's opinion was that the provincial papers of his time tended to reflect the views of their readers, while the London papers aspired more to form and influence public opinion. However that may be, the fact was that, as Croker remarked, after Parliamentary reform in 1832, public opinion, which formerly was only a subordinate factor in politics, became omnipotent. And that, in the absence of other means of expression, was the work of the press.

The new generation of Radical leaders that came to the fore in the Anti-Corn Law agitation was very conscious of the power of the press. They saw that the reduction of the Stamp Duty in 1836 from 4d. to 1d. had not had the desired effect. What with the advertisement and paper duties and the rise in costs of production since 1815, the selling price of a weekly newspaper fell only from 7d. to 5d., still beyond the means of the masses, especially considering the value of money in those days and the level of salaries and wages. The duty continued to prohibit the sale of a cheap newspaper and, as the Radicals saw it, almost entirely prevented the instruction of the working classes in town and country. Hence the emotional term 'Taxes on Knowledge', which was the slogan of Bright, Cobden and others through the 20 years' campaign for abolition that was waged in Parliament and on Radical platforms throughout the country. That the agitation in Parliament, associated principally with the name of Milner-Gibson, took so long was due to the fact that the taxes on newspapers brought in a substantial revenue. In 1849 the Chancellor of the Exchequer quoted a yield of £1,329,000 and said it would be an act of political suicide to surrender the annual income from these sources. Gladstone was thoroughly in favour of abolition and agreed with Bright and Cobden that a Government concerned for popular education ought to relieve the nation of all Taxes on Knowledge. But he in his turn as Chancellor could not dispense with the revenue. He brought forward the extraordinary argument that the working classes held the matter in their own hands and could get what they wanted by themselves cheapening the labour of newspaper production. The reformers, having failed repeatedly to carry the position by frontal attack all along the line, changed their tactics. They concentrated on the advertisement tax, a sector where they could count on assistance from allies outside the ranks of reformers and newspaper proprietors.

Gladstone still demurred, but Disraeli led the Tories into the lobby against the Government and the repeal was carried by a majority of 31. So, in 1853, the first breach was made in the defences and two years later the assault was launched on the central citadel.

The then Chancellor, Sir George Cornewall Lewis, introduced a Newspaper Stamp Bill to abolish the stamp duty and it became law in June, 1855. John Bright was moved to a burst of eloquence typical of progressive thinking of that time. 'I am willing to rest upon the verdict of the future', he declared, 'and I am quite convinced that five or six years will show that all the votes of Parliament for educational purposes have been as mere trifles compared with the results that will flow from this measure because, while the existing papers retain all their usefulness, it will call to their aid numbers of others not less useful, and while we enjoy the advantage of having laid before us each morning a map of the events of the world, the same advantages will be extended to certain classes of society at present shut out from it.' London newspaper proprietors of the day were not so enthusiastic as Bright over the prospect of penny provincial newspapers coming to their aid in the grand work of cultivating the masses. A hundred years later educationists may be disposed to question his confident appeal to the verdict of the future; though, seeing how few and small had been, by 1855, 'All the votes of Parliament for educational purposes', Bright's prediction was not unduly extravagant.

There remained one outwork still in the hands of the enemies of Knowledge, the Paper Duties, which applied, of course, to other users besides newspapers. In years to come Gladstone recalled that the economic freeing of the press had been one of the severest Parliamentary struggles in his experience. His selective memory overlooked the fact that he had resisted repeal of the advertisement tax and that abolition of the most onerous

26

impost, the Stamp Duty, had gone through quite smoothly. He was thinking only of the repeal of the paper duty, which he carried in 1861. It was, indeed, a most lively Parliamentary episode and a notable example of his tactical skill.

He introduced a Bill to repeal the paper duty in 1860, and the familiar arguments and Radical sentiments were brought out again to edify an acquiescent House of Commons. However, a young member on the Tory benches struck a discordant note. Lord Robert Cecil, the future third Marquis of Salisbury and Queen Victoria's last Prime Minister, rose to oppose the Bill. 'Normally, his thrusts are sharp rather than envenomed', his biographer, Lady Gwendolen Cecil wrote, 'and were probably less productive of exasperation that the superior pose of his principal adversary in these combats, Mr. Bright. He always fights on an equal footing and never claims against his opponents any exclusive proprietorship in religion or morality.' On this occasion, when his pugnacity had been roused by the parade of Radical righteousness over the last of the Taxes on Knowledge, Lord Robert was at the top of his form. A great deal had been said, he remarked, about the duties being a tax on knowledge. No doubt that was a grandiloquent, high-sounding and sentimental cry. But of the million-and-a-quarter pounds raised by the paper duty, only two-fifths were paid on books and newspapers, which reduced the 'taxes on knowledge' to £500,000. He was a little inclined to doubt whether the tax upon the penny papers could be said to be, in any proper sense of the word, a tax on knowledge. Could it be maintained that a person of any education could learn anything worth knowing from a penny paper? (Lord Robert at this time was making a passable income writing for the respectable *Saturday Review* and the *Quarterly*.) It may be said, he went on, that people might learn what had been said in Parliament. Well, would that contribute much to their education?

27

They might read the foreign intelligence, of which many would understand very little; and they might see the opinions of the editor of the paper on a variety of topics. No doubt all that was interesting to Honourable Members of the House of Commons, but it did not answer any true idea of education or carry any real instruction or true training to the mind. It was a prostitution of the word 'education' to talk of a tax on the penny papers as a tax upon knowledge. After this broadside, a shocked House passed the Bill, only to have it thrown out by the House of Lords. This precipitated a minor constitutional crisis. How, it was asked by indignant democrats, could the House of Commons be said to have control of taxation if the Lords could prolong or reimpose a duty by refusing its repeal when voted by the Commons? Gladstone, annoyed as he was, was not prepared to fight the Lords v. Commons battle on this minor issue. He was content to reduce the import duty on paper and to bide his time until the next Budget.

Then, in 1861, he produced a winning card from his clever hand. He embodied the remission of the paper duty in the Finance Bill, where the Lords could not touch it. This tactical move inaugurated the present practice of embodying all Budget proposals in a Finance Bill, which, being a Money Bill, is immune from amendment by the House of Lords. Thus are constitutional practices introduced under our infinitely flexible form of Parliamentary government. But Gladstone had not finished with his young Tory gadfly. When this device was brought before the House, Lord Robert Cecil declared it was 'worthy rather of an attorney than a statesman'. Gladstone was deeply offended, and so was the House. The Chancellor ponderously hoped Lord Robert would use the interval before the adjourned debate on the subject 'to consider his vocabulary'. Next morning the newspapers took up the point and administered heavy rebukes to the presumptious younger son.

28

Lord Robert accepted the invitation to consider his vocabulary and came down to the resumed debate with a personal statement in his pocket. The sequel, a famous Parliamentary occasion, is best told in Lady Gwendoline Cecil's words. ' "He had been very much taken to task", Lord Robert began, "for an expression he had ventured to use the other night to the effect that the course taken by the Chancellor of the Exchequer was worthy rather of an attorney than a statesman".

'The House composed itself to that hushed and expectant silence with which it enters upon a "painful personal incident"—a silence compounded partly of embarrassment and partly of the good boys' decorously subdued satisfaction in the spectacle of an erring comrade overtaken by retribution, Lord Robert pursued his way deliberately through the rounded phrases which custom prescribes for a House of Commons apology. "The expression was thought to be too violent—when any Hon. gentleman in the heat of debate dropped an expression which, on reflection, he felt to be stronger than was necessary, he ought to take the first opportunity to apologise or to retract"—and so on to the climax. "He felt that he was only doing justice to his own feelings when he avowed that on that occasion he did a great injustice"—a pause filled by an encouraging "hear, hear" from a kindly, if deluded, member—"to the attorneys". The half-dozen words of eulogy upon the profession which follow in Hansard's report witness to the momentary silence of stupefaction which ensued. Then the remainder of the sentence is lost in a storm of cries and exclamations. No doubt the performance was duly denounced at the time for its impertinent audacity; but though Lord Robert was to give and receive many a hard blow in the years that followed, it is not recorded that either speaker or writer ever employed against him the weapon of magisterial rebuke.'

So Parliament got rid of the last of the taxes on Knowledge, accompanying the concession with one of the brightest bits of 'copy' the newspapers have ever had out of the Palace of Westminster.

4

The First Proprietors

EVERY DAY AT THE HEAD OF THE leader column and under the title line, *The Birmingham Post* carries the legend, 'Founded by John Frederick Feeney, 1857'. Although by that date the founder had been in partnership with his editor, John Jaffray, for five years, there is no doubt that he is entitled to the credit for the new enterprise of a daily newspaper. In 1857 he was a man of fifty, ten years older than Jaffray, and with over twenty years' experience of journalism in Birmingham, twelve of these as a newspaper proprietor. He was the moving spirit, 'the Governor' to the staff, a man of bold initiative and, even by then, almost a legendary figure for immense industry and striking success in a calling notorious for failures. The paper is right to perpetuate his name as the sole founder. The point is worth making because his partner survived him by thirty years and succeeded to the credit, along with John Frederick's son, John Feeney, down to a time within living memory. Little enough is left about the original proprietor nearly ninety years after his death and the paper only does justice by perpetuating his name daily in a prominent position on the leader page. The office records preserve two original items; a small studio portrait typical of the mid-Victorian photographer's art, which was wonderfully good in spite of its technical handicaps; and a 'self' cheque for £18 15s. od. drawn on the Birmingham and Midland Bank, Union Street, dated 10th May, 1869. Pencilled on the back in an unknown hand are the words: 'This was the last writing of the Governor. He wrote this in the evening before he went upstairs ill and from this illness he never recovered.'

John Frederick Feeney came to Birmingham in 1835, at the age of 27, to edit a small weekly paper, *The*

Philanthropist, owned by Joseph Sturge. He was of Irish descent and it is assumed he learned his trade as a newspaper man in Ireland. His precise training is not on record, though office tradition has it that he was originally a compositor. There was no sharp dividing line in those days between the craftsmen of printing and journalism and it is more than likely that he had had experience as both printer and writer before he arrived in Birmingham as an editor and may well have continued to practice both crafts in his new appointment. *The Philanthropist*, first published as *The Reformer* by Benjamin Hudson, at 18 Bull Street, was a four-page weekly paper selling for 7d. in 1835, which was reduced to 4½d. when the Stamp Duty was reduced in the following year. *Showell's Dictionary* describes it as Liberal in politics, 'a staunch supporter of the Dissenters, who only supported it for about two years.' This is not quite correct. Joseph Sturge founded the paper to advocate the cause of Emancipation. When slavery was abolished on British territory in 1838, the paper had served its principal purpose; and the further campaign for international Abolition and Suppression of the Slave Trade passed into the capable hands of Lord Palmerston and the Royal Navy.

Feeney accepted an engagement as a reporter on the *Midland Counties Herald*, where he remained seven years, working industriously and saving hard until he was able to buy *The Birmingham Journal* in 1844. Sturge seems to have dropped out of newspaper enterprise entirely, but his career as Radical reformer and philanthropist is written large in the social history of the city and is commemorated by the memorial at Five Ways. He was a moderate, peace-loving politician, having much in common with the progressive, constitutional policy of the *Journal* under Feeney, who may have imbibed his political philosophy from Sturge. After the Chartist movement fell into the hands of the extremist, working-

New Street in 1829

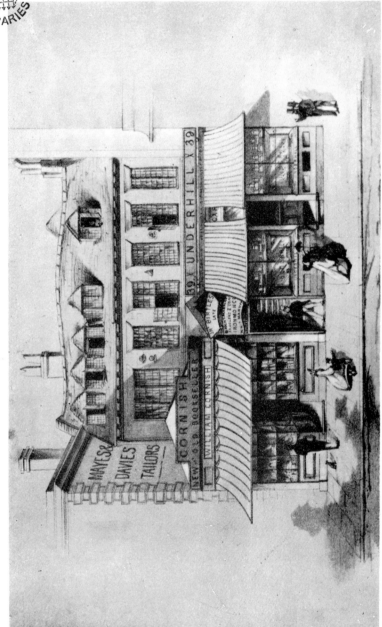

Site of the Office

class leaders from the North and disintegrated in quarrels and disorder, Sturge tried to restore the old alliance by issuing a notable pamphlet, *Reconciliation between the Middle and Labouring Classes*, in 1841. The rift had gone too far in the country at large for healing by pamphlet, but this appeal to reason remained the keynote of Birmingham Radicalism and of the policy of the *Journal* and subsequently of the *Post*.

Nine years later, Joseph Sturge and Feeney's *Journal* were again allied against a wave of popular excitement. The occasion was the turbulent agitation against what was called the 'Papal Aggression', when the Roman Catholic hierarchy in England adopted territorial titles. Tory Churchmen and Radical Nonconformists were equally indignant and the undifferentiated masses were ready to respond once again to the old cry of 'No Popery.' The *Journal* took a bold line in the teeth of popular agitation. It always needs courage to advocate toleration towards bodies that show none. The *Journal* paid for its convictions by a sharp loss in circulation, but by this time, in 1850, it was well enough established to take the shock and eventually to profit in public esteem for its independence and defiance of popular passions. The climax of the agitation in Birmingham was a town's meeting in the Town Hall on December 11, 1850, with the Mayor in the chair. The business was to adopt a strong resolution of protest against the 'Papal Aggression'. There were 8,000 people present and the 'No Popery' element was strong and vocal. Joseph Sturge intervened with an amendment advocating freedom for all parties and opinions. This so split the votes and confused the issue that the Mayor declared that the amendment was not carried and also that the original resolution was lost.

This was the first, but not the only, occasion when the papers under Feeney found themselves opposed to popular clamour on this issue of tolerance for Roman

Catholicism. In 1867 there was another outburst of anti-papal feeling, stirred up by a street-corner agitator and known to history as the 'Murphy Riots'. The newspapers stayed true to their old principles of Liberal tolerance and acted most powerfully for good on an excited and inflamed public. Any temporary unpopularity was soon forgotten and for this further display of courage, consistency and independence the papers and their conductors, proprietorial and editorial, received expressions of confidence and respect from leaders of public life in the city. The reputation thus gained stood the papers in good stead throughout the troublous political times to come.

One curious after-effect that has lasted right on to the present day is a propensity of rumour in the city to ascribe denominational leanings to newcomers to controlling positions on the papers. They crop up from time to time on the flimsiest pretexts. When Jaffray was standing as a Parliamentary candidate for East Staffordshire in 1873, and the Tories, it was said, 'got up a disgraceful riot', the *Post* found it necessary to publish the following:

'It is hardly worth while, perhaps, to take notice of personal rumours; but there are one or two erroneous statements diligently circulated by interested persons in reference to the Liberal candidate for East Staffordshire which should be corrected. Some people are pleased to say that Mr. Jaffray is a Roman Catholic—others that he is a Unitarian—others that he is something else to which they happen to object. Now, we do not think that a man's religious opinions ought to be regarded as any disqualification for Parliament. But in order to set right the false rumours in circulation, we may say that it is entirely untrue that Mr. Jaffray is a Roman Catholic. He is, and always has been, a member of the Church of England, and is actually churchwarden of his parish.'

34

A more recent incident was when E. W. Record became editor of the *Post* in 1933. In the course of the ambassadorial duties a new editor normally undertakes to meet leading members of the community and to make himself known to them, he paid an afternoon call on the then Roman Catholic Archbishop at Archbishop's House, Edgbaston. Afterwards, much to his amusement, he heard that a rumour was going around that he was a Roman Catholic. There was no call to issue a formal contradiction and the rumours soon died a natural death. Similar stories about other and later people associated with the papers have been known and have been quietly scotched in conversation. 'Scratch a Brummie' it has been said, 'and find a Roundhead.' As a matter of fact, most of the men who have held prominent positions on the papers have been Churchmen,—the Feeneys, and the great editor, J. T. Bunce, who nevertheless made most of his friends among the leading Nonconformist divines with whom he worked in the brave days of municipal reform. A newspaper serves the community as a social unit and seeks to give fair and impartial service to all sections, irrespective of party political or religious affiliations. Its staff is composed of men of all denominations, not only because religious opinions are no part of a man's professional qualifications, but because it is an advantage to have on the staff men capable of dealing knowledgeably with the affairs of the various churches and congregations that make up the religious life of the city.

To get back to the first proprietor, John Frederick Feeney had a hard struggle in the early years to keep the *Journal* going. The paper had lost much of its hold on the masses in the collapse of the Chartist movement; and the trade depression faced it with practical difficulties with which the former owners were not well equipped to deal. One catches a glimpse of the new proprietor throwing himself into the work of salvage with immense energy

and ingenuity, supervising and participating in everything from writing and printing to the arrangements for
street sales. It was said that within a matter of months
the circulation responded to his infusion of new life into
the paper. Then there came to his assistance a new
factor, the railway boom of the 'forties, which brought a
flood of advertising into all the newspaper offices. Feeney
had the necessary business acumen to take full advantage
of this windfall and, helped by the gradual revival of
trade, the paper was put on a firm economic foundation.
The circulation, which had been in the region of 1,200
copies a week when he took over became in a few years
12,000. The long Parliamentary notices that had to be
extensively advertised in the districts affected by
proposed railway developments were grist to the mill
throughout the critical years, the promotions on the
Staffordshire side of Birmingham being specially note-
worthy. By the time the Stamp Duties were repealed and
a daily newspaper became a possibility, the *Journal* was
quite a substantial property. It had been enlarged and
improved, was well filled with news and advertisements
and was counted among the leading newspapers of the
provinces. Compared with the struggling, poverty-
stricken circulations of earlier times, its weekly sale in
1857 of 23,000 copies was fabulous. The proprietor who
had made this property from such small beginnings was
ready to launch out into the uncharted seas of daily
newspaper production.

Meanwhile, the man he had brought to Birmingham
in 1844 to help on the literary side of the newly-acquired
Journal had developed a strong business capacity to go
with his writing ability. In 1852 Feeney had taken him
into partnership with a one-third share in the business
and John Jaffray had taken what he always described
as the first step on the ladder that led to his remarkable
success in life. The partnership agreement of 1852 was
for 21 years, with provision for determination earlier at

36

stated intervals and with customary arrangements for the sons of partners to succeed. The capital was to be divided with two-thirds to Feeney and one-third to Jaffray, and the profits and losses in the same proportion. It is interesting to read the valuation of the capital assets in 1852. They amounted to a total of £2,100. The copyright was valued at a nominal £5, the printing presses accounted for £600, book debts £300 and the remainder was assigned to the steam engines, type, plant, stock, etc. A curious arrangement was that the premises at what was then known as 37½ New Street remained the property of Feeney, who was to receive a rent of £150 per annum for them. This retention by the senior partner of the properties, the real essential assets, was repeated in the 1872 deed of partnership between Feeney's son and Jaffray and remained a feature of the accounting arrangements until the business was taken over by the present proprietors and turned into a limited liability company. It meant that when John Feeney and subsequently Charles Hyde were sole proprietors they paid themselves a rent from the business, a matter of transferring money from one pocket to another.

Within a few years of becoming a partner, Jaffray began to make his mark in the city as a business man and a public figure. It used to be said of him that everything he touched seemed to turn to gold and, later in his life, that there was no movement in Birmingham,— political, social, literary, artistic or philanthropical,—in which he had not been engaged. He was a tremendous worker, credited with at times passing fifty hours without rest or respite at his work and, in the early days of struggle, writing and setting up in type his articles for the paper. It was said of him that he could do anything on the paper, from stoking the boiler to writing a leader. Born at Stirling in 1818, he went to Glasgow High School and, therefore, received a better education than most of his contemporaries. He came to England to serve

37

as a reporter on a newspaper at Shrewsbury owned by a relative. According to his own account, he arrived in Birmingham in 1844 to take up the post on the *Journal* offered him by Feeney with £20 as his entire wordly possessions. He died fifty-seven years later a very wealthy man, a baronet with the tastes and possessions of a country gentleman. It was a success story typical of the expansive days of the second half of the nineteenth century. Barrie might have had John Jaffray in mind when he wrote that there are few more impressive sights in the world than a Scotsman on the make. Unquestionably, he was impressive; a forceful, striking figure, a good speaker, clear in statement, happy in illustration and earnest in manner. It would be wearisome to list the many public positions he held in the city. As early as 1857, when he was responsible for the editorial direction of the newly-founded *Post*, he was one of those who invited John Bright to accept a Birmingham constituency after the Radical leader had been rejected by Manchester because of his pacifism during the Crimean War. The association thus formed ripened into a close friendship. Bright was staying with Jaffray when he was offered a post in Gladstone's administration of 1868. He was reluctant to give up his freedom in the House of Commons and poured out his heart-searchings to his host. He walked up and down the room talking and talking till the hours flew past and it became late. Jaffray was an early man and could not conceal his growing weariness. Bright saw what was happening and, with a nice touch of humour, made for the chandelier and said: 'I see, Jaffray, that you will never go to bed till I turn off the gas.' It may be added that Bright accepted Gladstone's invitation to join the Government.

Jaffray's politics were unambiguously Liberal. He was an inner member of the party organisation and took an active part in the formation of the Liberal Association. He was invited several times to become a Parlia-

38

mentary candidate, but apart from the one unsuccessful candidature at East Staffordshire in 1873, he declined all such offers. He preferred, so it was said, the position of a political King-maker in the Midlands to that of a legislator at Westminster. But that was not the whole truth. He was a Liberal of the old school, who had advocated repeal of the Corn Laws, free trade, religious freedom, national education and extensions of the franchise. Despite his close connections with the 'Caucus' there were some aspects of the developing political scene in the late 'seventies and later that he found distasteful. It was typical of his liberal-mindedness and of the esteem in which he was held that he remained President of the Tory Blue Coat School at a time when such essentially non-political offices of a charitable and philanthropic kind tended to be filled on party lines.

Writing to his partner, John Feeney, in 1878, he spices a business letter with a piece of local gossip that reveals his concern with the direction of events. 'You will see by the paper I send you', he wrote, 'that there has been a pretty row between some of our great people here. There was a disposition to elect for the Grammar School Governors some who were not in the Town Council— Dixon amongst others. But Chamberlain opposed this; chose eight from the Council. Dixon exploded, attacked Chamberlain publicly at the School Board and the row is indescribable. I believe it will split up the party, as, outside, the people are profoundly displeased with the exclusion of Dixon. The affair will not be wholly useless if it checks that spirit of personal dictation that has been rampant of late'. He adds, playfully, 'So you see that though *you* are absent there is still a spirit of mischief left amongst us.' The split in the party came, sure enough, but not on the issue of Chamberlain's 'personal dicta- tion' over Grammar School Governors. When disruption over Home Rule came in 1886, the hesitations and dilemmas in the minds of faithful Liberals were all the

39

greater because they had had their doubts about the methods of the local party machine as long ago as this letter of 1878. It provides one reason why Jaffray was disinclined to seek Parliamentary honours after the one essay in 1873. True, he and the paper eventually followed Chamberlain into the Unionist camp, as will be told in due course; but the choice was made reluctantly and with much heart-searching.

Jaffray, the public man of affairs, tends to eclipse the newspaper proprietor and to outshine his retiring partners in business. He was the outward and visible symbol of the paper in the eyes of the public. It was to him that George Dawson and other leaders of Liberal thought presented an address and a collection of books in recognition of the steady stand the paper had made against the anti-papal scare; and he was publicly honoured for the sturdy independence that made the *Post* one of the few English newspapers to espouse, on Liberal principles, the then unpopular cause of the North in the American Civil War. No doubt these public tributes were well deserved and were meant to include his co-proprietor and the editor of the paper. All were jointly responsible for policy. No evidence exists to show how the decisions were arrived at or who, if anybody, had a major share in the inner councils of the office. It is, however, right to point out that the Feeneys, father and son, were men of the highest principles and that the editor, John Thackray Bunce, had thrown up his first editorship on a point of principle. One can deduce the influence of Jaffray in shaping policy from his public career, but the credit, whenever due, for policy decisions is to be shared among all concerned.

A friend who was intimately acquainted with him described Jaffray, after his death, as 'a curious mixture of shrewd commercialism and kind-heartedness'. He could be stern and exacting, but generous in ways which are often more serviceable to the recipients than gifts of money. An anonymous 'open letter' addressed to him

40

in the *Town Crier* of October, 1883, credited Jaffray with a keen appreciation of talent and perseverance and a readiness to help those who deserve help and show some disposition to help themselves. This 'open letter', impudently personal and critical, agrees that, 'in spite of your success and power, you are a modest, unaffected man'. To the end of his working life,—he retired in 1894 at the age of 75 and died in 1901—he was actively engaged in the daily affairs of the paper. Neither his public activities and extensive business interests, nor his great enjoyment of country life and farming on his estate at Skilts, near Redditch, and his delight in field sports, came between him and the newspaper. He remained to the end a newspaper man at heart, of whom it could be said, in the jargon of the trade, that 'he had printer's ink in his veins'. He was to be seen about the office at all hours, watching and commenting on the fascinating process of 'putting the paper to bed'. Mrs. Gertrude Bailey, daughter of a compositor, James Watts Gent, who served on the paper for over fifty years, recalls a story about Jaffray that illustrates his interest and humour:

'Sir John Jaffray was walking round the composing room and came to Dad. "Turn your back round, Mr. Gent, and look at me", he said. "You see that old man over there with the long whiskers? Well, he is fool enough to think I am fool big enough to think he is pouring tea out of that teapot, when I saw him, a little while ago, empty a bottle of beer into the pot." He said he was so amused, he had to share the joke with someone, and so he came to Dad.'

With all the serious, almost formidable, qualities that went into his make-up and fashioned his remarkable career, Jaffray was a genial man with a keen sense of fun. When he retired, neither of his sons succeeded to him in the business and the family departed from the Midlands. His name is perpetuated in Birmingham by the Jaffray

Hospital at Erdington, a branch of the General Hospital which he built especially for chronic cases. It was opened in 1885 by the Prince of Wales, later King Edward the Seventh. The City Art Gallery is indebted to him very largely for the celebrated 'Warwickshire Drawings' by David Cox and other possessions he was instrumental in securing for the public collection. Jaffray had a very sound judgment in works of art. He was a friend of David Cox when the painter lived in a cottage at Harborne and he made a choice collection of pictures for himself. The multifarious interests and wide-ranging activities and enthusiasms of these intensely vital Victorian businessmen are still something to marvel at and to envy.

5

The Daily Paper

FEENEY AND JAFFRAY HAD IN THE *Journal* of 1857 a sound foundation to build on. Two years before, when the Stamp Duty was abolished, the *Journal* was expanded into a twice-weekly paper, the main Saturday edition being reduced to 4d. and a smaller mid-week paper costing 2d. was published on Wednesdays. The partners were fully employed in bringing out and promoting the sales of this paper. On publishing nights Feeney himself helped with 'making up' in the composing room and getting the paper to press. After seeing the pages on to the printing presses, he went round the town visiting the newsagents and was particularly concerned to see that they had a sufficient supply of contents bills, which were studied carefully by the working people in those days and were the principal selling agency.

The *Journal*, with a sale of 23,000 copies, was making a substantial profit. Grant's *History of the Newspaper Press* (1871) is the authority. 'I do not at this distance of time,' the author writes, 'remember whether it was the late Mr. Feeney himself who mentioned the fact to me, but it was mentioned that the profits of *The Birmingham Journal* were for a long time not much under £5,000 per annum. This was a large sum for a weekly paper,'— and a large income for the Irish and Scottish proprietors who had built it up from such humble beginnings. The venture into daily production was a daring move, with no great body of general experience to draw upon. As always, London was no guide, as conditions in the capital were, and still are, very different from those in a provincial city. The partners were setting out on an uncharted sea. They may well have been anxious lest the daily should jeopardise the position they had won for the

43

weekly. 'The circumstances in which they did so (launched *The Birmingham Daily Post*)', says Grant in his *History*, 'have much of interesting history in them; but as I have not received the consent of the gentlemen by whom they were communicated to me to make them public, I forbear doing so.' This tantalising hint of interesting knowledge is rather typical of the whole story of the paper. Such discretion fourteen years after the event may have had some point at the time; but it meant that the 'interesting history' was lost once for all.

However, the outcome of the partners' deliberations was that the daily began in quite a tentative way, and with due regard to the interests of the flourishing *Journal*. Saturday was still kept sacred for the *Journal*, though the mid-week edition was dropped. The *Post*, a comparatively small four-page paper with six columns to a page, came out on the other five days of the working week. As experience accumulated, the *Daily Post* encroached on Saturday and, in addition, the proprietors issued another paper, the *Saturday Evening Post*, using for this purpose some of the matter that had appeared during the week and supplementing it with stories and light reading. By 1869 enough experience had been gathered to clear up the complications. The *Daily Post* was published on six days a week and the two Saturday papers were merged into one, called the *Birmingham Weekly Post*. The *Journal* ceased to appear as a separate paper, a decision scarcely taken without a pang after twenty-five years; though for some time its name was printed along with that of the *Birmingham Daily Post*. It survives to-day in the designation of the Journal Printing Office, the commercial printing works belonging to the firm. This reorganisation in 1869 cleared the way for another extension of newspaper enterprise the next year, when an evening paper was published in response to the demand for news of the fighting in the Franco-Prussian War of 1870. The *Birmingham Daily Mail*, as it was first called, proved to be in the true line of succession of Feeney-Jaffray enterprise. Being addressed to a mass readership, the evening soon outstripped its parents in circulation and became in due course the commercial pillar of the business structure.

In 1918, the word *Daily* was dropped from the titles of both papers, as by that time the novelty of issuing a newspaper every day had worn off. The *Post* was not the first daily paper to appear in Birmingham. Immediately after the repeal of the Stamp Duty in 1855, a small company was formed and launched the *Birmingham Daily Press*. The similarity of title has led to much confusion, especially as several of those concerned in this earliest daily paper enterprise subsequently were associated with the *Post*. The most prominent members of the company were George Dawson, the distinguished Nonconformist Minister; William Harris, Radical author and politician, who became a vigorous leader-writer for the *Post*; and Dr. James Freeman, an authoritative writer on statistical subjects, who also was a contributor to the *Post* in later years. The *Birmingham Daily Press* got away to a flying start and became well established in the first year or two. It was a serious, well-written paper, in tune with the radical, reformist atmosphere of the time; but none of those concerned with it seem to have had much practical experience in the business aspects of newspaper production. Its amalgamation in 1857 with the *Birmingham Mercury* appears to have provided a favourable opportunity for the *Journal's* proprietors to start their rival daily paper. For some time the *Post* made little impression, so Jaffray is reported to have said in later years. But a change came before long. The proprietors of the *Post*, being able and experienced newspaper men, 'drove the town, not from pillar to post, but from *Daily Press* to *Daily Post*', as Anderton puts it in *A Tale of One City* (1900). The *Daily Press* fell into a decline and expired somewhat suddenly in November 1858. Its victorious and unsympathetic rival remarked that 'it went out like the snuff of a candle, leaving behind it something of the flavour of that domestic nuisance.' George Dawson, who had lost money through the failure of the *Daily Press*, thought the *Post's* obituary notice spiteful. To crow over the vanquished in this fashion appeared to him worse than ungenerous; it was mean. He cannot have had much knowledge of the amenities of newspaper competition in the first half of the 19th century, when rivalries were fierce and personal, and the barbed comment of the *Post* in 1858 would have seemed feeble in the extreme. Dawson recovered from the disappointment and in the times to come he and the *Post* became the best of friends and devoted allies in the famous campaigns for municipal reform.

On Saturday, November 21, 1857, the *Journal* announced with a flourish the forthcoming publication of 'A Daily Newspaper to be called *The Birmingham Daily Post*,' price One Penny. The first issue was to appear on Friday, 4th December, the day following the opening of Parliament for a new session, with the Queen's Speech from the Throne as a principal feature for news and comment. The announcement goes on to develop into a proclamation of purpose, not without a note of challenge: 'The projectors of this new journal think they see in the circumstances of the times a necessity for the immediate communication to the Public, in a succinct and reliable form, of the current news of the day. Without disparaging in any way the efforts of those who have hitherto endeavoured to supply this want (a gesture in the direction of the *Daily Press*), it may be assumed that the public will be benefitted by that wholesome competition which rivalry provokes, and as the Projectors have had considerable experience in local journalism, they venture to think that they can, to some extent at least, render still more valuable to the commercial interests of the town and district, and to the general reader, the system

46

of cheap Daily Newspapers.

'The Proprietors of the *Daily Post*, while they will record the proceedings, advocate the interests, and reflect the opinions of the great community which constitutes the capital of this district, have made arrangements for the receipt of prompt and accurate intelligence from all the towns in the three counties with which Birmingham is more immediately connected, so as to render the *Post* as acceptable to the Manufacturer and Trader in Staffordshire and Worcestershire and to the Farmer in Warwickshire, as it will be to the varied interests in Birmingham. The Proprietors of the *Post* have also made arrangements for the fullest Telegraphic Intelligence, for Commercial and Trading Reports, for despatches from London, Liverpool, etc., and for original reports of all the Racing Meetings.'

They then go on to explain the other new paper, the *Saturday Evening Post*, price three half-pence. It will contain, they promise, 'a *resumé* of all the News of the Week, printed on a large and handsome sheet. This weekly publication is specially intended to meet the wants of the great body of the working classes, whose necessities, it is evident, are not to any great extent supplied by the existing papers.' (*The Birmingham Journal* still cost 4d.) 'Large as the circulation of *The Birmingham Journal* is,' the manifesto continues, 'it would be four times greater if it found its way into every working man's household in Birmingham alone; while the daily papers, useful as they are, record the news of the day only, and therefore do not supply the wants of those whose time and money limit them to a weekly acquaintance with public events. It is intended that the *Saturday Evening Post* shall supply this want. It will be published at a lower price even than the cheap London Journals; while in size and appearance it will bear comparison with any of its contemporaries. Great care will be taken to make its contents generally interesting and the

47

local news, which the London newspapers, of course, cannot give, and which is of the first importance to the working men of the town and district, will be fully reported. No pretence to dogmatism of opinion, and no sectarian views, will be pressed upon the reader. It will be a newspaper in the broadest sense of the word, a record of events rather than a vehicle of opinion. As its name implies, it has been resolved to publish the *Saturday Evening Post* at Five o'clock on Saturday afternoon. This arrangement, while avoiding competition with existing journals, will enable the Proprietors to publish all the news of Saturday down to a late hour, and thus make the paper a complete record of the week's news. The hour has been fixed so as to meet the convenience of the great mass of the public, as it is hoped that the working man after his week's labour will carry a copy home with him to his fireside, and enjoy with his family the cheap luxury of becoming acquainted with the incidents and opinions, the joys and the sorrows, the virtues and the crimes, which form the daily life of the busy world around him.'

After a brief recapitulation of the principal points of the announcement, including a statement that 'the *Daily Post* will be published at Five o'clock in the morning, and should be on the breakfast table of every subscriber in town and country,' the Proprietors address themselves to an important section of the community, the Advertisers. This paragraph throws an interesting sidelight on some newspaper practices of that day:

'The practice of filling a given space with advertisements day by day, whether these are legitimate or not, is in no sense of the word fair to the public. It is a disingenuous pretence, and it is an occupation of space with matter of no interest to the general reader. This practice the Proprietors of the *Post* will not adopt. They will be glad to publish all advertisements with which the public may favour them; and they hope to make their paper so universally acceptable as to

48

John Frederick Feeney

Birmingham News Room

justify the expectation that all announcements intended to reach the great body of the reading public of Birmingham and the district will be inserted in its columns.

'For repeated insertion of advertisements a liberal discount will be allowed; varying, of course, with the number of repetitions.'

This is a convenient moment to anticipate events and trace, as far as possible, the developments of advertising in the early critical years of the new daily paper's existence. For without a flow of advertising the venture could never have succeeded. The advertising public in Birmingham had been accustomed to weekly papers and apparently had no faith in, or saw no reason for, advertising in the ephemeral daily sheets. For some time they fought shy of the new medium and for the first year their announcements rarely occupied more than three columns, which appeared, not on the front page, but on the third, inside, page. The Proprietors announced that no wood engravings would be admitted into the *Post*. 'The advertisements, being limited in number and appearing in the best position in our columns, will obtain a prominence which can scarcely be enhanced by pictorial illustrations.' Nevertheless, they waived their own rule in the case of shipping advertisements. Already the shipping interests had established in the newspapers generally a customary right to embellish their announcements with diminutive woodcuts of paddle steamers with two masts and sails and a lofty funnel and three-masted full-rigged sailing ships, neither of which look very impressive to modern eyes. The *Post* conformed to tradition in this respect, much to the improvement, it may be thought, of its advertising columns.

The first anniversary of the *Post* was the occasion for a paragraph entitled 'A Word About Ourselves', which reflected the continuing anxiety of the Proprietors over the slow growth of advertising. 'Of course, there is not much margin of profit in a cheap publication like this,' it runs, in a burst of candour, 'and to some extent its success depends upon its advertisements. In the provinces —and, indeed, in the metropolis—the habit of daily advertising has not yet been acquired; while in America, and even in the colony of Australia, the newspapers are crowded day by day with announcements of the wants of the community and the markets for their supply. We have not yet been trained to the appreciation of the fact that the very essence of business consists in bringing buyer and seller together, and in no way can it be done so economically and effectively as by advertising. In Birmingham we are beginning to understand that principle, as our columns day by day convincingly show.'

Another twelve months were to justify the confident contradiction embedded in that last sentence. Birmingham advertisers overcame their suspicions of the new medium. Their announcements on page three steadily encroached on the news columns until they engulfed the whole page. Their number was greatly increased by a shrewd business stroke, the adoption of a cheap pre-payment rate for announcements of the 'Wanted' class. They overflowed on to page two and the time was ripe for a drastic change in the appearance of the paper.

New machinery,—the Hoe press, an American invention—was introduced. Its great feature was that the type itself was fastened to a central cylinder and the flat table was dispensed with. From about a thousand an hour with the old flat-bed Cowper machine, production went up to five thousand papers an hour. Printing was still on single sheets of paper, on one side of the paper only, and the sheets had to be passed through the machine again to print on the reverse side. However, the Hoe was a great advance on anything that had gone before. The *Post* was one of the first papers in the provinces to be printed on the Hoe press and two of these machines sufficed until 1873, when the revolutionary Walter press that prints from stereotype plates on a continuous band of paper came into use. Again the *Post* was the first English newspaper outside London to equip itself with the new invention, being beaten, in the British Isles, by the *Scotsman* by a short head; and, of course, by the inventors in London, *The Times*. The basic principle of the Walter press remains to this day the system of all newspaper printing. Speed of printing has increased many times and the motive power has changed from steam to electricity, but the newspaper is still produced on a continuous band of paper, the web, from semi-circular stereotype plates cast from the original type and bolted to the revolving cylinders.

Towards the end of 1859, then, the paper was equipped with new machinery, which incidentally produced a larger sheet, and the advertisements were bursting the bounds of page three.

On November 28 the paper came out with the entire *front* page filled with advertisements and assumed the characteristic appearance which it wore until September 23rd, 1946, when the usurper was ousted from the most prominent position and news resumed its sway on the front page. This piece of 'make-up' history is peculiarly interesting because the press as a whole endowed the changes of 1859 and thereabouts with an almost sacred significance. A solid front page of small advertisements came to be regarded as a mark of respectability, the equivalent in print of the Victorian frock-coat. When the popular half-penny newspapers defied sartorial convention towards the end of the 19th century, they automatically labelled themselves as 'yellow' and 'sensational'; though it is curious that Northcliffe, with one of his unexpected touches of conservatism, stuck to the old convention—and made a very good thing out of it. The same opprobious terms have been applied in turn to every serious paper that has discarded the frock-coat and put the principal news of the day on the front page,

51

where it can be seen at a glance and induce people to buy the paper to read on buses or in trains. The very English habit of investing practical and familiar things with moral qualities was never better illustrated than in this matter of news or advertisements on the front page. Advertisements won the day in 1859 for strictly practical and commercial reasons. In our time news has returned to enjoy its own again for similar reasons, dictated by changed public habits and a business-like appreciation of public tastes.

Looking back over the years, and looking through the files, one cannot avoid the conclusion that the press as a whole stifled initiative and hampered its development when it wrapped itself in a wet-blanket of respectability. The inside pages became as dull in appearance as the closely-printed front page. Efforts to lighten them and make them more readable were cramped by a supposed need to 'conform to style' and could never go beyond a certain modest degree of display. No matter how important and exciting the news, it had to be set out in sober, straight up-and-down columns, with headlines multiplied vertically and very rarely across even two columns. 'Any innovation whatever, though ever so much to their advantage,' wrote Captain James Cook in 1769, 'is sure to meet with the highest disapprobation from seamen.' One hundred years later those who conducted newspapers were sinking into the same state of mind as the sailors of Captain Cook's day. And they were forgetting the past of their riotous profession and smothering a great deal of good writing and vigorous journalism under a deadly typographical shroud. It would be a mistake to assume that the contents of these Mid-Victorian newspapers are as dull as they look. On the contrary, they will repay the effort of reading; but it is an effort. So, by the end of 1859 the *Post* had turned the corner and the owners knew they were making their fortune.

6

The First Post

AT ANY TIME FROM 1860 ONWARDS, the conductors of the *Post* would willingly have disowned their earliest papers, for they were sadly lacking in gravity. News, the life-blood of a newspaper, was a desperately scarce commodity until the Telegraph Act of 1869, authorised the Postmaster-General to buy up the several telegraph undertakings. Until then, provincial newspapers had to bargain with the competing companies; charges were high and the appliances for transmission were extremely primitive. Telegraphic news in the *Post* and other provincial papers amounted to no more than a column or so. A supply that was scarcely adequate for a weekly newspaper was wholly insufficient for a paper publishing on five or six days a week. It had to be supplemented by local news gathered by a small staff of reporters, by news articles sent through the post and by wholesale clippings from small weekly newspapers from all over the country. A great change came about when the Post Office took over the telegraph system. The provincial newspapers in 1870 formed the Press Association, a co-operative news gathering and distributing agency. The proprietors of the *Post* took part in the formation of this organisation and from that time the paper had access daily to news from all parts of the United Kingdom. The Press Association also distributed the foreign news service of Reuter's Agency, an organisation founded in 1847 by a Jewish bank clerk, Paul Julius Reuter, at Aachen and soon afterwards transferred to London. This was, in effect, a public extension of the private news arrangements of the great international banking houses in Europe that went back centuries and are best known from the famous Fugger Letters of 1568 to 1604, a priceless source of historical material.

53

The Press Association and Reuter's Agency transformed the news situation. From scarcity there grew an abundance of straight, factual news and reporting, kept on the highest level of accuracy and objectivity by the fact that the services were taken by newspapers of every shade of political opinion and with every variety of interests. Verbatim reports of all important speeches in the country and full reports of the proceedings in Parliament were circulated over the public wires. With them came a vast supply of miscellaneous news pouring into the newspaper offices. Before long, papers had to build up large staffs of sub-editors to select, revise and arrange this flood of material. Far from having to scratch around to find news to fill their columns, the papers were searching for space to print the news material that demanded admission. Towards the end of the 19th century another copious flow of news came over the private wires,—that is, wires hired from the Post Office for their exclusive use,—installed by newspapers, like the *Post*, with their own London Offices, which connected head offices in provincial cities with the metropolitan offices for as many hours in the day and night as they cared to keep the lines open.

These developments, however, were remote from the pioneers in 1857. They were thrown on their own resources to fill their four pages and they showed much ingenuity in doing so. The front page of the first *Post* contained six columns. The leading column was filled with small items of official news,—Foreign Intelligence, scraps from the Court Circular and formal reports of the social activities and bustle preceding the opening of Parliament. Lord Granville gave 'a grand Parliamentary dinner at his mansion in Bruton Street' and Lord Palmerston 'entertained his Parliamentary supporters at Cambridge House.' At both these gatherings the Queen's Speech, to be delivered the following day in Parliament, was read to the company. The Speech had been pre-

54

viously approved by the Privy Council, and the privileged gatherings were private. Nowadays a Prime Minister does not communicate the Queen's Speech to anybody except Cabinet Ministers; and the 'grand Parliamentary dinners', when they are held, are deprived of this *bonne bouche*.

Incidentally, the readers of the *Post* also had to curb their impatience, for the Queen's Speech was not printed on the front page, but on the back. There was, however, a solid bit of reading on the front, a long report of the monthly meeting of Queen's College and Hospital in the end columns. In the middle of the page was a jumble of small paragraphs of law reports, commercial and monetary intelligence, inquests and bankruptcies. Small type, close-set lines, diminutive side-heads and a very few stock headings across a column in black Gothic type, presented a formidable, but curiously inviting, mass of reading matter. There were some pearls to be found in this rag-bag. 'Extraordinary Case of Sacrilege', ran a small side-head. It was, indeed. A soldier from Chatham barracks had had a night out. 'I had been to a sort of free-and-easy with some sappers whom I knew at Sebastopol', he told the court at Maidstone Assizes, 'and they were going to India to-morrow. I had a drop of drink extra.' On the way back to barracks he grew thirsty, saw a church, thought of the water in the font, broke in, lit a fire in the vestry, burned his old shirt and put on two surplices. Disappointed of a drink, he emerged from the church into the arms of the law. Sentence, 12 months. No interest to Birmingham? Well, that's a matter of opinion and at least it was entertaining. By the bottom of column three, Birmingham comes into the picture with a 'Suspected Garotte Murder at Lozells.' There were plenty of these garotting crimes reported on the front pages of the early *Posts*, complete with grisly details. This first case, however, was memorable for the evidence given by a Mr. Goodall, house surgeon at the General

55

Hospital. He gave it as his opinion that the victim had died from 'a violent blow on the head, inflicted by some blunt instrument.' Failing any other claimants to the honour, we may venture to credit Mr. Goodall with the original authorship of this hallowed phrase.

Passing rather reluctantly over a Police Court report enticingly labelled 'A Blackguard Properly Punished', it is time to turn the page and get to the more serious affairs of life. Page Two was the heart of the paper, for it carried a leading article wherein the *Post* made its bow to the public and proclaimed the principles and practices it meant to follow. As this is an historic document, it deserves to be quoted in full.

'Nearly fourteen years ago' the article begins, 'the Proprietors of the paper launched to-day became connected with *The Birmingham Journal*. During these years they have continued to conduct that paper, with what result to the public the popularity it enjoys is perhaps the best evidence. This long association with the public interests of the locality, and the weekly proofs we have given of the spirit in which events are recorded and discussed, relieve us from the necessity of accompanying the first issue of a daily candidate for public favour with a profession of faith or an explanation of the mode in which it is proposed that the new journal shall be conducted. Fortunately for us we are the organ of no sect or party in politics, in religion, or in civic affairs, and can therefore exercise an independent judgment on all matters that come before us, without reference to the opinions of any individuals or parties. It is true that such a position sometimes involves an antagonism with those whose opinions coincide with our own, and it has secured for us no inconsiderable amount of obloquy. Still, we have chosen our course and we intend to adhere to it; for, besides being the more agreeable as it is the more honest, it is in the end the most profitable, a considera-

56

tion of which we are not ashamed, notwithstanding the good-natured sneers levelled at those who, like ourselves, expect to receive an equivalent for their labours.

'As the *Journal* has been conducted, so it is proposed to conduct the *Daily Post*, with this difference in favour of the public, that many local matters which we have either overlooked, or, from the small space at our command, treated more summarily than their importance required, will now have ample justice done to them. With this in view we have greatly increased our reporting staff, so as to ensure for the *Post* the same reputation for accuracy which has gained for the *Journal* the authoritative character it now enjoys as a chronicle of the sentiments of the public men, and of the occurrencies of the town and district. We shall also endeavour to maintain and enhance the character of our political commentaries, and, as we hope to show, the business department of the paper, that which possesses interest for the capitalist, the trader and the manufacturer, will be carefully attended to.

'In issuing the *Post* it is chiefly the intention of meeting the public demand for the news of the day, and we commence our daily career with a sheet that admits of indefinite expansion. At present and for some time we do not expect, we might almost say we scarcely hope, that the advertisements will press inconveniently on the space devoted to news. We pledge ourselves that so soon as the necessity arises for enlarging this sheet, either from an increase of advertisements, or from an influx of news which demands more space for its due treatment, that moment the dimensions of the paper will be increased. In the space at present at our command, we believe we can embrace all that is of essential interest in the current news of the day, and we have no intention of wasting our space, or the time of our readers, by the occupation of these columns with matter which is not useful, either in the sense of being amusing or instructive.

'We owe no apology, and we offer none, to those of our own craft who object to this extension of our influence and, as we believe, of our usefulness. We think that there is room enough for all of us, and if there is not, a preliminary trial of a few years will decide, as it has long ago decided in the case of the *Journal*, which of us best appreciates the wants of the public, and supplies them. We enter on our new duties in perfect good humour with our newspaper critics, and, we may add, in profound indifference as to whether that feeling is or is not reciprocated. There are abundance of common grounds of agreement and difference upon which we can co-operate or disagree without descending to the arena of personal recriminations, and to that limit we shall try to confine the commentaries of the *Post*.

'In another column we have ventured to publish a letter bearing upon the conduct of this paper, which anticipates to some extent the course we intend to pursue, and we notice it here to remark that while we cannot consent to disguise our own opinions in the form of letters, but will, as heretofore, treat minor topics under the head of "Local Notes," we invite the expression of individual opinion on all questions of public interest. No inconsiderable share of the interest which attaches to our London contemporaries is due to the stores of information contributed by private correspondents, and we shall be glad in like manner to make our columns available to all such who seek to address the public in a spirit of moderation and fairness.

'With these general remarks, demanded more by custom than by the necessities of the case, we set about our work, trusting that long before the expiry of another term of fourteen years we shall have many occasions to thank the public for their liberal appreciation of our services on their behalf.'

A straightforward, level-headed, businesslike statement. There is no starry-eyed idealism about it, no
parade of lofty sentiments or professions of high-minded
zeal for the public cause. The proprietors set out to
produce a paper which would be 'useful' and they did
not disdain to suggest that it might also be 'amusing'.
Their concern with the business interests of the community is manifest and, as businessmen addressing their
like, they were quite frank about expecting 'to receive an
equivalent for their labours.' At the same time, they
repudiated all forms of disguise or subterfuge, even the
comparatively harmless device of airing their own views
under the cloak of 'Letters to the Editor', written in
the office.

The correspondent whose letter provoked this declaration was the first of a company of friends who are always
with us in a newspaper office. In the kindest manner
possible, though at inordinate length, 'M. Justicia' of
King Edward's Road, Birmingham, proffered advice to
the editor on how he should run his paper. 'There is one
point to which I wish to call your attention with regard
to the leaders,' he wrote towards the end of his long
screed. 'Never introduce minor subjects into your
leaders; these degrade a paper perhaps more than anything else. They show the imbecility of the editor. Rather
than small subjects should occupy your leading space,
I would treat such subjects in letters written under
fictitious names; then they would not spoil the dignity
of your leaders. The leaders should assume a manly
dignity—something that the most intelligent can *look
up to* as the "higher powers"; and I would rather have
only one leader, *good and strong* in each paper than half-
a-dozen poor and weak.' It is to be hoped 'M. Justicia'
was satisfied with the 'Local Notes' proposed by the
editor, for he meant well and made some good points,
obvious though they must have been to the shrewd and

59

experienced newspaper men to whom they were addressed. He implored them to pay attention to the printing of the paper. 'You will not have failed to notice the causes which put an end to the *Daily Mercury*. It is my opinion that nothing contributed so much to, and hastened the annihilation of, the *Daily Mercury* as the bad materials of which it was composed, viz., its paper, ink, and typography. I gave up taking the *Daily Mercury* because I found it impossible to read it. I have taken the *Daily Press* in from the first, and this is not that I think its matter is better than was that of the *Mercury*, but because I could read it. Still, the *Daily Press* is very far from being up to the mark which I wish and expect the *Post* to reach.' He really need not have had any qualms. The early *Posts* are admirably printed on good quality paper which has kept its colour remarkably well. Those in the files are as legible to-day as they ever were and the setting is enviably free from typographical errors.

A very different tone was struck by another correspondent who hid his identity under the simple initial, 'B'. He gave the new paper a hearty, not to say flamboyant, welcome. 'Holding, as we all do, the great cosmopolitan creed that the nation alone is unfettered that has an open Bible and a free newspaper, there should ever be a ready recognition of the friends of the one and an honest and spontaneous welcome to the originators of the other. Whether it be a *Little Pedlington Gazette* in arms against the tyranny of a parish vestry or wrathfully rebuking the superciliousness of a local lord, or whether it be a metropolitan censor, dignified, severe and just, correcting the impertinences of continental critics, it is alike the national broadsheet, and has the foremost claim on our sympathies and help. The press is, after all, our true strength,—thinking for us, fighting for us, working for us, suffering for us,—a fine type of the great restless, agitated heart of this mighty empire, and the fit guarantee of its aspirations and destinies . . . .

60

'Locally there is surely a sphere for your labours in representing the wishes and requirements of a quarter of a million of people. Birmingham is a long-tongued town, and if it has forgotten its greatness, it has still its loquacity, and contrives at least to manifest traditional animation by its everlasting talk. If you will help to report this, we may see ourselves as others see us, and a little improvement may be the result. Our counsels, however, are superfluous, as we have the fullest confidence that you will give us a paper of which, neither as citizens or countrymen, we shall have cause to be ashamed.'

Under 'Notices to Correspondents' one finds a tactful answer to a certain 'H.C.' that will find an echo in the hearts of most modern editors. The earnest enthusiast is always with us. 'It is quite possible' the editor in 1857 reflected, 'to degrade things sacred by the familiar treatment of them in a newspaper, and, therefore, while we appreciate the earnestness of our correspondent, we do not feel justified in adopting his suggestion. We may be week-day preachers without importing religion as such into the *Post*.'

Page Three is conspicuous for the three columns of advertisements that foreshadowed greater things to come and reflected some facets of contemporary life in Birmingham. At the head was an announcement by Lambon & Sons that was of particular concern to the paper. They begged to state 'that they have organised "*Post* traps" to enable them to supply the *Daily Post* in time for the Breakfast Table, throughout Birmingham, Edgbaston, Harborne, etc.' The embryo, in fact, of our present fleet of motor vans that distribute the paper far and wide during the small hours and much beyond 'Edgbaston, Harborne, etc.', the limits for pony traps.

The entertainments available to Birmingham folk at that time were severely limited. At the Theatre Royal 'Sir William and Lady Don will appear in comedy, melodrama and farce.' Pell's Opera Troupe (nine in

61

number) 'will continue their elegant Drawing Room Entertainment every evening at 8 at the Gallery of Illustration, New Street, including a lecture on mesmerism, burlesque opera and acrobats.' A third and last choice for an evening's dissipation was offered by the Concert Hall, Coleshill Street, where a 'powerful attraction" was a 'grand ballet divertissement.' For those of a more serious turn of mind there were lectures on religion and temperance, and cattle and poultry shows. Interspersed with these announcements, and with no attempt at classification, were some singularly unalluring trade advertisements, of which 'Gentlemen requiring very superior hats by the most eminent makers should apply at Paris House, 13, Snow Hill,' was the least alarming. Not ladies' hats, be it noted, at Paris House. The feminine market was ignored by the first advertisers. One could obtain from traders patent medicines, goloshes and waterproofs and one shop proudly offered 'Artificial teeth at 10s. each. Never change colour or decay.' An entirely local product that, it is safe to guess, would not be found advertised in any other city, was 'A Patent Metallic Air-tight Coffin' the advantages of which were described in terms we should consider a trifle macabre. At the bottom of the column came the light relief in the shape of the only illustrations in the paper, the small woodcuts of the shipping announcements. The Steamship Companies and White Star lines of ex-Royal Mail Australian Packets offered passages to emigrants. The ship *Sultana*, 4,000 tons, would take passengers to Melbourne for a minimum fare of £14, while one could go in a steamer to New York or Canada for as little as Eight Guineas. These fares, of course, were for the passage only; emigrants had to make their own arrangements for food and bedding.

Over to the back page and the big news of the day. 'Opening of Parliament (From Our Own Reporters)' led the page and spread through two columns. The

62

Queen's Speech was given verbatim, and, it is interesting to note, the proceedings in Parliament were described and reported in the flowing style of a Parliamentary sketch. This was probably the work of Edward Bernard Neill, who had written a London Letter for the *Journal* and carried the feature over to the *Post*. He was described as the *doyen* of London correspondents, a brilliant writer who virtually lived in the Lobby and Gallery of the House of Commons, and was a *persona grata* in political circles. He also was credited with knowing everything of interest in the social world of London. A memory of him survives from the *Journal* days, because, like so many busy journalists, he wrote an almost illegible hand. There was only one compositor on the *Journal* who could decipher it. This man was looked after with precious care, so that, when the night train came in on Friday, the *Journal's* press night, he might be in readiness to turn Neill's copy into type.

The remainder of the back page was filled with a variety of miscellaneous material, testifying to a hurried make-up to fill the uncertain gaps left after the Parliamentary news had been dealt with. This did not apply, perhaps, to the commercial and monetary information, which was remarkably full. The London Stock Exchange report, an article contrasting the 'late panic and present crisis' with a similar occasion in 1847, an account of the panic on the Hamburg Exchange and lists of failures, showed the importance the proprietors attached to authoritative intelligence for the business community in Birmingham.

The political aspects of the first number of the *Post* require another chapter. They are of first-class importance as an index to the future.

7

The Political Scene

TYPICAL OF THE PERIOD AND THE temper of the times was the only point in the Queen's Speech that moved the *Post* to comment—a passing reference to reform. A short second leader seized on the point with the avidity of a terrier after a rat. Palmerston's government had been returned to power in the previous April with an increased majority at the General Election. 'Members of all parties from whom his Lordship had, one time or other, seceded,' the *Post* declared, 'enquired disdainfully whether it was probable that a placeman of fifty-two years' standing would begin at the age of seventy-four, for the first time in his life, to keep his word one instant beyond what individual interest or convenience suggested?'

True, reform was mentioned in the Queen's Speech, but nobody took it seriously, not even Lord John Russell, for whose benefit and comfort the passage had been inserted. Palmerston's 'principal parasite of the press,' the *Post* exclaimed with a snarl at Delane of *The Times*, 'deliberately intimates as much yesterday, that though reform is introduced in the Speech, it is certain to remain a dead letter.' All the same, the *Post* insisted that reform was the paramount issue. The Speech 'has put on record, through the mouth of the Sovereign, the conviction of our rulers that we are imperfectly ruled.' So, clinging hard to this scrap of comfort and without any confidence in its worth, the paper welcomed the Queen's Speech. It viewed Palmerston's faint admission with the deepest distrust; and was justified by events. There would be no reform—which meant, on Radical lips, extension of the franchise—while Palmerston lived; and the *Post* had to put up with him for another eight years. But the real reason for the irritable tone of this comment was that the

Joseph Sturge

Sir John Jaffray, Bart.

Radicals had just received proof that the country was not interested in reform at that moment and was ready enough to accept a further instalment of Palmerston's very capable administration.

The penny provincial dailies,—all Radical in complexion—had come on the scene at a time of momentous change. There was a pause in public affairs, a society poised, as it were, on a watershed between a familiar landscape and the unknown countryside beyond. Despite the Reform Act of 1832, government and administration were still the preserves of the landed aristocracy; but the ruling class had been deeply discredited by its incompetent conduct of the Crimean War. The Indian Mutiny was raging in the winter of 1857-58, giving another shock to official complacency. The press had played a notable part in exposing the ineptitude of military organisation in the Crimea. William Russell's despatches to *The Times* from before Sebastopol had not only shattered the reputation of the military authorities and brought down the feeble Aberdeen government; they enhanced the power of the press and provoked the newborn penny newspapers to virulent attacks on the existing regime and the spirit it embodied. They gave voice to a public demand for full investigation of the military administration and went on from that to call for an end to the reign of aristocratic favouritism. Personal merit, irrespective of birth, should be recognised as the sole qualification for public appointments. The language of the press became unusually violent. It attacked everybody and everything in the most unsparing manner. The *Greville Memoirs* reflect the alarm felt in ruling circles. 'The press, with *The Times* at its head, is striving to throw everything into confusion,' he wrote. 'They diffuse through the country a mass of inflammatory matter.' A spirit of opposition and criticism swept through the country on the crest of the wave of cheap newspapers and was reflected in the literature of the day. In Birmingham, as in other industrial cities, this general onslaught on the existing regime was sharpened by political grievances. Still with only two members of Parliament, the middle classes were grossly under-represented and the working classes were not represented at all. Given time and sound leadership, the material was there for a revival of that union of the dispossessed classes which had carried through the reform agitation of 1832 and had been shattered by the dissensions of the Chartist movement in the 1840's. But the time was not ripe in 1857. By one of the most curious paradoxes of political history, one man, Palmerston, without any intention of doing so, stood between one age of reform and the next and staved off that fusion of classes that alone could generate heat for a major reconstruction.

The *Post* leader abused Palmerston as a placeman who had deserted every party in turn and was an untrustworthy reactionary. That may have been the Radical view, but the country as a whole, and particularly the working classes, simply adored Palmerston. He was the last survivor of the Whig society that dominated the 18th century; and had held office as Secretary at War, a subordinate position, when Wellington was fighting his Peninsular campaigns. He was not attached to either political party, and judged every question on its merits. As a man he was quite exceptionally attractive, a handsome, cheerful country gentleman who went into politics without ambition, because it was the thing to do for men of his privileged class. Above all, he was a supremely industrious and competent administrator. At the age of seventy he became Prime Minister for the first time to get the country out of the mess of the Crimea. And the country gratefully acknowledged him as the 'man who won the war'. In 1857 he grappled with the Indian Mutiny with the same cool resolution and confidence. Eighty ships and 30,000 troops were sent out in good time and he cleared up the confusion afterwards by transferring the dominions of India from the East India Company to the Crown. Whatever Radicals might say, here was a man who got things done, not on high principles, perhaps, but with a firm grasp of practical affairs and in the light of a unique experience of the business of government. Efficiency, however, is not in itself an endearing quality. Palmerston was impregnably rooted in popular affections because his character was admired and his brisk, hearty manners were loved. His loud laugh rings through the memoirs of the times, his racing colours shone on the turf, and his wit and elegance were proverbial.

When the good people of Rugeley petitioned him for leave to change the name of their town because of its undesirable association with Palmer, the Rugeley Poisoner, Palmerston blandly suggested they should adopt his name. As is often the case with hereditary aristocrats, he got on better with working men, his tenants or craftsmen and labourers, than with the middle-class rising industrialists. This relic of the Whig Oligarchy, who had been rejected by Cambridge University owing to his resolute support for Lord Grey's Reform Bill, worked diligently with Lord Shaftesbury for the regulation of the labour of women and children and for control of hours of work in factories. He was no reactionary in social reform. The key to his policy and practice was that he hated cruelty and oppression, at home and abroad, and, when he had the opportunity as Foreign Secretary, he used the power and prestige of Britain for righteousness. He was lukewarm over Parliamentary reform because he simply did not believe the country would be better governed under an enlarged franchise that would give more power to the middle classes. He saw the inevitability of changes in the future. At the age of eighty, during his last administration, he surveyed the House of Commons with unclouded vision and delighted his colleagues with shrewd prophecies. 'Gladstone will soon have it all his own way; and whenever he gets my place, we shall have strange doings,' was one remark often quoted in the years to come. 'Beware of that young man,' he remarked to his neighbours on the Treasury bench, indicating Lord Robert Cecil. 'He is master of one great secret of success in debate. Instead of defending himself, he attacks you.'

Within a year of Palmerston's death in 1865, the dam burst and the Radical reformers, backed by the *Post* and the rest of the provincial press, swept on towards reform. Russell and Gladstone brought in a temporizing Bill which was scorned by the Radicals and defeated with the help of Disraeli. Agitation was worked up throughout the country under Bright and from Birmingham as the power house. The Whig 'Adullamites' under Robert Lowe roused the lethargic working classes and re-knit the old alliance of middle and working classes by a classical ineptitude. They opposed extension of the franchise on the grounds that working men were unfit to have a vote, owing to their intellectual and moral deficiencies. The storm which nothing could raise while Palmerston was alive, raged furiously and resulted in that astonishing *volte face* of 1867, which Disraeli mischievously described as 'dishing the Whigs.' For it was a Conservative Government that carried the Bill giving the vote to industrial workers in the boroughs. Lowe and his Whigs had given the agitation a basis of class union by their attacks on the fitness of the working classes for responsibility and Bright's Radicals had seized the opportunity.

'In vain the country houses were filled that Christmas with ladies and gentlemen abusing Bright,' Trevelyan has written. 'In their hearts they were afraid, with that wise old fear of their countrymen when thoroughly roused, which has done as much to save England as many more heroic virtues.'

The battle was won and the *Post* led the Radical jubilations in Birmingham. But there was a flaw in the victory. As the Bill went through Parliament, Disraeli

68

abandoned one after another the checks and balances tartly described by Bright as 'Fancy Franchise'. One, however, remained, of peculiar import to Birmingham. The city was selected as one of the boroughs for an experiment in minority representation. Birmingham was given three seats in Parliament, but Birmingham electors (it was still a single constituency), were given only two votes. That meant in theory that a minority candidate,— that is, a Tory,—would slip into the third seat despite an overwhelming Radical majority. The Radicals were determined to defeat this device and to elect all three Radicals as members. How they did so belongs to history and to another chapter.

In many other fields besides politics, society in the late 1850's and early 1860's seemed to be at pause and, under an apparent calm and indifference, to be gathering its strength for the next period of turmoil and achievement. Looking back with all the advantages of hindsight, men are prone to fasten on certain dates and events as turning-points, to ring down the curtain on the Middle Ages on Bosworth field in 1485, or to fasten on the invention of the steam engine or the smelting of iron with coal as the moment of the Industrial Revolution. But even the greatest of changes is a slow process and not an event. Men did not wake up one morning in a New Age; nor at the time were they conscious of the forces working to transform the shape of society. Modern history, however, is peculiar for the pace of change. It is, in Trevelyan's phrase, 'a series of dissolving views,' in which in each generation a new economic life half obliterates a predecessor only a little older than itself.

Newspapers have no higher gifts of prescience than the rest of humanity and it is vain to look in their files for recognition of the really significant developments of the day. Three years before the first numbers of the *Post* appeared, a young man of 18 came to Birmingham from London to join a family screw-making business and in the same year, 1854, a new minister arrived at Carr's Lane Chapel. Dawson, at the Church of the Saviour, was already preaching a Radical doctrine of civic responsibility when Chamberlain and Dale arrived in Birmingham. But no hint of the coming explosion of energy is to be found in the papers of the 'fifties. Two years later John Stuart Mill's treatise *On Liberty* was published, to give force and direction to liberal thought, and in the same year Darwin's *Origin of Species* started a disruptive process of scientific thinking which was to have repercussions far beyond his intention. Of more immediate import to contemporaries, particularly in Birmingham, was the advent in 1858 of the Bessemer process, which changed steel from a scarce and costly metal into the basic commodity of structural and mechanical engineering. This was one of the few recognisable turning-points apparent to people at the time. In the world of art, a group of undergraduates at Oxford, including a lank, pale, fair-haired young man from Birmingham, Edward Burne-Jones, were decorating the walls of the Oxford Union with frescoes. It was a great, hilarious rag, inspired by Dante Gabriel Rossetti, and the frescoes were slapped on over the whitewash with no regard for permanence. Eighty years later the faded, flaking pictures were lovingly restored under the direction of Professor Tristram. The movement that was to give Birmingham Cathedral its fine windows and the City Art Gallery its collection of Pre-Raphaelite paintings thus got under way at Oxford, unregarded, in the same year as the *Post*.

All these movements, artistic, literary, scientific and technical, were to bear fruit in the future. The immediate present in the Birmingham of 1857, was not at all exhilarating. The picture was one of lethargy, inefficiency and indifference. The city had been incorporated in 1839, but there were crippling legal defects in the first charter which were not put right until 1842. Even then, the Town Council shared responsibility with no fewer

70

than eight other bodies, none of them elective, for government of the town. It was not until the Improvement Act of 1851 swept away these bodies and vested their powers in the elected Town Council, that Birmingham had a fully-endowed representative municipal authority. The attainment of free, popular local government, however, was followed by disillusionment. This was the notorious 'Woodman Era' when the affairs of the town were run from the parlour of a public house in Easy Row, over a pot of beer and a churchwarden pipe. The credit of the Town Council was deeply impaired. 'So many efficient members had been sickened of public life,' Bunce wrote in his *History of the Corporation*, 'that the status of the governing body had been lowered.' Birmingham was governed, in Anderton's words, by men of 'the unprogressive tradesmen class,—many of them worthy men in their way, but of limited ideas. In their private businesses they were not accustomed to deal with big transactions and high figures, so that spending large sums of money, if proposed, filled the brewer, the baker and the candlestick-maker with alarm'. The conduct of Council debates was disorderly and scandalous and earned the contempt of all decent men. The result was that nothing effective was done. In 1852 and the following year the Council removed the turnpikes from Moseley Road, Bristol Road, Pershore Road and Hagley Road,— and rebuilt them a quarter of a mile outside the City boundary, where they remained in existence for another 30 years. In 1859, in another burst of reckless energy, the Town Council decided to provide a borough cemetery, which was opened at Witton in 1863. There was growing need for it.

For the horrid truth was that Birmingham was sinking beneath its own midden. The community that was Birmingham settled where it did because this was the nearest spot with a good water supply to the coal and iron resources of the Black Country. Unlike most settlements,

71

it had no strategic importance and was not favoured by situation on a river linking it with a seaport; nor did it lie at an intersection on the system of Roman roads that is still the skeleton structure of our land communications. Water is always a necessity for a human settlement: in Birmingham's case it was the very reason for existence. The geological sub-strata held abundant water supplies. As recently as 1869, there were 150,000 Birmingham people dependent on wells for their water,—nearly half the total population. And those wells were being poisoned. An enquiry into the sanitary conditions in 1848 noted that Birmingham was 'not so healthy as it may be' owing to unpaved streets, confined courts, open middens and cesspools, and stagnant ditches. In the next twenty years conditions, far from getting better, became worse. Birmingham was growing rapidly, not in area but, what was far more dangerous, in density. A sanitary census in 1874 found that 24,000 houses, out of a total of 70,500, derived their water from wells contaminated by middens and ashpits. 'The public health in Birmingham,' the report said, 'has been gradually declining for some years.' No such studied moderation of language marked the indignant oratory of those keepers of the civic conscience, the campaigning Nonconformist ministers. 'Our people are ill-taught; our children die at a rate which is shameful and disgraceful,' George Dawson thundered. 'Our people live in filth and disease. Large parts of our great city are a shame and a disgrace, and the odours of corporeal nastiness interfere even with the propagation of the Gospel.'

Nor was it only in the over-crowded inner wards that water supplies and sewerage were breaking down under the weight of population. In Edgbaston, the select residential district of the well-to-do business and professional classes, the main Bristol Road was flanked by open ditches carrying crude sewage. If those were the fruits of popular government, it is not surprising that the better

72

classes of citizens held aloof from public life. But they were recalled to their civic duties by the pulpit preaching and platform oratory of the remarkable group of ministers,—Dawson, Dale, Crosskey and Vince—who initiated the civic renaissance of the seventies. 'One by one the leading citizens came back into the Council,' Bunce recorded, 'and the first work they had to do was to combat the leaders of the dominent section.' Dawson, who knew that exhortation alone would not bring down the walls of the Woodman, looked around for the best and ablest men in the business community to undertake the task of saving the city from its own improvidence. He found a leader in Joseph Chamberlain, an ally in pulpit politics in Dr. Dale and a tremendous instrument of propaganda in the greatest editor of the *Post*, John Thackray Bunce.

The newspaper that reported sermons and speeches at length and hammered away in its leader columns with the doctrine of municipal reform was an essential partner in the enterprise. It was the connecting link between the active men of affairs amongst themselves and a public mouthpiece that carried their message into the homes of the people, where in those days the voices could not otherwise penetrate. The triple alliance of moral force, business and administrative capacity, and press propaganda stimulated the community to throw off the lethargy of the 'fifties and to gird up its loins for the convulsive heave of the 'seventies that made Birmingham 'the best governed city in the world.' Once again, the perspective of history foreshortens the scene. It looks to us as though the walls of Jericho fell at the blast of the trumpet and that all was over in a trice. But the files of the *Post* are a corrective. The fight was long and stubborn: the 'enemy', as the opposition was invariably called, put up a stout resistance; and public opinion was slow to respond to the call to action. Behind the oratory and action, astute organisers built up the necessary

73

machinery of mobilisation and planned the detailed moves in the campaign. The *Post* offices witnessed many staff conferences and several of those associated with the paper occupied key positions in the inner council of the movement. Jaffray began to make his mark as a public speaker: Bunce seemed to be everywhere as adviser and inspirer; and William Harris, the Radical leader-writer with a flaming enthusiasm for the cause, developed into a shrewd political tactician. This period from 1857 to about 1877 was the 'glad, confident morning' of municipal politics, with the *Post* laying the foundations of its power and influence in the city.

8

John Thackray Bunce

JOHN THACKRAY BUNCE WAS EDITOR of *The Birmingham Post* for 36 years, from 1862 to the end of 1898. Such records and memories as have come down to us relate to the final years of his editorship, when he was an old man, full of years and honour, a bearded patriarchal Elder Statesman and something of a pundit. He was the historian of an era even then receding into a half-forgotten past, one who remembered a Birmingham without railways or public transport other than canals. He had played a prominent part in the municipal regeneration that had transformed Birmingham into a modern industrial city and had just crowned his services to the community by throwing all the weight of his influence as leading citizen and editor of the principal newspaper into the project for a University of Birmingham, which he did not live to see. On his retirement he was made an honorary Freeman of the City, one of the few to be thus honoured outside the ranks of civic dignitaries and national figures. That is the wholly worthy and honourable portrait that is remembered by posterity; but it is obviously incomplete. One would give a great deal to have a sketch of Bunce as a young man and in his prime, to have his own account of the stirring events through which he had lived and to catch even one glimpse of him among his office colleagues when large decisions were in the making. But none of his books help to recover his personality. He began the volumes of the History of the Corporation and he wrote about old St. Martin's, the Triennial Musical Festivals and the General Hospital and the life of Josiah Mason,— all sound and useful standard works of local reference. The only digressions that throw some light on the author are a couple of slim volumes of fairy stories, one an

75

original tale reminiscent of Charles Kingsley and the other a collection of Christmas lectures given at the Midland Institute in 1877.

Like so many of the men who come into this historical sketch, Bunce was not born in Birmingham. His early years were spent on a family estate at Longworth, near Faringdon, in Berkshire. The property apparently passed to another branch of the family and Bunce's father came to Birmingham to seek a living in 1839, when Bunce was eleven years old. One can gather that these early years in the country left happy memories from the fact that when, in the days of achievement, Bunce built a house for himself in Priory Road, Edgbaston, he named it Longworth. His father set up in business as a watchmaker and silversmith in Digbeth and the boy was entered as a pupil at the newly-established Gem Street school of King Edward's Foundation. This was one of four branch schools set up by the Governors 'for the free education of boys and girls of the humbler classes,' and from them evolved in time the present King Edward's Grammar Schools. Bunce was among the first entry and went to the Gem Street school on the day it opened. It was a most fortunate start. A great headmaster of the Foundation, Prince Lee, who subsequently became the first Bishop of Manchester, took a real interest in the branch schools and Bunce attracted the notice of Prince Lee himself. After he left school at the age of fourteen to be apprenticed to the trade of printing, Prince Lee continued to advise him in his course of reading and study and accorded him the privilege of making use of his own private library. In after years Bunce repaid his debt to Kings Edward's by becoming 'a most valuable Governor,' to quote the words of Mr. T. W. Hutton in the official school history, *King Edward's School, Birmingham, 1552-1952*, and in 1890 was appointed Bailiff. In an eloquent speech he made on receiving the Freedom of the City in 1899, Bunce looked back to those days. 'Though not a Birming-

76

ham man born, I am proud to trace back to early boy-
hood my adoption into a community than which there is
none nobler in the Queen's dominions, and none which
has a happier faculty in receiving and absorbing all who
come to her, in drawing their affection, in developing
their highest qualities, in securing their devotion to her
interests, in commanding and employing their services;
in a word, in grappling them to herself with hooks of
steel.' Many citizens of Birmingham, not native-born,
could echo this tribute to the influence of King Edward's
School and not a few have had a share in the life and
development of the city comparable with that taken in
his day by Bunce.

He was apprenticed to a printer, Thomas Barber
Wright, who also was proprietor of a newspaper, the
Midland Counties Herald. That he was an industrious
apprentice can be taken for granted; and subsequent
events confirm that he was a studious young man who
continued his education and enlarged his mind while
learning his trade. During these seven years he started
writing and first saw himself in print as the writer of an
anonymous letter to his own paper. The subject, rather
surprisingly from a young man in his 'teens, was a suggestion for establishing a public Art Gallery and Industrial
Museum in the town. He recalled in after-life the thrill
of the printer's apprentice in setting up his own letters
in his employer's type and reading them in the paper.
Quite a long correspondence followed; but nothing was
likely to come of it at the time—somewhere before 1850.
However, this early concern for art bore fruit in due
season. Not only was the Art Gallery established, with
Bunce a member of the Museum Committee and a
trustee of the Public Picture Gallery Fund founded by
Clarkson Osler, but in 1879 an article from Bunce in
the *Post* drew a letter from Richard Tangye, addressed
personally to the editor, offering £10,000 towards a
building for the School of Art. This was made conditional

77

on the School being taken over by the Corporation, as Bunce's article had suggested. From the abortive and anonymous suggestion of the apprentice printer to the ability, thirty years later, to charm such a munificent donation from an industrialist for an artistic and civic purpose, is one measure of Bunce's progress. His success as a letter-writer attracted the notice of his proprietors and before long he was commissioned to write a series of articles for the paper on the trades of Birmingham and other topics. By 1851, when he had finished his apprenticeship, he was sufficiently well regarded as a writer to be given the task of 'covering', as we should put it to-day, the Great Exhibition. The qualified compositor emerged as a reporter and from that time onwards his career and calling was that of a journalist.

Bunce was a loyal Churchman, and remained so all his life, so it was natural that he should gravitate towards the high-and-dry Tory daily newspaper, *Aris's Gazette*. The Tory Party in Birmingham was entrenched in privilege and reacted vigorously against the rising tide of Radical reform; but it had lost all hold on the masses since the time in 1791 when it could rouse the mob with the cry of 'Church and State' in the ugly Priestley Riots, which incidentally extinguished the brief intellectual eminence of Birmingham in the civilised world. Bunce became a reporter on the Tory paper, then Assistant Editor, under John Caldicott, and in 1860 succeeded his chief in the editorial chair at the early age of 32. There is a great difference between working on a paper in a subordinate position and occupying an editorial post with responsibility for its policy. Bunce was always a moderate-minded man and it was noticeable even at this period of his life that he made his personal friends mainly among Liberals and Nonconformists. George Dawson, R. W. Dale, Charles Vince and others of that circle he found most congenial company. It was not surprising that his employers apparently felt some reservations over

78

his moderation and Bunce himself had to take stock of his position. The crisis came, according to his own account, one evening when he was persuaded to attend a Town Hall meeting addressed by John Bright. Powerful and lucid oratory combined with evident sincerity of purpose to convince him that he could not conscientiously continue to advocate a Tory policy. The conversion was evidence of a maturing mind. He could do no other than resign his editorship and he prepared to pack up and go to London in search of employment.

Shortly before this time, Jaffray had relinquished the duties of editor of the *Post* to devote himself to the business affairs of the paper and to a career in public life. For a brief period he was succeeded as editor by a Mr. Silk, but when it was known that Bunce had resigned from *Aris's Gazette* and was leaving for London, the editorship of the *Post* was offered to Bunce, who promptly accepted. Thus in 1862 an association began that lasted for 36 years. 'I was considered rather young for the post', Bunce related, 'and for about six weeks my two proprietors narrowly watched me, wanted to know what I proposed to write, what I had written and so forth. Then one day Mr. Jaffray said to Mr. Feeney, "I think we can trust him," and from that day to this I have had practically a free hand.'

Ten years later, when new articles of agreement were drawn up between Jaffray and John Feeney, son of the original proprietor, Bunce was made a salaried partner. He was to receive a salary of £700 a year or one-twelfth of the net profits, whichever was the greater. 'The said J. T. Bunce' the articles read, 'shall fill the position and discharge the duties of Editor, Leader Writer and General Superintendent of the literary, political and general news department of the newspapers called *The Birmingham Daily Post* and the *Birmingham Weekly Post* and shall attend to and do all matters and things appertaining to the office of the Editor of a newspaper.'

79

The principal partners retained their absolute control over the contents of the papers. Nothing was to be inserted in the papers to which a majority of the partners objected,—no 'article, intelligence, advertisement matter or thing of a particular nature, purport, bearing, tendency or effect, or calculated to enforce any particular opinion or line of opinion.' Nor could there be any 'engagement or determination of engagement to which a principal partner shall object.' This attempt to define in legal language the relations between an editor and his proprietors is interesting, but largely irrelevant to the day-to-day conduct of a newspaper. To carry it out literally would be impossible. To apply it in practice calls for another factor not capable of legal definition,— mutual confidence and understanding. That this existed in full measure between Bunce and his proprietors the long story of his editorship proves beyond doubt.

Bunce threw himself into the work of the Liberal party, locally and nationally, with special reference to educational policy. He became a member of the Managing Committee of the Birmingham Liberal Association and was one of the founders of the National Liberal Federation, drafting its earlier reports. When the split came in 1886, however, he withdrew from active participation in political organisation, always in the hope that the rift might be healed and that the paper might play a part in reuniting the two sections of Liberals. He continued his association with the National Education League, along with George Dixon, Joseph Chamberlain, Jesse Collins and others and had charge of the League's publications and most of its circulars and manifestoes. It was, however, in the municipal reform campaign, before these unhappy political differences arose, that his influence was greatest and most fruitful. Dr. Dale's tribute was emphatic. 'The new movement was fortunate in securing, from the first, the able support and wise guidance of the *Daily Post*. Its Editor (Mr. Bunce) was the trusted friend

80

John Thackray Bunce

The Daily Moralist

Dr. R. W. Dale

Unimproved Birmingham

and adviser of the leaders, and the intimate personal friend of the most important of them. Through the columns of the most powerful newspaper in the Midland Counties the new ideas about municipal life were pressed on the whole community.'

Bunce's principal achievement as an editor was to raise the level of newspaper controversy well above the scurrility, violence of language and personal abuse which were accepted as normal before his day. In his writing he observed 'an almost Addisonian tone,' it has been justly said, and tried to preserve and inculcate an attitude of reasonableness and courtesy. It was a notable contribution to a community at a time when feelings on all sides ran high and violence was never very far below the surface. How powerful feelings were may be gathered from two quotations. The first illustrates the religious fervour behind the campaign. Speaking of one alderman friend, Dr. Dale, of Carr's Lane said he believed ' he was trying to get the Will of God done on earth as it is done in heaven just as much when he was fighting St. Mary's Ward, just as much when he was speaking in the Town Council, as when he was teaching his Bible Class on the Sunday morning.' Down in the heat and dust of municipal electioneering this lofty fervour could take on a tone of personal denunciation worthy of an Old Testament prophet. George Dawson, supporting the candidature of W. H. Dixon for the Town Council, said this of Dixon's opponent. 'Mr. Hayden appears to have some vested interest in filth and fever. Mr. Hayden resists the appointment of sanitary inspectors and to do that is to throw protection over dirt: and dirt means disease and disease means death. When men get wise they will sweep disease out of the world. They will put down cholera, kill smallpox and kick out many maladies that they now drivel and cant about as though they were the inevitable condition of humanity. They are the inevitable condition of dirty humanity,—but not of humanity sweet, clean

81

and wisely instructed.' Under the impetus of pulpit and platform oratory of this calibre, gas and water politics, as it has been contemptuously called, excited strong passions and bitter hatreds. For the editor of a paper sympathising with all his heart with the campaign and committed by faith and friendship to active, personal support, it can have been no easy matter to maintain a tone of reason and moderation and seek to keep public excitement within bounds.

It is, however, from a non-political occasion that an illustration may be drawn of the *Post* in action against popular passions. In June, 1867, the town was visited by an itinerant rabble-rousing lecturer, by name Murphy, preaching a virulent brand of anti-Catholicism. From Sunday, 16th June, until the following Tuesday night, the centre of the town was given over to disturbance, riot and looting. The scene in the neighbourhood of the Bull Ring is vividly described in this report from the *Post*:

'The third day of Mr. Murphy's campaign in Birmingham dawned upon a scene of ruin. A stroll through the Park Street district in the first grey light of morning just as the last shouts of the rioters had died away—while the mob exhausted and scattered was tumbling to its drunken rest and the injured and captured were watching the first streak of light as it fell athwart the sick room or the cell—revealed destruction and distress as great as if the place had been bombarded by a military force instead of having been protected by one. Houses doorless, windowless, and in some cases almost roofless—pavements and roadway strewn with stones, brick ends, broken glass, fragments of wearing apparel and furniture—women and children huddled into corners, crooning and crying amongst the wreckage of their homes—such were the sights and sounds to be seen and heard on every hand in Park Street . . . . But it was not to Park Street alone that the rioting and work of destruction were confined.'

82

That day the *Post* came out with a leader that became historic. At the time it served its immediate purpose of steadying public opinion and shaming an excited populace into restraint. For the future it laid down principles for the guidance of editorial policy in similar circumstances that have endured to the present day. The line drawn between rights of free speech and public discussion and incitement to violence by provocative utterance and action is firm and clear. The distinction has become horribly relevant in our own time throughout Europe and the world at large. It is not too much to claim that some of the responsibility for the triumphs of violence in other countries rests on the failure of influential newspapers to speak out courageously in the early stages.

This is what the *Post* wrote:

'As our readers know but too well, Birmingham has within the last day or two been disgraced by riotous proceedings of a serious character. The present aspect of the centre of the town recalls its appearance in the Chartist disturbances of 1839. The Bull Ring and several of the adjacent streets are in something like a state of seige—every avenue guarded by soldiers, police and special constables, the military picketed in the roads, the Riot Act read, the Magistrates sitting *en permanence*, every available means for the maintenance of peace called into full activity. While we write the town is restless and excited, the walls are placarded with appeals of a more or less incendiary character, the cells at the police station are crowded with prisoners and the hospital surgeons are busy with wounded men. Between thirty and forty people injured —some of them seriously—between seventy and eighty prisoners at the police station or in gaol, dozens of houses battered into ruins; this is the aspect of affairs in Birmingham at the present moment; and, full of dismal forbodings, everyone asks his neighbour what is going to happen next—what new outrage, what fresh

83

discredit? This is a strange and melancholy picture of the chief town of the centre of England, in the middle of a century which we used to boast of as the brightest development of "progress" and "enlightenment". But still more strange and melancholy it is to find when we come to look into the matter that all this has arisen out of religious disputes, the too familiar antipathy of Protestant and Catholic, the wretched quarrels of professedly Christian people.

"Fighting like devils for conciliation,
And hating each other for the love of God."

'Miserable and discreditable as the retrospect undoubtedly is we may, however, hope that it *is* something to be simply looked back upon; and that the worst is over. But for the wise and vigorous measures taken by the Magistrates, and the prompt assistance of the military, the town might have witnessed last night still worse excesses than those of Monday. However, the day passed off quietly and up to the time at which we write there has been no renewal of disturbances, though the streets are greatly crowded and all kinds of alarmist rumours (nine-tenths of them obviously unfounded) are or have been in circulation. For the sake of the reputation of the town we hope the present quietude is earnest of a return to an ordinary condition of peacefulness; and this is to be hoped still more fervently on account of the sacred names dragged through the mire by the miserable transactions of the last two days.

'As yet we scarcely know how the rioting actually began, which party was first in the fray or which gave earliest opportunity to the roughs and thieves abounding in all large towns to begin their work of outrage and plunder. It is, however, of little consequence to determine this point at present; we can wait until fuller light is thrown upon it by the magisterial enquiries at the Police Court. But whoever began or whoever is responsible, whether the outbreak was due to organisation or to impulse the whole affair is irredeemably disgraceful. It cannot fail to bring discredit on the town, to shame the cause of religion and good order, and—though this is least of all—to entail heavy cost upon the ratepayers who will have to make good the damage inflicted upon property. The only satisfactory features of the transaction are that, no person of respectability or position in Birmingham has in any way countenanced or taken part in the proceedings which have led to this lamentable exhibition. All the mischief is due to the intervention of strangers to the town; no local clergyman or minister, or laymen of note, having hand or part in the doings of Mr. Murphy and his associates. It is due also to the Roman Catholic clergy to say that at no slight personal risk they have done their utmost to restrain their people; and but for their exertions much more serious disasters would doubtless have occurred.

'While expressing a hope that all who are proved to have been concerned in the riots will be severely punished we regret to say that the persons who are proximately and morally responsible, seem likely to escape the legal consequences which ought to fall upon them. These persons are unquestionably the lecturer, Murphy and his abettors, most of them, as we have already said, being strangers to Birmingham. They come here without the least necessity amongst a population heated by strong religious partisanship, and with full consciousness of the inevitable results, they behave so to speak, as men who wantonly cast a burning match into a powder magazine. Wherever the lecturer has made his appearance his advent has been immediately followed by "religious" riots. However greatly these disturbances are to be condemned—and nobody can reprobate them more severely than we do —they are well nigh inevitable. The indiscriminate

85

circulation of indescribably filthy books, the use of language unparalleled for violence, incessant attacks upon everything which Roman Catholics hold sacred —the doctrines of their Church, the honour of their clergy, the purity of their wives, their sisters, and their daughters—what are these but direct and almost irresistible means of provocation to forcible retort? If it were designed to cause a breach of the peace, a surer method could not have been devised. Whatever may be the intention, the result is always the same— personal violence, damage to property, general disturbance of the community, stirring up all the baser passions of humanity, exciting bitterness and hatred which the lapse of years will scarcely allay. It was so in the Potteries and in South Staffordshire, it is so now in Birmingham and it will be so wherever the provocation is repeated.

'Surely by this time, Mr. Whally, Colonel Brockman, and the other strangers who confess themselves the employers of this lecturer, have had opportunity enough to learn what is the natural issue of their proceedings. If these persons stand legally clear— which is by no means certain—they are morally chargeable with very heavy responsibility. They pretend a desire to "vindicate the freedom of discussion". The pretence is little less odious than the discreditable results, to which it gives rise. In this case it is not freedom but license, that is in question. Any number of lecturers, in any part of England might declaim against the "errors of popery" till they were black in the face, and yet cause no disturbance, provided they set to work with common decency and observed the customary methods of controversy. But the subjects dealt with and the mode of treatment adopted, put these proceedings altogether out of the pale of decent controversy. If the object of the lecturer and his associates is really that which they profess, the first step towards accomplishing it must be a change of method. As the campaign is at present conducted, Romanists will never be convinced but only exasperated by such harangues; while public morality is outraged by the circulation of indecent books, and the cause of Protestantism injured by the reaction certain to spring from a mode of proceeding which it would be an abuse of terms to describe as controversy.'

There were no more disturbances after this, though the 'lectures' went on for another three days,—and were noted in the *Post*, without further comment.

Finally, two personal reminiscences from men who remember Bunce's time. One who knew him testifies to the fact that 'Bunce was a splendid citizen and a fine character all through.' Another veteran, Mr. Harry J. Stirrop, a compositor for 50 years who joined the firm in 1892, recalls a glimpse of the distinguished Editor inside the office. He was, Mr. Stirrop says, 'a genial gentleman' and used to visit the composing room without fail every New Year's Eve, shortly before midnight. As soon as the New Year was born, he would take out his snuff box, an ornate affair, and pass it round the compositors, who were, and often still are, inveterate snuff-takers. With this agreeable domestic scene, we may appropriately take leave of a famous figure in the history of the paper and of Birmingham.

9
Second Generation

JOHN FREDERICK FEENEY, THE FOUN-
der, died in 1869 at the age of 62. The *Post* and the
Weekly Post had consolidated their positions and his
first paper, the *Journal*, had just been merged in the
other two. The following year the evening paper, the
Mail, was launched to complete the trio of Feeney newspapers. For several years before his death his health had
been undermined by a bronchial affliction that led to his
retirement from active management. The conduct of the
papers passed into the hands of his younger partner
Jaffray and his second son, John Feeney, who joined the
business in 1863 soon after Bunce became editor. Apart
from his profession, John Frederick Feeney 'lived a peace-
ful and uneventful life; contented with the discharge of
his private duties and in the enjoyment of domestic
happiness,' Jaffray wrote in a touching tribute to the
memory of 'one of the purest minds that God ever
created, and as kind a heart as ever beat in human
breast.' Thus on a note of affection that breathes sincerity the long and successful partnership of twenty-five
years came to an end.

It had been intended that the founder's eldest son
should succeed his father. Memories grow dim and some
writers of recollections have taken it for granted that this
is what happened, and that John Feeney was the eldest
son. Actually there was a brother two years older, by
name Peregrine Feeney, who outlived them all and
appears to have had a happy life as a moderately successful painter. That a man should prefer to paint pictures
and live in Devonshire to the prospect of becoming a
millionaire newspaper proprietor in Birmingham is so
perplexing to some minds that they give up the puzzle
and tend to forget. But this independent-minded man

who knew what he wanted from life and apparently sacrificed golden prospects for a comfortable whim becomes thereby an interesting, and rather enviable, character. Peregrine Feeney was apprenticed to journalism on the *Scotsman* under the editorship of Alexander Russell, and joined his father's paper in Birmingham in 1862. In addition to work on the journalistic side under Bunce, he assisted his father in general management. But he soon found a newspaper office uncongenial to his temperament and within twelve months he suggested that his place should be taken by his younger brother, John. Whatever disappointment his father may have felt was evidently swallowed up in the family affection that was so notable in all the Feeneys. Peregrine went off to London to become a painter and John stepped into his place. He never lost interest in writing, however, and was an occasional contributor of verse to the papers throughout his life. He did one considerable service to the papers by recommending to them a remarkable journalist, D. Barron Brightwell, a London schoolmaster who became editor of the *Weekly Post* and well-known locally as a writer under the pen-name 'Rufus'. The abiding friendship between the Feeney brothers was happily shown in after years when John, who was something of an amateur architect, prepared the plans for a house which Peregrine was having built for himself at Croyde, in Devonshire.

Peregrine Feeney's career as an artist scarcely comes within the scope of this historical sketch. It may be put on record, however, that he kept a studio at Primrose Hill, London, had a large circle of friends among artists in the capital, exhibited at the Royal Academy and was a regular contributor to the exhibitions of the Royal Birmingham Society of Artists. His Academy picture of a Devonshire headland, Baggy Point, was presented to Birmingham General Hospital, and the City Art Gallery owns a picture of Llyn Idwal, Wales, presented by Sir

89

John Jaffray. In this office hangs a large oil painting of Saunton Sands, to tantalise night-working journalists in the small hours with rebellious thoughts of sunshine and sea breezes and endowed choice of careers. Peregrine Feeney's striking appearance was turned to good account by his artist friends. Logsdail, whose pictures of London Street scenes were once very popular and may still occasionally be found in coloured reproductions from old Christmas Numbers, used Peregrine Feeney as his model for bearded, genial horse-bus drivers and policemen.

The second half of the 19th century was a golden age for artists not unduly afflicted with an aesthetic conscience. The new wealth from industry and commerce was spent lavishly on patronage of the arts. Men of position were expected, according to the doctrines of Ruskin, to cultivate artistic appreciation, to collect pictures to hang in their oppressive houses and to make presentations to public galleries and other institutions as evidence of their taste. In the seventeenth century that kindly gossip, John Aubery, sometimes had to admit reluctantly that a gentleman was not much of a hand at a sonnet or a madrigal. Seventy or eighty years ago no man of means liked to be thought insensible to the arts of painting and sculpture. The cellars,—and not only the cellars—of public art galleries are littered with the unappreciated relics of this age of taste; but while it lasted, artists flourished exceedingly and life for them was agreeably and prosperously strenuous. Peregrine Feeney lived through this genial age and never had cause to regret his renunciation of the prospect of becoming a wealthy patron of those artists whose congenial company he shared. He died in 1913, at the age of 76.

John Feeney who thus came unexpectedly to the throne in New Street, was born in 1839 and at an early age was sent as a boarder to the High School at Stirling, the town where Jaffray started his education. Jaffray's influence and advice may be deduced from the fact that

90

his partner's eldest son went to Edinburgh to start in journalism and his second son to Stirling to start his schooling. The pre-eminence of Scottish education in those days was recognised and by none more forcibly than those who had themselves enjoyed its advantages.

However, the father seems to have had second, and wiser, thoughts, for in due course the young John was brought back to Birmingham to become a pupil at King Edward's School, New Street. He does not seem to have shown a scholastic bent, nor at that time was there an opening for him in his father's office. So he left school and was put to the business of learning a trade. First he went into the warehouse of a merchant's, Scholefield, Goodman & Co., to become acquainted with business methods. Then at the age of 18 he entered a firm of art metal workers, Messenger and Sons, in Broad Street. This is the first episode in his career that seems to have had a lasting influence on his life and interests. It was a profound influence and must have been invaluable as a contrast to the actual working life that ultimately became his lot. He shared with his elder brother a natural aptitude for drawing, which he turned to advantage as a worker in the firm's modelling department, and cultivated at every opportunity at the School of Design and elsewhere. This interest brought him in contact with W. C. Aitken, an industrial designer in the firm of Hardman and Sons, who became a foremost authority on the subject. A close friendship sprang up between the two young men which lasted until Aitken's death. John Feeney thus acquired his life-long interest in industrial art, especially as applied to metal work. Had he not been called upon to inherit his father's proprietary interest in newspapers he would probably have become an industrial artist and designer of distinction, for he had the technical capacity and initial training and his heart would have been in the work. Instead, it became his chief hobby and object of patronage.

As a newspaper proprietor he was in a position to keep the subject of industrial design constantly before the public. His friend, W. C. Aitken, became a regular contributor to the *Post*, which thereby won a reputation in its turn as an authority. John Feeney himself became a considerable traveller in his middle years. He visited most of the famous cities of the world and wherever he was, he studied the local applied arts and sent home specimens which almost all ultimately found their way into the Municipal Art Gallery or other public collections. He held the principle that a work of art was the property of all mankind and should not be hidden from the general public in a private collection. Consequently his own collections of pictures and art objects were never long in his possession. He was one of the best friends the City Museum and Art Gallery has ever had during his life and it is very appropriate that his name should be perpetuated in the Feeney Gallery and the Feeney Trust established under his Will. In his travels he developed a particular partiality for Oriental jewellery and metal work. On one journey to Tiflis in 1888 he made an interesting collection of old Turkish, Persian and Armenian armour and weapons, illustrating the old art of decorating steel by processes of Damascening and inlay. His chief enthusiasm, however, was for the art of Japan, which was not so well-known in this country seventy years ago as it is to-day. Indeed, he was one of the pioneer collectors and his interest did much to stimulate the movement of specialised study and collection which has completely opened up Japanese art to the Western world. He believed that the Japanese artificers were the finest metal workers in the world and his only regret was that he was not long enough in that country to make a truly representative collection of the best examples. In pictorial art his tastes were catholic, ranging from the Pre-Raphaelites to the Impressionists, and the City is indebted to him for some of its examples of the work of

92

Burne-Jones, William Morris and Rossetti. One of the very few public offices he held was that of a trustee of the Public Picture Gallery Fund founded by Clarkson Osler. All these benefactions and legacies to art were ultimately the fruits of his early training for a career in industrial art, which likewise implanted in the newspapers he came to control a tradition of concern for the arts and of competent, scholarly criticism. This has naturally embraced all the arts and set a standard in dramatic and musical criticism also, of which the *Post* is justifiably proud. It is in the nature of journalism, and newspaper ownership, that all's grist that comes to the mill; for a newspaper must touch the community at every point and reflect all possible interests. There is much to be said, therefore, for having on the staff men who have early experience in some quite different walks of life; it would be a sad day for newspapers if a narrow specialisation were to rule out recruitment from other trades and professions.

In 1862 John Feeney, industrial designer in the making, represented his firm of art metal workers at the International Exhibition in Hyde Park. Within a twelve-month he was learning to become a newspaper man and was heir-apparent to the proprietorship. His training in the office was strictly in a commercial capacity, for that was where the firm needed strengthening. His father's health even then was giving some cause for concern and Jaffray was beginning to take an interest in public affairs which in the next decade were to absorb much of his time and energies. John Feeney soon showed that he possessed high commercial capacity and that necessary quality of shrewd judgment and grasp of essentials described as 'strong common sense.' When he succeeded to the partnership six years later, he was well equipped to carry the responsibilities. The *Post* triumvirate in 1869 was a strong and a young team,—Jaffray at 51, with a quarter of a century's newspaper experience behind him; Bunce as editor, an established figure in the office and outside,

93

aged 41; and John Feeney, only 30, but with a varied career behind him and a fresh outlook. They were to remain together for twenty-five years. The two older men were more fortunate than they may have guessed in at least one respect. Their colleague was a man of most retiring disposition, so there was never any suggestion of rivalry in the public eye. Indeed, John Feeney's hatred of publicity was an obsession that makes it difficult to do justice to his memory. In some notes for this sketch by an unknown hand it is remarked that 'John Jaffray, unlike his partner John Feeney, took a great interest in the life of Birmingham.' The implication in this unhappy phrase is wholly false; though that may have been the impression of those who did not know John Feeney well during his lifetime or have failed to study his Will. Unlike Jaffray, he shunned public life and public offices.

An old-fashioned progressive Liberal, he supported the Birmingham Liberal Association and, after the Home Rule split, he was for a short time treasurer of the Chamberlainite National Liberal Union. But political organisation did not interest him; his concern was with the broad principles of freedom, justice and progress. He held that a newspaper proprietor should hold aloof from party commitments sufficiently to preserve the paper's freedom to criticise any party or government and to advocate any policy it thought right in the interest of the country. This did not mean that the paper under him was given to sitting on the fence, as its history abundantly proves. It did mean that politics were treated on their merits, issues were weighed carefully—and nobody could count on the support of the *Post* as a matter of course. Consequently, the paper's influence, when it did make up its mind and come out for a particular line, was all the greater, was valued or execrated accordingly and was often decisive. John Feeney's jealous independence was all the more useful because his partner was so deeply involved in party political affairs. Whatever ties of

94

friendship and commitments of office Jaffray might acquire, the paper remained uncompromised. That was well understood in political circles, though outsiders did not always grasp the distinction. The *Post* was never the instrument of Chamberlain and those who said and thought it was ignored the facts and overlooked the senior partner in the background. It came in due course to support Chamberlain over Home Rule and Tariff Reform, but the files show that neither policy was adopted precipitately, as later chapters will make clear.

Aloofness from politics, however, certainly did not mean lack of interest in the life of the city. John Feeney was always ready to sponsor works he thought were for the good of the city and he was a generous, indeed lavish, contributor to the hospitals and other charitable institutions and to special appeals like that for the University endowment fund. But always, if that were possible, it was under the cloak of anonymity. Leaders in public life looking for money for worthy objects, knew one man to whom they could go with some confidence; they also knew that it would probably be fatal to future prospects if they let it be known where the money had come from. An outstanding example was Aston Parish Church which in the 1880's had become wholly inadequate for the needs of the large population that had grown up around it. A rebuilding on a big scale was put in hand, but the building fund progressed so slowly that it was feared some modifications would be necessary. One day the architect, J. A. Chatwin, received a call from John Feeney, an old family friend, who asked to see the plans. He had an idea of contributing a window or windows as a memorial to his father, who was buried in the churchyard. The architect explained his troubles and the fear that his plans would have to be curtailed. The upshot of the conversation was that John Feeney undertook to bear the entire cost of restoration of the Erdington Chapel and the rebuilding of the whole chancel-end of the church.

95

The architect was given *carte blanche* as to cost and he alone knew who was providing the means. His son, Mr. Philip Chatwin, has related how the secret was kept. 'The money to pay the builders and the various craftsmen,' he has written, 'came from the Bank of England in London in £1,000 bank notes. On one day half a note would arrive at the office and on the next day the other half came in a registered envelope to our home address. I remember feeling it was a kind of magic; two apparently worthless bits of paper were joined together and at once became an enormous sum of money.'

There was much curiosity at the time as to the identity of the anonymous donor, but it was not until years later, in 1898, that a clue was given. John Feeney then obtained a faculty for the removal of his parents' bodies from the churchyard to a vault under the Erdington Chapel. Even so, every effort was made to keep the arrangements private and the removal of the remains took place at night. He kept this part of the proceedings all too much to himself. Next morning he was horrified to see in his own paper a short paragraph headed 'Vandalism in Aston Churchyard,' stating that during the night bodies had been exhumed from a grave. Since his day, a wit has coined the paradoxial aphorism: 'If you want to keep a secret, tell the Press.' It is a maxim much open to abuse by politicians who want to conceal something the public has a right to know. To the left of the altar in the Erdington Chapel is a mural monument designed by George Frampton, R.A., with an inscription disclosing the fact that 'the chancel and chapel of this church were built in 1883,' as a memorial to John Frederick Feeney, 'by one of his sons.' To the last the donor kept his own name out of it.

In his younger days, John Feeney was a man of remarkable vigour and robust health. He looked much more of a countryman than his partner, the Squire of Skilts, but his taste in country pursuits was very different

George Dawson

'Our People Live in Filth and Disease'

John Feeney

Site of Corporation Street

from Sir John Jaffray's. He had no love for field sports with rod and gun, nor did he hunt. His recreation was walking and his interests were in scenery, architecture and places of antiquarian appeal. Long rambles in Warwickshire and Worcestershire gave him an intimate knowledge of the countryside and its buildings. It was on one of these walks that his eye was taken by an old property at Berkswell, known as the Moat Farm, a finely situated house with a commanding view of the gentle Warwickshire countryside. Shortly afterwards it came on the market and he bought it at auction. He extended and practically reconstructed the house and laid out the grounds, all to his own ideas and plans. Magnificence or display were foreign to his character. The Moat, Berkswell, was and remained essentially a homely country residence, and a considerable tribute to his taste. English domestic architecture around 1880 was at a low ebb, but the Moat transcended its period of reconstruction and belonged to the best tradition of unostentatious comfort and seemly design. It remained in essence a farm-house, a likely residence of a prosperous yeoman, and seemed to reflect the character of its new owner. For many years John Feeney had lived practically over the office, in Stephenson Chambers, New Street, and kept on these town quarters all his life; but his heart was at Berkswell. He lived there almost exclusively when not on his travels and entered into the life of the neighbourhood. The lovely parish church owed to him a new organ and peal of bells. He became a Justice of the Peace for Warwickshire and for some time sat at Coleshill Petty Sessions. In his prime he would think nothing of walking in from Berkswell to the office in the morning and walking back in the evening. He was also a keen tennis player. A former employee who joined the staff in 1892, has a vivid recollection of the contrasting appearances of the two partners. Whereas Jaffray always used to come to the office wearing a frock coat and top hat, Feeney

97

regularly wore a velvet jacket and looked more like a country squire than a city businessman.

His vigour, high spirits and hearty companionship in his younger days need to be recalled, because a very different and sadder picture has been left by those who knew him only in later life. Soon after Jaffray retired in 1894 on the expiration of the partnership agreement, John Feeney showed the first symptoms of a progressive and crippling malady that afflicted the last years of his life. Some elderly men remember as boys seeing the proprietor arrive at the office, not walking in full vigour but in a carriage, from which he had to be helped, almost carried, into the building. These visits steadily became rarer and he spent much time searching for health in the milder climate of South Devon. He was now sole proprietor and struggled hard to retain control of the business. Until the end all major decisions had to be referred to him. In 1892 he had brought into the office as assistant, J. R. H. Smyth, who later became general manager and, shortly before John Feeney's death in December, 1905, a salaried partner. The day-to-day management in the office passed progressively into Smyth's hands. Yet it was in these years of declining capacity that several important major developments took place.

Linotype machines were introduced in place of the traditional hand-setting of type and new printing machinery came into use. The complex reorganisation of labour, involving some displacements and transfers, was successfully carried through. John Feeney was personally responsible for the considerate arrangements for those adversely affected. It was due to his wise and generous provisions that the changes were made amicably and that the pleasant relationships that had always obtained between management and staff were preserved. In 1902 he embarked on a large enterprise, buying from the Corporation of London a freehold site by St. Bride's Church, in Fleet Street, and building a new London office which, in its day, was one of the finest belonging to a provincial newspaper. It was linked by private wire to head office in Birmingham, additional agency news services were installed and the staff of London representatives, editorial and commercial, was expanded. These and other developments showed there was no diminution of mental vigour in the proprietor, though his physical strength had failed and he was a pathetic shadow of his former self. He had married late in life and there were no children. The question of the succession was present to his mind soon after he became sole proprietor. He was intensely proud of the papers and determined to ensure, as far as was humanly possible, that they should be carried on in accordance with his own ideals of service to the community and independence.

He turned naturally to consideration of his two nephews, one of whom, he felt, might be suitable for the position. One was John Alexander Inglis, eldest son of one of John Feeney's sisters who had married a Dr. Inglis, a well-known Edinburgh physician. The other was Charles Hyde, younger son of his favourite sister, Mary, who had married Dr. George Hyde of Worcester. Eventually his choice fell on Charles Hyde, at that time (1897) an undergraduate at Oxford. As a result Charles Hyde left Oxford and came to Birmingham to start a steady course of training under his uncle's guidance. He always said he was unaware of his uncle's intention to leave the properties to him, and that is borne out by the fact that John Feeney's Will is dated in 1903, with codicils making substantial alterations in December, 1904, within twelve months of his death. In 1897 Charles Hyde came into the office as a junior managerial assistant and was put to work in all the various departments in turn to gain a thorough understanding of the internal working of a great newspaper undertaking. Regarding the other nephew, John Alexander Inglis, one is happy to be able to record that he took a high degree at Oxford,

99

read for the Bar and made a successful career in the law, becoming a K.C. in Scotland and eventually King's Remembrancer for Scotland. John Feeney followed his nephew's early progress with keen family interest and appreciation. This he showed by appointing him as Senior Trustee under his Will, a post which, when the time came, John Alexander Inglis filled with distinction and marked ability for a number of years.

John Feeney died at Torquay on 16th December, 1905, and was buried at Berkswell Parish Church. He had been sole proprietor for eleven years, and a proprietor for thirty-six years. He left the newspaper and other properties, valued at £952,998, in trust. His nephew Charles Hyde was given a right by beneficial purchase to acquire the business on 1st January, 1913. In the Will there was a clause, later revoked by codicil, that deserves mention. 'As I desire to perpetuate the name of my father and myself in connection with the establishment and development of the before-mentioned well-known newspaper, I make it a condition that my nephew Charles Hyde shall not be entitled to purchase the business on the terms hereby fixed unless within six months after my decease he shall formally adopt the name Feeney as a sole surname (not to be used in conjunction with the name of Hyde as a surname) and shall continue to use such surname thenceforwards on all occasions and for all purposes.'

Whatever persuaded the testator to change his mind, second thoughts have proved the wiser. Charles Hyde never married, so in any case the name of Feeney in association with the newspapers would have died again within a generation. His substantial legacies to the Art Gallery, to the Trust for art purchases and to the University will preserve the name of Feeney for a while; and, what is closer to his wishes, the *Post* prints his father's name daily as its founder. John Feeney was a keen reader. Did he ever, one wonders, read Sir Thomas Browne, and,

100

if he did, could it have been when he was revising his will and revoking that clause about the name? 'Diuturnity is a dream and folly of expectation.'

10

Shakespeare and All That

IN THE 'SEVENTIES AND 'EIGHTIES OF the last century Birmingham was still a comparatively small, compact and homogeneous community, where a man of character and ability would be known to everybody and could make his mark on the lives of his fellow-citizens. A writer in the *National Review* of May, 1899, deploring the growing unwieldiness of the expanding city, pointed this contrast with the earlier times. 'A generation ago it was a more manageable, and in some respects more gratifying, field for the display of great abilities than the metropolis; a clever man was not lost in it; he was the common possession of his townsmen and within their easy reach. It is open to question whether anyone will again make a great and general position in Birmingham.' For an objective study of the Birmingham at that period one may turn to a remarkable work by a French scholar, *Democracy and the Organisation of Political Parties*, by M. Ostrogorski, a book long out of print and not readily obtained. In its day (1902) this massive study in 'the pathology of party government,' as Lord Bryce called it in an introduction, was well thought-of, for it was a first attempt to examine the working of democratic institutions in Britain and the United States scientifically and in a philosophical spirit.

The author took Birmingham as a specimen of tendencies in political organisation and management which he deplored but thought worthy of detailed scholarly examination. 'A quarter of a century ago', he wrote in 1902, 'the capital of the Midlands was anything but a well-ordered city. It still bore the stamp of the great manufacturing centres which had developed with extraordinary rapidity in the north of England and which exhausted their energies in huge buildings with tall chimneys vomiting forth clouds of smoke from dawn to sunset; absorbed in the task of production, the inhabitants were not only little open to intellectual and artistic ideas, but were even indifferent to the material well-being of their city. In spite of the growing prosperity of Birmingham, everything in the town was in an unsatisfactory state, from the street pavements to the sanitary conditions of the dwellings'. This was the environment upon which Chamberlain, 'the most brilliant representative of a group of remarkable men whom chance brought together there', made his initial impact. It is of this group, all more or less associated with the *Post* in the first flush of its young manhood, that this chapter deals.

'They were all very advanced Radicals', Ostrogorski wrote. 'Their Radicalism had nothing speculative about it. For the most part active and intelligent men of business, they were not much encumbered with reading. They had a few men of literary education among them, but were little inclined to philosophic doubt. The picture of the Athenian democracy drawn by Grote had imbued them with a Radical enthusiasm of an uncompromising stamp; they did not understand the scruples of a John Stuart Mill, who tried to discover counter-checks for democracy; for, they believed, if democratic government is a good thing, it is so without restriction, without reserve. A very important position in this group was held by some Unitarian ministers, animated by a generous and overflowing enthusiasm which lifted every question into the higher regions of morality and civilisation. The humanitarian zeal and public spirit of one section as well as the desire of others to make their mark in public life after having succeeded in business, found a sphere of activity in the municipality of Birmingham.'

Making allowances for a savant's poor opinion of the intellectual standing of men who had not had the advantages of an academic education, this is a fair picture of the

103

Radical group that set out to make themselves masters of the Town Council and to transform the squalid city. Apart from Bunce, who had as editor to preserve a certain degree of detachment, the most active journalist in the group was William Harris, an ardent Radical and a brilliant political organiser. By profession Harris was an architect and he continued in practice as a senior partner in a firm of architects all his working life. How he found time to attend to his professional work is beyond understanding, for he was Bunce's principal leader writer for many years. He was so highly valued in this capacity that after the Home Rule split, when Harris returned from the losing battle for conciliation to the Gladstonian fold, Bunce retained his services, on the understanding that he was not to be asked to write on the forbidden topic. It must have required much diplomacy, for Harris was a fiery partisan. His trenchant Radical leaders in the brave days of the 'Unauthorised Programme' still breathe the fires of conviction. He is remembered as author of a *History of the Radical Party in Parliament*, published in 1885, a work still not wholly superseded even by the two-volume history of *English Radicalism* written by S. Maccoby in 1938.

Harris's greatest claim to remembrance, however, is his name as 'Father of the Caucus' and his greatest triumph was his celebrated scheme for defeating the Minority Clauses of the 1867 Reform Bill. Birmingham was a single constituency and was given three Members by that Bill; but each Birmingham elector was given only two votes. Harris invented the ingenious and highly controversial 'Vote as You are Told' device. By a preliminary canvass the central committee ascertained the exact number of Liberal voters in each municipal ward and the minimum of votes necessary to secure a majority at the poll. The electors in each ward were then told which two of the three Liberal candidates they should vote for. In this way no Liberal votes were wasted in

104

piling up a needlessly large majority for the most popular
candidate. He received just enough to ensure his election
and the surplus was distributed over the other two
Liberal candidates, ward by ward, to give them majori-
ties over the Conservatives. The scheme was completely
successful at the General Election in 1868, the three
Liberals, Bright, Dixon and Muntz, receiving the same
number of votes within a few hundreds, and the nearest
Conservatives not much over half the Liberal poll.

The scheme was furiously denounced by Conservatives
as a negation of democracy and the gloomiest prophecies
were made about the threat to freedom under 'Caucus
tyranny'. But the device was freely accepted and
operated by the Liberal voters; and it was only workable
in a small constituency with three Members. The votes
cast in 1868 for the whole of Birmingham were only some
30,000,—fewer than in some of the thirteen constituencies into which the enlarged city is divided to-day. A
rather similar attempt to organise the Liberal vote two
years later to capture the School Board broke down and
the Liberal Association was soundly defeated. Political
wire-pulling, however, was not Harris's chief occupation.
He appears in all sorts of contexts as a spokesman for
advanced Liberal opinions, on platforms and in the *Post*.
The cause of oppressed nationalities found in him an
indefatigable champion. He took a great interest in the
Hungarian struggle for freedom under Kossuth; Gari-
baldi engaged his sympathies; and he was the leading
spirit in a committee to organise moral support for the
people of Poland in their fight against 'the protracted and
systematic cruelty and bad faith of the Russian Government.' There is a sad topicality to-day in the causes that
excited the generous enthusiasm of Harris and his Radical
friends a century ago. With advancing years he witnessed
the decline of the old Liberal Radicalism and he withdrew from active politics. But he lived to see its revival in
new forms before he died at the ripe age of 85 in 1911.

105

It is a relief to turn from obsolete politics and battles long ago to catch a glimpse of this remarkable group of men, the 'Dawson circle' as it was called, in a happier setting. 'Our Shakespeare Club' was the intellectual centre of the community, the nineteenth century equivalent of the famous Lunar Society. It arose from the informal meetings once a month of a handful of friends of George Dawson, the first prophet of reform, who dined together and discussed at their ease everything under the sun of interest to intelligent men. In 1862, after two years, they formed themselves into a club, which they first thought of calling the Crown Club, because it sounded 'superficially loyal' and also was the price of the dinner at the Hen and Chickens, or the Stork. But as their interests were predominantly literary the name, 'Our Shakespeare Club', was adopted. Dawson, Thackray Bunce, William Harris, Sam Timmins, J. H. Chamberlain, the architect, T. Edgar Pemberton, and a score of other men of parts were the leaders and at one time or other most of the principal figures in the city were members or associates or guests. William Harris wrote a history of the club in 1904. 'The defence of freedom of thought and speech and the promotion of intellectual intercourse in the town were more or less consciously the actuating impulses in the minds of the two men (Dawson and Timmins) who may fairly be called the founders of the Club,' he wrote; and that defines its spirit. They established the principle 'that all subjects, however serious their nature, however deep and earnest the sentiment by which they were inspired,— political, social, philosophical, ethical or religious,—may be treated without animosity or disturbing the closest bonds of true friendship if the discussions are carried on with a due respect to the feelings of others and with the one desire to arrive at the truth.' None of these discussions has survived, since the meetings were strictly private; but it is impossible to over-estimate the influence of 'Our

106

Shakespeare Club' in the life of the community and, one may confidently add, in the columns of the *Post*.

In a material sense, and through individual members, the club had a principal hand in founding the magnificent Shakespeare Library, on the basis of a collection of books presented to the town by Timmins, who also was mainly responsible for the selection and purchase of books for the Reference Library. J. H. Chamberlain and Bunce, in their turn, practically reorganised the School of Art. Of the Club's members through the years, five were Members of Parliament, three of them Ministers of the Crown; eleven served on the Town Council, of whom five became Mayor and eight served on committees having charge of the literary, artistic and scientific departments of the Council. The first Recorder of the Borough, Matthew Davenport Hill, was an Honorary Member. This honour was conferred on the Recorder in 1866, when he presented the Club with a case of champagne; for high thinking did not go altogether with plain living, nor serious discussion with undue solemnity. The members, in fact, enjoyed themselves, as may be gathered from some minutes privately printed 'for Members only', which may be seen in the Birmingham Library, Margaret Street. A year after the Recorder's gift it is minuted that 'Piano provided and Ingleby sang and Anderton played.' Then follows a recurrent note, not unknown to club secretaries in the present day: 'Dinner very bad. Hon. Sec. to complain.' Sometimes members came to the rescue of the hotel commissariat, 'Thanks to Pemberton for a fine pike, 16lb. and to Mathews for champagne,' runs a minute of 1869, and again in 1873 Pemberton provided 'a pair of perfect pike.' In 1870 Bunce moved and Harris seconded the election of Joseph Chamberlain. A year later the Club had a positively frivolous debate on the Tichborne case, the losers to provide game for dinner and C. E. Mathews champagne cup. The believers in Tichborne included Joseph Chamberlain and the believers in the claimant were Dawson, Aitken, Timmins and Tonks. Bunce did not vote. Editorial prudence, no doubt. The losers eventually paid up and Hill promised a box of cigars, to be chosen by Bunce,—a nice tribute to editorial judgment. On another occasion Bunce and the Hon. Sec. were instructed 'to provide a tobacco jar and snuff box for the use of the club.' A feature of the club from its earliest days was a Summer Excursion to places of interest, often far away from the Midlands. It is interesting to note that the practice of visiting country houses, cathedral cities and historic sites on day trips in organised parties was already established a hundred years ago.

An outstanding member of this coterie and one of the Club's founders was the remarkable Sam: Timmins. Characteristic of his pleasant eccentricity was his insistence on signing himself in this fashion with a colon after the diminutive christian name, which was never expanded to full length. He and Bunce were inseparable cronies and Timmins was a prolific contributor to the *Post* of literary articles and dramatic criticism. He was a picturesque figure with fine wavy hair hanging almost in ringlets from his massive head, a full beard, cherry wood pipe and velvet jacket. The two old friends could usually be found of an afternoon with a few companions, puffing away at their pipes, in the 'select' room above the Chaucer's Head bookshop in New Street. A perfect picture, one would think, of the Victorian 'lit'ary gent', and one would not be mistaken. Literature was the passion of his life, especially Shakespeare and Byron. Before the days when Eng. Lit. fell into the hands of the academics, Sam: Timmins was an inspired student of Shakespeare and a scholar whose reputation spread far beyond his native city and even overseas. Yet he was in fact a Birmingham manufacturer of steel 'toys' and proud of it. He inherited a family business and began life in a narrow nonconformist atmosphere where the idea that

108

there could be any connection between business occupations and literary culture was utterly foreign. To the parental mind, time devoted to literary studies was diverted from the serious business of life; and it was almost by stealth that he made himself acquainted with the treasures of that literature of which he became a master and, in some branches, an authority. In later life when his name and fame as a Shakespearean scholar was established, students and critics from Germany and America would seek him out and find in a small warehouse in a Birmingham back street the man they had come to recognise as their equal in exegesis and store of information. It is not perhaps surprising to learn that he was less successful as a manufacturer than as a literary man. Towards the end of his life,—he died in 1902 at the age of 76—he was dependent on the earnings of his pen as much as on the profits of his business. He had always been lavishly generous with his means as with his knowledge in the public interest and he has left a fragrant and honourable memory in the city.

There was within the office another link between commerce and the arts in the person of Alfred Feeny, for many years the commercial editor of the *Post*. He came from a collateral branch of the family (hence the different spelling of the name, without the third 'e') and was a nephew of the founder, John Frederick Feeney. His father was an Irish journalist who came to London early in the century, and Alfred was born in London in 1834. Like many another journalist before and since, Patrick Feeny determined to put his son to a commercial career. After a wide education which included some years abroad at Cologne and Louvain, Alfred Feeny started business life in the manager's office of the old Eastern Counties Railway and later became assistant manager to the London General Omnibus Company, one of the ancestors of London Transport. When the *Birmingham Daily Post* was launched in 1857, J. F. Feeney needed help on the business side and thought of his nephew in London. In that year Alfred Feeny came to Birmingham, the first of a distinguished family that has played, and is still playing, a conspicuous part in the life of the city, notably in the Roman Catholic community. He joined the commercial department of the newspapers but the printer's ink in his veins soon found other outlets. He began writing musical, theatrical and art criticisms for the columns of the *Post*, and his literary inclinations were doubtless eagerly fostered by his contemporary, the young editor, John Thackray Bunce. One can only speculate over the adroit and conspiratorial manoeuvres of the two young men, the commercial assistant with an itch to write and the editor on the look out, as always, for literary talent in any quarter. Be that as it may, within ten years Alfred Feeny became recognised as a member of the editorial staff and the management had to look elsewhere for a business assistant.

He went over to the editorial side with the title of commercial editor and he remained responsible for all the commercial intelligence in the *Post* for close on forty years. His business talents and training, therefore, were not wasted, and in addition to his work for the *Post* he acted as Birmingham correspondent of *The Times* and was associated with the leading organ of the hardware trade, the *Ironmonger*. But he developed a quite remarkable versatility as a writer. 'He was equally at home in finance and in commerce, in music and the drama, and in fine art and in fiction,' a colleague wrote, adding, as one might guess, that 'he had the faculty of turning out his work with extraordinary rapidity.' He read widely, travelled much on the Continent, acquired an apparently inexhaustible fund of information on all sorts of subjects and astonished his colleagues with his ability to turn out brilliant 'copy' from the most unpromising material. He became, in fact, a first-class all-round journalist of a type that is of incalculable value to a newspaper. He would crop up in the most unexpected quarters,—as a military commentator on the campaigns of the Franco-Prussian War of 1870 and the Turco-Russian War of 1877-78; as the author of the short stories that it was the custom of the *Post* to published in its Christmas Day issue; and as a writer about great and mysterious crimes, which he delighted to analyse with shrewdness and insight. Probably his best work, however, and that from which he derived the greatest personal satisfaction, was his musical criticism. He was the first regular music critic of the *Post* and covered the Triennial Musical Festivals from 1858 to 1900, besides the more important subscription concerts and performances of opera at the theatres.

In his time a concert notice was a massive undertaking. Before the days of mechanical reproduction, a critic could not assume public familiarity even with the most famous works, such as Beethoven's nine symphonies. Nor was there likely to be an opportunity for a second hearing of an important new work for a long time after its first performance. A concert notice, therefore, consisted of two parts, a descriptive and analytical essay on the composition, which might be written, at least in part, beforehand from study of the score; and a critical notice of the actual performance. And this process had to be repeated for every concert, and for every major work as though it had never been heard before, as it probably never had been by a considerable part of the audience.

Alfred Feeny's musical writing was recognised and appreciated far beyond the Midlands where the paper circulated. He may be said to have established the tradition that criticism of the arts in the leading provincial newspapers, whether of music, drama, literature or the fine arts, should be in no way inferior in scholarship or literary merit to the best to be found in the metropolitan newspapers and reviews. It is a tradition that has been jealously maintained by the *Post* to the present day. The work of the critics on a newspaper stamps upon that paper its individuality and sets its standards of taste and responsibility more surely than any other feature. It is a good paper, indeed, that lives up to the level set by its critics.

So abnormally useful and versatile was Alfred Feeny that a time came when his other work had to be allowed to encroach on his musical writing. He never gave it up, but he called into partnership a local organist and music teacher, Stephen S. Stratton, who eventually succeeded him as music critic and carried on until he died in 1906, when the first whole-time music critic, Mr. Ernest Newman, was appointed. From 1877 to 1904, when Feeny retired, they shared the heavy work in a manner only possible between like-minded friends. 'We were jointly concerned in the musical work of the *Post*,' Stratton wrote years afterwards, 'and when our views did not quite coincide, there was always the endeavour to be just. The Festivals were at times hard work. Occasionally, one of us would write the analysis of a composition and the other the critique of the performance, an arrangement which required delicate handling. At the great meeting of 1885, when Dr. Richter conducted for the first time, all the *Post's* preliminary articles were ascribed by some London papers to that *facile princeps* of musical journalists, Mr. Joseph Bennett. That was a great compliment, and was duly appreciated. Mr. Feeny's first Birmingham Festival notice was written in 1858; his last in 1900. For he took a great interest in these celebrations and gave a helping hand long after he had ceased, owing to other duties, to act as musical critic. Of late years his work at the office ended just as mine began and I saw comparatively little of him; but formerly we finished at about the same time and, as our road home was the same, the walks and talks at "midnight's starry hour" were interesting and profitable to me. His range of topics was wide. He had read much and he had travelled. In the early days of the School of Art many a young

112

SUNDAY-SCHOOL TEACHER. 1864.

TOWN COUNCILLOR. 1869.

MAYOR 1874.

MEMBER OF PARLIAMENT 1876.

PRESIDENT OF LOCAL GOVERNMENT BOARD. 1886.

The Evolution of Joseph Chamberlain

Frank Schnadhorst

Out in the Cold

The Tide Turning

student had been encouraged by his kindly criticisms of the School's yearly exhibitions of work. Long before I knew him I had met with the same genial treatment with regard to one of my first published efforts. In music the great masters were naturally his idols, but he had an open mind in regard to modern developments.'

From the manager's office of the Eastern Counties Railway to an editorial position of consequence in Birmingham was a notable progress. Alfred Feeny's career however, was by no means unique. It was as good an example as could be cited of the twin facts that a born writer cannot be kept from writing and that a born journalist will turn all his interests, experiences and enthusiasms into 'copy'. He was unusual in being able to exploit all his talents and all his knowledge. Nothing in a journalist's life is ever wasted; but some things, like an early business training, are often uncongenial memories which he is glad to forget. But Alfred Feeny, the music critic and short story writer, was, after all, first and foremost the commercial editor of the *Post* and in that capacity he built the paper's reputation as the leading organ of the business community of Birmingham and the West Midlands. His knowledge of the region's trade and industry was both wide and deep. Business men and manufacturers looked to him as an authority, not only in print but as a man. Many of them would never have known of his other work and interests and quite likely they would have had less respect for his commercial acumen if they thought of him as an authority on Beethoven. Anonymity in journalism has its advantages, both for the journalist and his paper.

11

Home Rule

THE DECADE FROM 1880 TO 1890
saw Birmingham's maturity as a modern industrial city and an expansion that first strained
and then burst the old bounds and loyalties and
intimacies of the community's social and political life.
The great work of municipal reform had been accomplished. The reformers who had found Birmingham a
'rotten borough' in more than the traditional sense had
cleared the ground for rebuilding, both literally and
metaphorically. The mass of the working population now
had the vote and was asserting its claims to government,
locally and nationally, and to a larger share in the
abounding prosperity. It looked for leadership to those
who had led the city itself from squalor to decency and
above all to the dynamic chief, Joseph Chamberlain.
Gratitude is among the rarest of virtues in public life.
Birmingham has shown an unexampled loyalty to the
Chamberlain tradition for two generations, due in part
no doubt to the continuing gifts of leadership in the
family but basically to a simple gratitude for services
rendered.

Those services were not only to the material well-being
of the city and its inhabitants but, perhaps more endur-
ingly, to the people's pride and sense of importance. For
Chamberlain had graduated from the Council House to
Westminster, had soon established for himself and his
Radical friends a commanding position in the councils
of the nation and was making the name of Birmingham
heard with respect and admiration on the one hand and
fear on the other throughout the country. His methods of
political organisation spread all over the country, the
National Liberal Federation operated from Birmingham
and the city became the head and front of all that was

progressive in the life of the nation. Chamberlain's hold on 'his own people', as he always called the Birmingham folk, reached its height in the 1880's, and so did the city's influence and proper sense of self-importance. With it all, *The Birmingham Post* became one of the most important political newspapers in the land; not because it was 'Chamberlain's organ', as opponents disparagingly called it, but because it voiced the Radical faith in all its vehemence and determination.

The *Post* was inevitably the best informed Radical newspaper in the country and politicians of every shade of opinion scrutinised its news columns and leaders for hints and portents. Its relations with the Radical group were intimate and Chamberlain and Bunce kept up a running correspondence which punctuates Garvin's 'Life' at this period. In a typically Garvinesque phrase he remarks that '*The Birmingham Daily Post* was well able on occasion to vaticinate from the tripod',—in plain English, to prophesy. As a matter of fact these 'vaticinations' in the *Post* often caused trouble in the Cabinet. The Radical Three Musketeers, Chamberlain, Dilke and John Morley, used the Press without compunction to advance their cause against Whig colleagues in Cabinet and to put steady pressure on Gladstone himself. Chamberlain asserted that nothing underhand or unfair was ever done and claimed that without special intercourse with the Press it was impossible to secure an adequate defence of the decisions and policy of the Government. He admitted, however, that it was a matter of opinion whether in any given case the confidences given to the Press overstepped what was right. Ministers who found themselves and their policies embarrassed by Press disclosures that could have come only from one or other of their Radical colleagues naturally held rather strong opinions on the subject. 'The case of leakage is the most scandalous that has yet occurred and has most appearance of purpose.' Gladstone wrote indignantly to

115

Lord Granville about something in the *Post*. 'Shall I speak of it in Cabinet, when we meet, in rather strong language?' Whether he did or not on this particular occasion is not on record; but he often had to while the young lions of Radicalism were stalking their Whig quarry and treating them as little better than Tory enemies,—which, in fact, the Hartington Whigs were. Meanwhile, of course, the political stock of the *Post* soared.

'The enclosed extract from *The Birmingham Post* has been sent to me this morning,' wrote Gladstone coldly to his President of the Board of Trade. 'Statements of this nature form a heavy addition to other cares. I am at a loss to conceive how anything of this kind can have oozed. But on account of the local origin I refer it to you.' This time, however, Chamberlain was not guilty. It was the *Post's* indefatigable Parliamentary correspondent, H. W. Lucy, who had written about troubles in the Cabinet in a manner suitable to his Birmingham market and on the basis of common gossip in the Lobby. Gladstone could be very simple-minded over newspaper reports and the methods of clever political correspondents in putting two and two together to make a hard story. When a government is sick unto death, as Gladstone's was in the Summer of 1885, the symptoms are clear enough to shrewd observers.

The Radicals were at loggerheads with the Whigs on almost every subject and were making an all-out bid for the succession to the leadership of the Liberal Party, which everybody expected to fall vacant when the seventy-six years old Gladstone finally carried out his frequent hints of imminent retirement. They had incurred his displeasure with their 'unauthorised programme' of reform by agitation and, most ironically, by their advocacy in Cabinet of a liberal Irish policy involving the abandonment of coercion and the granting of a large measure of Irish self-government. Chamberlain had

116

agreed to tone down his Radical campaign in the country for a while and was trying to negotiate a settlement with the implacable Parnell, to remove the Irish obstacle from the path of domestic reform.

That Radical campaign had opened the year with Chamberlain's notorious 'ransom' speech to a working-man's demonstration in Birmingham Town Hall. 'What ransom will property pay for the security it enjoys?' he demanded; and a shudder passed through the propertied classes throughout the country. Such language from a responsible Minister of the Crown had never been heard before; it was not to be heard again for another twenty years, when another Minister, who had been inspired in his Welsh youth by the Chamberlain trumpet, took up the call at Limehouse. To-day the items of the 'unauthorised programme',—principally, graded income tax and compulsory acquisition of land for public purposes, —sound mild enough and have been carried far beyond anything intended or visualised by Chamberlain. But in 1885 they appeared revolutionary and the blunt eloquence of Chamberlain an incitement to the overthrow of Church and State.

Next morning the *Post* leader-writer,—probably that old Radical warhorse William Harris,—drove home the challenge. The speech 'took a wide and wise view of national policy ' from the point of view of 'the interests, the fortunes and the desires of those great masses of the population now, for the first time, to be entrusted with a predominant voice in the formation of the Government of the Country . . . the increase of the recognition on the one side of the rights of the people and on the other of the duties of property is put by Mr. Chamberlain as the keynote of the new policy. Last night he could indicate no more than the broad lines on which the policy should be founded; but he said enough to induce the people to believe that they need not go beyond the ranks of their old and trusted friends to find leaders who will

117

direct the new constitutional forces towards the legitimate objects of democratic desire.' The last sentence went to the root of the matter. That was the issue,—the leadership of the urban masses enfranchised by the reforms of 1867 and of the rural workers who were to exercise the vote for the first time at the forthcoming general election. Chamberlain and his friends had no sentimental illusions about the supposed political wisdom of 'the people'. Many were old enough to remember the Chartist debacle when a genuinely democratic movement drove on to the rocks for lack of skilled pilots. The Radicals with their experience of platform agitation and their incomparable machinery of the Caucus felt themselves to be predestined leaders of the new democracy; at least until such time as the universal, unsectarian free education that occupied a prominent place in their programme should create a people fit for self-government.

Chamberlain himself had every reason to believe in his personal power over the masses in Birmingham. The great mass meetings of this period were acts of adoration. If the accounts in the *Post* are suspected of partisan enthusiasm, there survives one remarkable picture of a Chamberlain Town Hall demonstration from the pen of an observer of unquestioned impartiality. It is an extraordinary piece of word-painting by any standards; but it is simply amazing coming from a young woman of 25. Beatrice Potter, however, was no ordinary young woman and this extract from *My Apprenticeship* foreshadows the qualities of the famous Fabian partnership of Sidney and Beatrice Webb,—keen sighted observation, powers of analysis and description and an almost inhuman detachment from mass emotion. Here is her account of a Birmingham meeting in 1884, committed to her private diary.

'Below us, packed as close as may be, stand some thousands of men. Strong barriers divide the hall into sections, and, as a newcomer pushes in or a faint-hearted

118

one attempts to retire, the whole section sways to and fro. Cheers rise out of the general hum as a favourite member of the "nine hundred" seats himself; and friendly voices from the crowd greet the M.P.'s from neighbouring constituencies, or delegates from other caucuses, as they take their places on the platform. The band strikes up, and the three members for Birmingham enter. John Bright is received with affectionate and loyal applause, as he stands for a moment before the children and the children's children of his old friends and contemporaries. Muntz, a feeble-looking elderly gentleman, with rabbit-like countenance and shambling gait, forms an interval between Bright and Chamberlain; and, in his weak mediocrity, looks comically out of place—a materialised vacuum—between these two strong embodiments of humanity. Chamberlain, the master and the darling of his town, is received with deafening shouts. The Birmingham citizen (unless he belongs to the despised minority) adores "our Joe", for has he not raised Birmingham to the proud position of one of the great political centres of the universe?

'I was disappointed in Bright as an orator. Still, there was something nobly pathetic in the old old story of Tory sinfulness told by the stern-looking old man, who seemed gradually to lose consciousness of the crowd beneath him, and see himself confronted with the forces of the past. The people listened with reverence and interest, and as one looked down upon them, and one's eye wandered from face to face, this mass of human beings, now under the influence of one mind, seemed to be animated by one soul. Perhaps the intoxicating effect of the people's sympathy is due to the great fact of the one in the many.

'While Philip Muntz meandered through political commonplace, and defended himself from charges of lukewarmness and want of loyalty to the Radical programme, the crowd once more became a concourse of disconnected individuals. The subtle bond was broken which had bound man to man and fused all into one substance worked upon by an outside force. Laughter and loud-toned chaff passed from neighbour to neighbour. Conflicting cries of "Speak up, Philip", "Make way for a better man", "We'll hear you", and hissed-down attempts to clap him into a speedy end, showed the varying tempers of the mixed multitude. As the time advanced, the backward portion became more and more unruly, whilst the eyes of those in front gradually concentrated themselves on the face of the next speaker. He seemed lost in intent thought. You could watch in his expression some form of feeling working itself into the mastery of his mind. Was that feeling spontaneous or intentioned? Was it created by an intense desire to dominate, to impress his own personality and his own aim on that pliable material beneath him; or did it arise from the consciousness of helpful power, from genuine sympathy with the wants and cravings of the great mass who trusted him?

'As he rose slowly, and stood silently before his people, his whole face and form seemed transformed. The crowd became wild with enthusiasm. Hats, handkerchiefs, even coats, were waved frantically as an outlet of feeling. The few hundreds of privileged individuals seated in the balcony rose to their feet. There was one loud uproar of applause and, in the intervals between each fresh outburst, one could distinguish the cheers of the crowd outside, sending its tribute of sympathy. Perfectly still stood the people's Tribune, till the people, exhausted and expectant, gradually subsided into fitful and murmuring cries. At the first sound of his voice they became as one man. Into the tones of his voice he threw the warmth of feeling which was lacking in his words; and every thought, every feeling, the slightest intonation of irony or contempt was reflected on the face of the crowd. It might have been a woman listening to the words of her lover! Perfect response, and unquestioning receptivity. Who reasons with his mistress? The wise man asserts his will, urges it with warmth or bitterness, and flavours it with flattery and occasional appeals to moral sentiments. No wonder that the modern politician turns with disgust from cantankerous debates of an educated "House" to the undisputing sympathy of an uneducated and like-thinking crowd. Not extraordinary that the man of passionate conviction, or of the will which simulates it and clothes it in finely worded general principles, who ignores all complexity in things, should become the ruling spirit, when the ultimate appeal, the moving force, rests with the masses whose desires are prompted by passion and unqualified by thought.'

Beatrice Webb was a personal friend of Chamberlain's, —all her life she was something of a connoisseur of public men,—and after the public meeting she went behind the scenes to dine with the chief in company with a few intimates of the Caucus. Her comments on this private occasion are equally illuminating, but one only will suffice, for its shrewdly prophetic quality. 'In his treatment of some members of the Association,' she noted, '(I noticed this particularly in his attitude towards Schnadhorst) he used the simple power of "You shall, and you go to the devil if you don't."' Thus already to this alarmingly acute girl the Achilles' heel was apparent, when, in Mr. Julian Amery's lambent phrase, 'the edge of persuasion would be dulled by the habit of command.' When the rupture came the little nonconformist draper, Schnadhorst, the organising genius of the Caucus, turned into Chamberlain's bitterest enemy and carried the National Liberal Federation against him.

Stale politics can be as tedious as old sermons and the details of the Home Rule Split and the disruption of the Liberal Party have been worked over time and again by industrious and often brilliant writers. The consequences were tragic enough for England and Ireland and have

121

not yet worked themselves out. Our concern, however, is with the part played by the *Post* when Chamberlain parted company with the Gladstonian Liberals and the first Home Rule Bill and led his band of Unionists over to the Conservative camp. At this distance of time it all seems so unnecessary and the margin of disagreement absurdly narrow. That was in essence the attitude of the *Post* in the 1880's. The paper fought steadfastly for accommodation, compromise, reconciliation in the Liberal Party and the fight lasted from the launching of the so-called 'Harwarden Kite' in the Winter of 1885 well into the Summer of 1887. But the material for compromise was lacking in the minds of the leading figures and one cannot escape from the conclusion that the Home Rule Split was only the occasion for the release of a disruptive tidal force that was carrying men into a new era without their knowledge or understanding.

Gladstone's ineptitude at this period has bewildered admirers, biographers, historians and political writers. 'Old age had had on him a strange effect' writes G. M. Trevelyan, 'It left his gifts and energies as wonderful as ever and his mind no less open to new ideas, but it diminished his tact and prudence.' He accomplished the 'almost incredible feat' of driving out from the Liberal Party on this Irish issue not only the Chamberlain Radicals, but their most hostile opponents, the Hartington Whigs and the venerable John Bright. His most recent biographer, Sir Philip Magnus, decides that 'Chamberlain could have been kept loyal if he had been more wisely handled.' Writing of Disraeli and Salisbury, Dr. Traill acidly said that 'both enjoyed the inestimable advantage of being opposed by a politician (Gladstone) whose influence in undesignedly healing feuds among his political adversaries has often earned him the benediction pronounced upon the peace-makers.'

If only Gladstone had consented to include in the first Home Rule Bill continued Irish representation at Westminster—as he did spontaneously in his second Home Rule Bill of 1892,—the *Post*, at any rate, would have been satisfied. Whether Chamberlain would is another matter. However, in hopes of securing an amendment in this sense, the *Post* supported the Bill on second reading, when Chamberlain voted against it. 'The supremacy of the Imperial Parliament must be preserved; and with this firmly secured, all else is possible', the paper wrote at the very start of the controversy; and to that principle it adhered with hope and gathering despair until the bitter end. At the general election in the Summer of 1886, when Chamberlain advised his supporters to vote Tory against Liberal Home Rule candidates, the *Post* vigorously contradicted him. 'Vote, say these advisers in effect, for any candidate, whatever his political views, who is against the Irish policy of the Prime Minister. Put party aside, let general principles go to the winds; only, for this time, give a majority pledged to prevent Mr. Gladstone from giving a legislative assembly to Ireland. Now, we most earnestly ask all electors whom our words can reach to put aside, to disregard, to entirely reject these lamentably mistaken counsels. We ask them to do so because the only possible result of putting Mr. Gladstone in a minority is to hand over to Lord Salisbury power, not only with regard to this one question, but as to all questions.'

This is a significant leader. It shows that the *Post* was not opposed to Home Rule for Ireland *in toto* or on principle, but only to the particular method embodied in Gladstone's Bill. The paper had supported the second reading of the Bill and was still satisfied that it could be amended to meet the ostensible objections that had led Chamberlain to vote against the second reading. It repudiated the very idea of voting Tory to destroy the Bill, because that would also destroy Gladstone and the Liberal Government. This was a shrewd prediction. The electors took Chamberlain's advice, not the *Post's*, and the result was to put the Conservatives in office for the next twenty years, apart from the brief and sterile Liberal interlude from 1892 to 1895. In Birmingham two Tory Members were returned with the help of Liberal votes. 'The mischief is done for the present' the *Post* sadly commented, 'and the familiar proverb that it is no use crying over spilt milk conveys a calming lesson even in the heat and conflict of a political contest.'

Out of office, there seemed a fair chance the Liberals might compose their differences over details. We know to-day, in the light of subsequent disclosures, that it was a forlorn hope. Chamberlain meant to destroy Home Rule and Gladstone and also Parnell, whom he wrongly supposed to have played him false in their secret negotiations twelve months earlier. But the intensely dramatic background of intrigue which culminated a few years later in the Parnell divorce case and the Irish leader's downfall was unknown to contemporaries. Men of good-will laboured for reconciliation within the Liberal Party and the *Post* threw all its weight on the side of compromise in leader after leader.

By the Spring of 1887, however, things were looking desperate. It was borne in upon the peace-makers that there were obstacles to agreement between Liberal politicians that they did not know about and could not understand. A note of exasperation crept into the *Post's* leaders. 'The chief need of the situation is mutual frankness,' it exclaimed bluntly in April, 1887. 'At present the party is wasting its strength in civil war; and the worst of it is that not a single person, from top to bottom of the party, can tell us precisely what we are fighting about.' A month later matters came to a head. The Gladstonian Liberals were asked to define the details of a Home Rule Bill which they would introduce when returned to power and especially on the question of Irish Members in the Imperial Parliament. The reply was entrusted to John Morley, who, with Charles Dilke, had been Chamberlain's closest friend in the days of Radical reform. The bitterness of a personal quarrel gave a cutting edge to Morley's speech. He refused to give any pledges, not even on Irish representation, which was in fact included in Gladstone's Bill of 1892, and he made a wounding attack on Chamberlain and the Unionists. 'This, we take it, is the official answer,' the *Post* wrote, 'a refusal of concession, a refusal even of reply, an imputation of base motives and of deceitful professions. There is only one thing to be said. It is a most unhappy speech and one that is fraught with mischief alike to the interests of Ireland and to the reunion of the Liberal Party.'

It only remained for the Liberal Unionists to table their ideas for an Irish settlement, which they proceeded to do, and to present them for acceptance at a Town Hall meeting. They can be summarised as Home Rule with safeguards and they were elaborated in the *Post* in a series of articles, reprinted as a pamphlet, which was ascribed to Chamberlain but actually was written by Bunce. In a long and closely argued leader on the 2nd of June, 1887, *The Birmingham Post* aligned itself with the Unionist minority. 'They have a policy of construction, it is clear and frank, and in its main lines we believe it to be one that will commend itself to the approval of the country and to ultimate acceptance by Parliament.' All hope of Liberal reconciliation was abandoned. 'It is a saddening confession to make, but there is no avoiding it; and perhaps on the whole it is better that the fact should be admitted and that no further effort should be made to patch up a delusive agreement certain to fall to pieces on the first real strain to which it may be subjected.'

On the delicate and troublesome subject of collaboration with the Conservatives, the leader-writer seems to have lost his sureness of touch. He toys wordily with a notion that if Lord Salisbury were to retire (he continued to lead the Conservatives until 1902) the Whig leader, Lord Hartington, who had also broken with the Glad-

125

stonian Liberals over Home Rule, might become Prime Minister in a Conservative-Unionist Government. 'When once the bonds of party union are severed, and when one great question dominates all others, there is ample room for conjecture. Under such circumstances it is possible that combinations may become feasible, or even inevitable, which under ordinary conditions would never be so much as dreamt of.' As events turned out, the 'one great question', Home Rule, sank below the horizon in the confusion following Parnell's ruin and Irish nationalism ceased for a time to dominate British politics. The Imperialist movement, scarcely discernable in 1887, rose in the firmament and incidentally effected the integration of the Liberal Unionists with the Conservative Party. The Radical programme sank virtually without trace. Stalwarts like William Harris reverted to Gladstonian Liberalism, disheartened and discouraged; 'never glad confident morning again.' The *Post*, however, clung obstinately to its claim to Liberal origins and never ceased to make respectful obeisance to the shades of Gladstone and John Bright. This was no empty gesture. In social policy the *Post* has been progressive and liberal (without a capital letter) and almost aggressively independent of party ties.

12

London Office

APIED-A-TERRE IN FLEET STREET
probably existed earlier, but the first mention
of a London Office occurs in the paper for 2nd
November, 1877. An office had been opened at
138, Fleet Street, it was announced, 'where files of the
paper can be inspected and copies purchased. Advertisements for the *Post* received at the London Office not later
than five o'clock p.m. will be in time for next morning's
publication.' No indication is given of editorial use of
this office, but the *Post*, and the *Journal* before it, took
a variety of London correspondence and several well-
known names in journalism were among the contributors
of regular features. The earliest writer of a London Letter
was E. B. Neill, who has already been mentioned in connection with the *Journal*. It continued as a weekly feature
and it was not until 1888, in fact, that a London Letter
was started daily, when A. F. Robbins (later, Sir Alfred
Robbins) gave his exclusive services to the *Post* as London
Correspondent. Until then London Letters, Parliamentary articles and other features were contributed by
journalists serving on London newspapers or as free-
lances. Neill introduced to a share in his work one T.
Frost, whose *Reminiscences of a Country Journalist* (1886)
contain some references to the early days. Frost was a
leader-writer and reporter, who began by sending reports
of Select Committees and other public enquiries on
subjects of particular interest to Birmingham. He
developed into a specialist in industrial and labour affairs
and also wrote articles of a technical nature on extension
of the franchise before the big reforms of 1867. He never
met the Birmingham proprietors, but he records 'one
pleasant recollection' of the founder, John Frederick
Feeney. Through Neill, he had done a 'trifling service' in

connection with the erection of a monument in Kensal Green cemetery to one of the founder's brothers. 'I think,' Feeney wrote to Neill, 'you told me Mr. Frost is a married man. He shall have the best goose in Warwickshire.'

Among the better-known contributors was William Hale White (Mark Rutherford) who wrote a weekly column of *Sketches in Parliament* for the *Post* from 1866 to 1880. For many years before he became editor of the *Daily News* in 1885, a famous Parliamentary journalist, H. W. Lucy ('Toby M.P.' of *Punch*) wrote a weekly London Letter for several provincial newspapers, including the *Post*. His account of those years gives a vivid picture of the crowded working life of an industrious Parliamentary journalist. 'Among other work carried on through these days of drudgery,' he wrote in his reminiscences, 'I wrote a weekly London Letter which appeared simultaneously in seven or eight of the principal country papers.' He had his salaried work for the *Daily News* and, later on, also a daily London Letter for the provinces. 'After luncheon I went straight off to the House. On most nights, with an interval for dinner, I was in my box in the Gallery in close touch with what was going on till the House was up. At this stage my work was simply doubled. I was a dual personage; summary writer for the *Daily News*, London Correspondent for eight important daily papers, each wanting the best. In addition, no slight addition, I spent an hour, sometimes two, in the Lobby in conversation with multitudinous friends on both sides of the House. As a result, I wrote for the *Daily News* in addition to 'Pictures in Parliament,' a separate London Letter, rarely less than half a column in length. After all, it was easy enough. I made it a point of honour never to touch my country work till I had done my best for the *Daily News*. That copy despatched with full record up to the current moment, I approached my London Letter from a fresh point of view, wrote in a different

128

Sam: Timmins

T. Edgar Pemberton

style and, though necessarily dealing with the same incidents, produced an article which no one not privy to the fact would know was the work of one and the same person. Taking up the wondrous tale at a later period of the sitting, the process was repeated, the *Daily News* always being first served.'

Lucy wrote with a marvellous fluency and sparkle and was in consequence in great demand; but he was by no means unique in the volume of work he undertook. Capable and hard-working Parliamentary journalists nearly always supplemented their meagre salaries by doing additional work for other papers or for periodicals in the days when Parliament was the staple diet of the reading public. It was, however, no easy task to turn out a sketch of the night's proceedings while they were actually taking place, a London Letter in, as Lucy points out, a different style, and miscellaneous other items for one or more papers. The practice of the more important newspapers of appointing their own exclusive London Correspondents, Parliamentary sketch writers and Lobby Correspondents was of slow growth and the roles are often doubled to this day. Lengthy and partly verbatim reports of debates have been supplied for many years by the news agencies. Sometimes newspapers would employ a reporter of their own to supplement the agency reports on subjects of particular interest to a paper's locality or to follow questions put to Ministers by local members. Nowadays the agencies undertake specialised work of this kind when it is required. *The Times* maintains its own team of shorthand-reporters in the Gallery. Other large papers generally rely on the agencies for their extended reports and on their own London staff for a sketch-summary and for Lobby news. Until the drastic newsprint rationing of the Second World War destroyed the old pattern, a leading provincial newspaper habitually carried on its 'leader page' a London Letter running into two columns and a full column Parliamentary sketch.

On a strict assessment of news value, Parliament did not always deserve this measure of space and prominence every day. It was a sketch-writer's business to make it appear deserving and to keep it interesting.

For more than half the life of the *Post* the paper has had its London Office at 88, Fleet Street, with a side frontage on St. Bride's Avenue, a shallow, paved way leading up to one of the most beautiful of Wren's city churches. The shell of the church, with its lovely spire, is now being restored, having been gutted by fire in the blitz. Building activities always seem to have been a feature of this part of Fleet Street. A print of 1745 shows St. Bride's Church and Churchyard plainly visible to anyone walking down Fleet Street across an open space to the west of what is now No. 88. In the next half-century mean buildings engulfed and hid the church. They were destroyed by fire in 1824. Rebuilding and clearances took place alternately until, in 1900, the building line was set back between Salisbury Court and Bride Lane. Renumbering makes it difficult to identify the present site with former buildings in the vicinity; but No. 88 and its newer, towering neighbour across St. Bride's Avenue, the headquarters of the Press Association and Reuters, may be content to share the honour of standing on a site that deserves to be called historic in the annals of the Press. For hereabouts, at what was then called No. 84, were the premises of Richard Carlile, printer and bookseller, who, in the words of the distinguished historian, G. M. Trevelyan, 'suffered and achieved more for the liberty of the Press than any other Englishman of the nineteenth century.' He was not an endearing character, for he had all of Cobbett's radical vanity without Cobbett's touch of genius. But he endured fines and persecution and unjust imprisonment in the cause of freedom. He and his like bore the brunt of the early struggles with authority for the right to republish the works of Thomas Paine and other deistic writers of

130

the eighteenth century, whose influence had been snuffed out in the repressions of the Napoleonic Wars. The revival of the submerged doctrines of Tom Paine by Carlile and others was the beginning of the Radical Movement which dominates so much of this story of a Radical newspaper. 'Thanks to these sturdy predecessors,' Trevelyan says, 'the decorous and well-to-do philosophers of the Victorian era were able without fear of the law to write whatever they thought about the relation of science and literature to dogmatic belief' and the scientists of the Darwin-Huxley period vindicated 'the right of science to investigate and teach, without having first to square its results with Mosaic theology.'

It is not only the fact that Carlile occupied the site that qualifies the corner of St. Bride's Avenue for a commemorative plaque. The use he made of it in time of trouble should touch the hearts of good churchmen disposed to disapprove of the man and all his works. When in 1824 a fire destroyed Carlile's house and the adjoining properties, the churchmen of St. Bride's saw an opportunity to improve the view of their hemmed-in church and regain a frontage on Fleet Street. The owner of the house, however, was in jail in Dorset, where he had lain for five years on a trumped-up charge of libel. He made his release the chief condition for parting with his house to St. Bride's. The churchmen would seem to have been in something of a dilemma, but, very sensibly, they put the interests of their church above any reluctance to plead on behalf of an 'infidel' printer and bookseller. Besides, Peel was Home Secretary and Peel was growing heartily sick of coercion. No official record exists of the transaction and we have only Carlile's word for it that in May, 1825, a committee of churchmen interviewed Peel. In November of that year, however, the sheriff of Dorset received two Royal Warrants concerning Richard Carlile. The first said: 'We do hereby remit so much of the said fines as may still remain unpaid.' The second was rather more flowery of speech and still more acceptable. 'We, in consideration of some favourable circumstances presented unto us in his behalf, are graciously pleased to extend our grace and mercy unto him, to remit unto him such part of his said sentences as directs his finding security for his good behaviour.' Mr. William Wickwar, who has rescued this episode from oblivion in his admirable history, *The Struggle for the Freedom of the Press*, is moved to a poetic epilogue. 'After six years' imprisonment for libel Carlile was at last free as the wind that blew upon him as he rode away on top of the coach across the Dorset Downs to his native Devon.' Prosaically we may add: 'And that is how St. Bride's Avenue came into being.'

A corner site made available by the clearances for the street-widening in 1900 was bought at auction for £15,000, a large sum even for London City land fifty years ago, and the task of designing the new building was entrusted to John Belcher, A.R.A. It was to be an investment and the greater part was to be let off to business tenants until such time as the expanding needs of the paper called for the whole accommodation. A water-colour drawing of the building as designed was shown by the architect at the Royal Academy in 1902. Fleet Street was, and still is, an architectural muddle, but the designer of *The Birmingham Post* building had the beautiful spire of St. Bride's Church as a nodal point to restrain any tendency towards exuberance. The style he adopted was described at the time as 'a quiet, but strong, type of Renaissance architecture.' The resulting building was a considerable improvement on the general level of architecture in a street that could do with improvement. It was much praised in its day and, though it has been over-topped by many later buildings in the Street of Ink, it remains a rare and conspicuous example of tactful modesty and decent regard for good neighbourly conduct. In the light of subsequent developments in

132

newspaper production, which could scarcely be foreseen fifty years ago, the interior lay-out could have been better; but that could be said of almost any functional building erected in the first years of the present century. On the ground floor are the public office and the offices of the London Commercial Manager and his staff. Above that are the editorial offices, including the room housing the agency teleprinters and other instruments that pour out 'copy' for the attention of the sub-editors. The London Editor, the City Editor and their assistants have their abodes on the editorial floors and higher still is the vital 'Wire Room' where a staff of telegraphists transmits 'copy' to the Birmingham head office and also, nowadays, wired pictures. The London Office serves all three newspapers, editorially and commercially, and functions by day and night. The building opened in January, 1903, had cost £9,000, over and above the cost of the site. It continues to be adequate for its purpose.

Before the custom arose of designating many departmental heads with the title of 'editor', accompanied by a descriptive prefix, the head of the London Office was known by the traditional name of London Correspondent. In 1903 the new office was taken over by a distinguished journalist, Alfred Farthing Robbins, who is most fittingly commemorated on a monument in St. Bride's as 'Lobbyist in the Palace of Westminster and London Letter writer in the parish of St. Bride.' He had been whole-time London Correspondent of the *Post* since 1888 and he was to continue as such until he retired in 1924, a period of 35 momentous years. His intimate acquaintance with public affairs and public men began in the days of Gladstone, Salisbury and the Home Rule controversies and closed in the post-war era of Lloyd George, Baldwin, and Ramsay MacDonald. Already, by 1903, he was doyen of Lobby correspondents, a confidant of party leaders, including Joseph Chamberlain, and a valued friend and adviser of the young Austen Chamber-

133

lain, about to take office for the first time as Chancellor of the Exchequer in Balfour's Government while his father stumped the country in the cause of Tariff Reform. Sir Alfred Robbins (he was knighted in 1917) had come to the top of his profession by the hard way. Son of a Launceston Town Councillor and born in 1856, he was apprenticed to a local chemist on leaving the Grammar School at the age of fourteen. Three older brothers, George, Edmund and John, were already in journalism, on the road to successes in Fleet Street that were to make the Robbins family famous in the newspaper world for two generations. The young Alfred gave up virtually all his spare time to writing for the local paper, the *East Cornwall Times,*—leading articles, letters, reports of evening meetings and notes on local history, for none of which he received any payment. His first salaried job in journalism was on the *Western Daily Mercury,* which he left after eight months when his request for an increase of his salary of 9s. 8d. a week was refused. After further provincial experience, he came to London in 1879 as one of the chief sub-editors of the Press Association. His first connection with the *Post* came in 1885, when he succeeded his brother G. F. Robbins, as contributor of a weekly London Letter. His appointment as London Correspondent in 1888 inaugurated the daily London Letter which he was to stamp so firmly with his personality. It became the inspiration and model for the London Letters of other provincial papers. Politics was his abiding interest but he set an example to London Correspondents of cultivating a wide field. He was an enthusiastic playgoer and dramatic critic and his writing was seen at its best in descriptions of great scenes of pageantry in the capital.

His greatest satisfaction, however, was derived from the universal trust he won from politicians of all shades. Nothing pleased him more in the whole course of his career than a remark made by the aloof and imperious

134

Irish leader, Parnell: 'I like Robbins; he never leaks.'
When the time came for public tributes, they were heart-
felt and unstinted. 'I have often heard my father speak of
him in the warmest terms,' Neville Chamberlain wrote
to Lady Robbins. 'He held him in the highest regard as a
man in whom the most absolute confidence could be
reposed and who combined the keenest political flair
with a sound discretion and a perfect sense of honour.
Their association was very close, and though my own
acquaintance with him came much later he always
showed me a kindness and consideration which I deeply
appreciated. It was always a rare pleasure to talk with
him. I have known few men whose minds were so richly
stocked with interesting experiences, and he always
seemed able to draw upon them without effort and as he
wanted them.'

A letter in the possession of the family which Robbins
received from Austen Chamberlain in reply to a note of
congratulation on his 'coming of age' as a Minister,
reflects the feeling for the man and his work. 'Twenty-
one years seems a long spell of work and life, but on the
whole they have been very interesting and if I had my
choice of career to make over again I should not make it
differently. I hope that you feel able to say the same. In
days when, more and more, both the news and the
comments in the daily papers seem written to order, the
value and the interest of independent writing increase.'
From a politician of a very different party and character,
Lord Morley, came a note of congratulation when
Robbins received the honour of Knighthood. 'Never was
journalistic honour more worthily bestowed,' wrote this
old opponent of everything political that Robbins and
the *Post* stood for by 1917.

'You began the Lobby five years after I entered the
House. As a contemporary I can testify to the high
standard of your work and to the wise, kindly and
honourable feeling that went through it all.' Then

135

in a postscript John Morley added an acute observation. 'Not many people know as I do your special
difficulties in steering a straight course from a rather
sensitive and imperious city.'

Away back in 1899, when Joseph Chamberlain was
about to pay a visit to Ireland, Robbins heard of the
existence in Dublin of a sinister organisation known as
the 'Transvaal War Committee,' which might be expected to make trouble during the Colonial Secretary's
stay. He did not deem it sensible to allude to the fact
publicly, but, in case the British authorities were unaware
of the organisation, he dropped a private note of warning
to the Minister. Joseph Chamberlain's reply was characteristic. 'I am much obliged for your friendly hint,' he
wrote. 'I have no doubt the local authorities will make
all safe, but if not, I am quite ready to take my chance.'
At another time Robbins had occasion to send a copy
of the *Post* to Lord Milner containing a reference to him.
Milner's reply was an adroit compliment from one who
had no reason to be friendly towards the Press in general.
'I may say that, on various occasions in the past, my
attention has been called to the London Letter of *The
Birmingham Post*, and I have had occasion to appreciate
its well-informed and judicious tone, without knowing
who was its author. It will now have additional interest
for me.'

There are many more letters in the family papers to
testify to Robbins' close and friendly relations with
leaders in public life and to their regard for him as man
and journalist. This evocation of one of the most eminent
servants of the *Post* cannot close better than on a quo-
tation from an eloquent address given by Sir Austen
Chamberlain in 1932, when he unveiled the tablet in
St. Bride's. 'Here in St. Bride's, and in Fleet Street, we
think of him first and foremost as a journalist. He did not
occupy one of those commanding positions in the Press
that gives at once an introduction to whatever society

136

the occupier of it desires to enter in any country in the world. His was a humbler sphere, but, for many years, as Lobbyist in the Palace of Westminster and Letter-Writer in the Parish of St. Bride, he occupied a position which must have exposed him to many temptations, a position all the more open to abuse because he was, like the great mass of journalists, anonymous to the public who read his work and known by name only to a comparatively limited circle. In that position, watching and living in the midst of the fierce conflicts of party that broke out more than once in his time with quite exceptional acerbity, it is true of him to say he never said an unfair thing, and that, writing in haste, as he was bound to do, he still was able to restrain his pen, and that, whatever his own views, his own predilections, his own hopes or his own fears, he never made an unfair comment on an opponent and never twisted the truth to serve a friend.

'I doubt whether any other journalist in Sir Alfred's position was received on a footing of such complete confidence by so many different men. He inspired trust in them all. His judgment was worth listening to; his views were worth ascertaining. You gave him what you had to give in order that in return you might receive from him the contribution which he could make. However fierce their conflict and their differences, leaders of all parties gave him their confidence as a man whose integrity was above suspicion, one who would never take a mean or unfair advantage, and one in whom loyalty to any confidence confided to him could be placed in perfect trust.'

This tribute from a statesman who was himself accounted the soul of honour is quoted at some length because it describes so admirably the ideal relationship that should exist between a Lobby Correspondent and leaders in public life and gives a perfect picture of the work and duties and obligations of a Lobby Corres-

137

pondent in those days. Since Robbins' day conditions in the Lobby have changed. He had to get the news by assiduous 'lobbying' of Ministers, Opposition leaders and private Members, picking up clues and hints here and there, putting two and two together and drawing his own conclusions,—often working under a sense that something important was afoot which was being concealed from him or that some of his informants were flying kites for their own purposes and trying to mislead him. Nowadays the dissemination of political information has been systematized. There is no lack of news, of a sort. Press conferences, Public Relations Officers, departmental 'hand-outs,' embarrass political correspondents with a wealth of material. But it is all material the suppliers want to be published; and therefore has to be taken with the caution proverbially advisable in dealing with those who come bearing gifts. The modern Lobby Correspondent needs a cool, discriminating mind, a habit of reading between the lines for unacknowledged motives and a determination not to mislead his editor and his readers by a too-ready acceptance of information at face value. At the same time he must possess the traditional virtues of integrity and reliability eulogised by Sir Austen Chamberlain and direct them as heretofore to the creation of mutual confidence and the elucidation of the truth. Were he alive to-day, Alfred Robbins probably would not approve of the indiscriminate dissemination of information; but almost certainly he would see in it greater opportunities for exercising his old gifts for discovering 'the news behind the news' and presenting a balanced account to readers of the *Post*.

Outside his work as a journalist, Sir Alfred Robbins had what was virtually a second career in Freemasonry, which brought him into association with a great variety of men in all walks of life. He devoted himself wholeheartedly to the business and charitable interests of the craft. For many years he was President of the Board of

138

General Purposes of Grand Lodge, a position which has been described as that of the Prime Minister of Free-masonry, and at the end of his life he was a Past Grand Warden. These and other positions of honour and dignity he filled with an assurance and high competence derived from his experience of public life as an observer in the Lobby. A last word on the man himself is most appropriately to be had from a letter to the family from his colleagues of the Parliamentary Lobby Journalists Committee: 'Every political journalist admired and loved Sir Alfred Robbins. His distinguished career was an inspiration and an ideal to all of us. He had that happy quality, which only the best of men possess, of giving cordial comradeship to his juniors and treating them as equals, which they never felt themselves to be.'

The Robbins tradition in Fleet Street has been most worthily carried on by the present generation. No fewer than three of his four sons have been engaged on the editorial staff of *The Times*, one of them, Mr. Alan Pitt Robbins, as political correspondent for several years in the Lobby where his father worked and later as News Editor. On his retirement from *The Times* Alan Robbins, who had begun his London career on *The Birmingham Post*, became Secretary of the General Council of the Press.

April 1. 1913. EGERTON PLACE.
S.W.

Dear Mr Robbins,

Many thanks
for your kind wish.
Twenty one years seem a
long spell of work & life
but on the whole they
have been very interesting
& if I had my choice
of a career to make
over again I should

From Sir Austen Chamberlain (1)

not make it differently. I hope that you feel able to say the same. In days when, more & more, both the news & the comments in the daily papers are written to order, the value & the interest of independent writing increase. So I very heartily reciprocate your wishes & express the hope for long continued life & activity for you

Yrs sincerely

Austen Chamberlain

From Sir Austen Chamberlain (2)

Highbury,
Moor Green,
Birmingham

Dec: 8/99

Dear Mr Robbins

I am much obliged for your friendly
hint, I have no doubt the
local authorities will make all
safe but if not I am quite ready
to take my chance.
Believe me
yours very truly,
J. Chamberlain

From Joseph Chamberlain

```
                              47 Duke St,
                                 St James's,
                                    S.W.

Private                       4 April, 1913.


Dear Mr Robbins,

          Many thanks for your letter and for the two
copies of the Birmingham Post, which you kindly sent
me.
          I may say that, on various occasions in the
past, my attention has been called to the London
Letter of the Birmingham Post, and I have had occa-
sion to appreciate its well-informed and judicious
tone, without knowing who was its author.  It will
now have additional interest for me.

                    Believe me,

                    Yours very truly,

                         Milner
```

From Lord Milner

Privt:

June 5. 17.

FLOWERMEAD.
WIMBLEDON PARK.
S.W.

My dear Robbins,

I congratulate you with warmth and sincerity. Never was journalistic honour more worthily bestowed. You began the lobby five years after I entered the House. As a contemporary I can testify to the high standard of your work, and to the wise, kindly, and humane

From Lord Morley (1)

feeling that weak
through it all

with all cordial good
wishes

Yours

Morley (ALS)

Not many people know so
well as I do, your special
difficulties in selecting
a straight course from
a rather censorious and
imperious city.

From Lord Morley (2)

11, DOWNING STREET,
WHITEHALL. S.W.

22nd November, 1921.

My dear Robbins,

I must send a line of thanks
to you for your note in your London
letter appearing in yesterday's "Post".
I wonder how many people besides you and
me realize how closely I was following
in my father's footsteps?

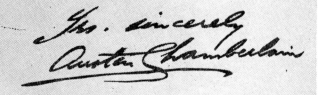

From Sir Austen Chamberlain

13

A Personal Note

WHEN FIRST A CENTENARY HIS-
tory of *The Birmingham Post* was contem-
plated, older members of the staff were
asked to contribute their reminiscences
for use as raw material by the late, and deeply lamented,
T. C. Kemp, who had undertaken the task of preparing
a history.

Among the material he received was the following
memorandum written by myself. It was meant only as
raw material to be polished, if used at all, by a more
accomplished hand. On reading it again, I feel it has the
small merit of spontaneity and may help to convey something of the zest and enjoyment a former member of the
staff, my father, found in work for the *Post* under the
wise and tolerant editorship of G. W. Hubbard.

*　　*　　*　　*

Local antiquaries must supply the dates when I first
knew Birmingham and *The Birmingham Post*. I am writing
away from books of reference, as scholars say when they
cannot be bothered to verify their facts. It must have
been between 1906 and 1908 that my father, Harry
Whates, was appointed leader writer and assistant
editor. By 1909 he was back in the Gallery at the House
of Commons, writing a Parliamentary sketch to the day
of his death in 1923. Here are some clues from a retentive
and capricious memory of school holidays spent in
Birmingham about the time the *Post* was fifty years old.
Wilkie Bard was in the Theatre Royal pantomime, wearing a sailor suit (was it 'Sinbad the Sailor'?). He sang
the current popular song with additional topical verses
composed for him by a member of the *Post* staff. One
verse that convulsed the audience turned on a question
whether the trams should be extended to Harborne. I

couldn't see the joke, but the vociferous citizenry found it the height of humour. Which reminds me that Birmingham stationers' shops were showing mourning cards in memory of the deceased steam trams. The barrel organs were flooding the streets with the 'Merry Widow' Waltz. Finally, there were gudgeon in those days in the canal at Edgbaston. I know, because I caught one from the bottom of our garden in St. James's Road, and have never recovered from the infection. That should be enough to date the occasions, with the proviso that more than one holiday contributed to these clues.

My acquaintance with the inside of the office was slight and awe-struck. I believe I met the Editor, G. W. Hubbard, who was to appoint me reporter in the London Office some fifteen years later. My clearest recollection, however, is of the Literary Editor (if he was called that in those days before every other person in a newspaper office was an editor of some sort). He passed on to a small boy occasional adventure stories and I am not sure he did not have some responsibility in this way for sending me to sea, and so out of this narrative.

Some time before the Liberal landslide of 1906, Arthur Pearson bought the *Standard*, the leading Conservative morning newspaper in London, in the Tariff Reform interest. The staff dispersed and the *Standard* wilted and died. Men have bought newspapers from various motives other than financial and journalists in the past accepted the risk as a normal part of their precarious profession. My father resigned his post as assistant editor, along with the rest, not altogether without relief, I suspect, and became a free man again. Like Kipling's character in *The Light that Failed*, who was always saying 'There'll be trouble in the Balkans in the spring', he looked around for trouble. He bought a sturdy bicycle and made for Russia by way of Germany and Poland. Post-Napoleonic Europe was breaking up. The Austrian Empire, the Balkans and Turkey were attractive fields for adven-

148

turous English journalists. He chose Czarist Russia. Then he went steerage in an emigrant ship to Canada, took up a 'free farm' on the prairie with a partner, and finally wrote a book with a challenging title, for that time, 'Canada, the New Nation'.

That brings us back to *The Birmingham Post*, which gave him the chance to return to his old love, English Politics and the Houses of Parliament. In retrospect, I realise that G. W. Hubbard, besides being a great editor, was a man of courage. My father was an Asquithian Liberal, a Free Trader and Home Ruler. The *Post* was Chamberlainite, Unionist and Protectionist. He never was called on to compromise with his principles and he was not the man to hide them under a bushel. Yet he worked happily for the *Post* as Parliamentary Sketch Writer through the tempestuous years of the People's Budget, the House of Lords controversy and the climax of the Irish Question. He had the political journalist's gift of detachment allied with humour and a deep-seated devotion to Parliamentary institutions. His Editor trusted him and must have fought many a skirmish on his and the paper's behalf against politicians less appreciative than readers of the virtues of independence and candour. His proprietor, too, enjoyed the occasional flurries stirred up by the Parliamentary Correspondent and, as a marked individualist himself, had much in common with his sketch writer. Their relations were on a plane of confidence and friendship. 'You're a cantankerous old devil, Whates', Charles Hyde said at the close of a private conversation, 'but you tell me the truth'. My father treasured that characteristic compliment from one who was even more outspoken than he was. One reason for their understanding of each other may have been that my father had no ambitions beyond steadfast fidelity to his work in Parliament and elsewhere.

He was satisfied with the trust extended to him and the unusually large measure of discretion allowed him in carrying out his work. The Parliamentary Sketch in those days was a daily column on the leader page, an almost sacrosanct feature of the paper. Yet on occasions when Parliament was dull even to his indulgent eyes, he was known to send a curt message, 'No Sketch to-night'. At other times he would ignore the House of Commons altogether and write an absorbing column on a Lord's debate that everyone else ignored. It was always a temptation to him when their Lordships were discussing an obscure matter of colonial administration. As a young man he had edited a paper in British Guiana and never lost his interest in colonial affairs. Among other subjects he would inflict without notice on *The Birmingham Post* and its readers were ecclesiastical debates, particularly when they had a socio-theological flavour.

This hobby-horse earmarked him for the annual Church Congress during the Parliamentary recess. He applied the Sketch technique to these meetings with zest and candour. One year when the Church Congress met in Birmingham he was detailed to cover it and he wrote of the opening session that the presiding Bishop's address was 'painfully diffuse'. Any who still remember Dr. Russell Wakefield will reflect that the comment was probably just. It gave much glee to the diocesan clergy; but the Bishop, a kindly man with a sense of humour, had the last word. At the dinner marking the end of the Congress the Bishop was in the chair. After the loyal toast, Dr. Wakefield said, 'Gentlemen, you may smoke. Not even *The Birmingham Post* will call *that* diffuse.'

Another annual undertaking during the Long Recess was to visit Ireland and write articles on the steadily worsening state of affairs. These visits went on throughout the 'troubles' and to all parts of the country,—unplanned wanderings carefully avoiding official contacts. The only time he admitted running into danger was once in Belfast, when a friendly German hotel keeper who had had a hand in the pre-war Ulster gun-running, smuggled him aboard the boat at night with a warning not to return until his hair had grown again. A suspicious Orangeman barber had cut a mark at the back which was an invitation to loyalists to use a gun. After one of these visits *The Birmingham Post* (still, of course a Unionist paper) reprinted as a pamphlet a series of articles advocating a possible settlement. The suggestions were much on the lines of partition, with a separate Parliament for Ulster, and attracted some attention, coming from *The Birmingham Post*. The writer was invited to discuss them with a Cabinet Minister; but by that time any reasonable compromise had been overtaken by events and the final settlement, when it came, went far beyond the suggestions in the pamphlet. The incident is worth recalling as an example of the courage of the Editor and of the political influence of the paper at the time.

Perhaps these reminiscences may conclude on a lighter note of more particular concern to newspapermen,—a question of expenses. My father would never keep a reckoning. Before going off into the blue he would draw more than enough for his needs from the cashier in the London Office. On his return three or four weeks later, he would empty his pockets on the cashier's desk and leave that long-suffering person to make out an expenses claim,—and make his peace with Birmingham in the formidable shape of Sir Bertram Ford. It seemed to work to everyone's satisfaction,—except perhaps the London cashier's.

* * * *

To resume the tale of the London Office, when Robbins retired at the end of 1923, it seemed to mark the end of an era. A London Correspondent and a Parliamentary Sketch Writer whose memories went back to Gladstone, Salisbury and Joseph Chamberlain in his prime, had gone. The dominance of politics was yielding to the competition of many other public interests. Though always the major concern of serious newspapers,

151

Parliament and Whitehall had become only one of several public topics and their treatment in the papers tended to move away from the spacious solemnity of earlier times. The new London Correspondent had to reflect this change of emphasis. An admirable appointment was made in the person of E. W. Record, a seasoned Parliamentary journalist but at heart a brilliant reporter with the invaluable background of early experience on the *Manchester Guardian* under that great trainer of journalists, C. P. Scott. Ten years later, Record was called to Birmingham to succeed G. W. Hubbard in the editorial chair and his work and personality in that high office is a subject for later consideration. Here he shall be treated as London Correspondent and London Letter Writer.

It may be said without a hint of disparagement that with Record personality was everything. It made a sharp impact on all who met him and shone in his writing with many bright hues. His appearance was striking,—a tall, handsome man with a clipped, military moustache, keen, twinkling blue eyes, and a natural air of command. One would put him down without hesitation as a country gentleman, a Colonel, probably, living up at the Hall and Master of the local Hunt. It is not a type commonly encountered in Fleet Street. Nor did appearances belie one side of his delightful character. He was a countryman born and his principal recreation was country walking in company with congenial companions. That last phrase evokes another and better-known characteristic, for he was a companionable man who loved good company. A bachelor who lived in chambers in the Temple, he fitted exactly Dr. Johnson's ideal of 'a very clubbable man.' He was, indeed, a great talker and an inveterate gossip and was never happier than when seated in his club, the centre and inspiration of a lively group of stimulating listeners. He took far more than a professional interest in 'the best club in the world,' the

House of Commons.

It may seem strange to say that he was not profoundly interested in politics, but that was the root of the matter. Not principles and policies absorbed his mind, but rather the practitioners of politics, the individual politicians of all shades, whose careers, vagaries, passions and ambitions he delighted to study. One of his earliest contacts was in Manchester in 1906 with the young Winston Churchill, then campaigning triumphantly on the flood tide of the Liberal revival. Record followed the fortunes, the very abrupt and diverse fortunes, of a vivid personality through the years. He gathered a rich store of anecdotes such as a journalist acquires, and can seldom write, which he could draw upon at any time for the entertainment of a suitable audience. And they seldom bore any relationship to the policies Winston Churchill was pursuing at the time. Always it was the man in action, the clash of personalities and the oddities of behaviour and play of repartee that furnished the material. This was typical of his attitude to all men. He had no wish to be a political pundit or propagandist. If serious-minded readers found a lack of solid nourishment in Record's London Letter they were compensated by the light and easily digestible nature of the diet.

He brought to the *Post* something of the style and temper of C. P. Scott's great newspaper. In particular, he insisted that serious topics need not be made dull and that a London correspondence should reflect a wide range of interests, and be written with zest and evident enjoyment in the many-sided life of the metropolis. When things were dull and unpromising, he would take a stroll in the park or through Covent Garden to pick up a paragraph about the wildfowl, the trees, the flowers or the exotic produce and write of his discoveries in his own individual style. He had some personal idiosyncracies of style that stamped a hall-mark on all his wrote. John Morley once offered the advice to an aspirant after style

153

to read through his copy and turn all the 'whichs' into 'thats'. E. W. R., as his colleagues called him, was an enthusiastic 'which-hunter'. He was also twitted by a friendly critic with 'adverbial eccentricity', a habit he had of placing adverbs in unorthodox positions in a sentence,—and he enjoyed a criticism that in his eyes was a compliment. He could be a difficult taskmaster and a severe critic of anything that seemed pompous, cliché-ridden or obscure; but his appreciation of all that pleased him was frank and heart-warming. His impulsive generosity could be quite overwhelming.

James Lawton Nixon, a reporter in the London Office, was suddenly called on in an emergency to write the Parliamentary Sketch. He had had no experience of Parliament, but he filled the breach so competently that he was confirmed in the appointment and held it for ten years, until he succeeded Record as London Correspondent in 1933. He laboured under the disadvantage of having been a junior reporter in Birmingham, who was sent up to the London Office in 1914. A hard-headed Lancashire man with no pretensions to brilliance, his merits were those of a thoroughly sound reporter. His pertinacity, shrewdness and utter reliability were invaluable virtues and he served the *Post* with devotion to the day of his retirement in 1952.

Until recent years the principal work in the London Office was the sub-editing of agency copy, Stock Exchange reports, official publications, and other material originating in London. A staff of sub-editors under an experienced chief prepared this material ready for the paper, including summarising, paragraphing and head-lining, in close liaison with the Chief Sub-Editor in Birmingham, and their completed work was transmitted over the private wire to head office. For several years the Chief Sub-Editor in London was Bernard Twinn, who later was promoted to the senior post in Birmingham. He will be remembered by those who knew him, for his sound judgment of news values, his massive imperturbability in times of stress and, above all, for his loyalty to his staff. He was to be seen at his finest when something had gone amiss in the sub-editor's room, when he would stand stubbornly between the errant member of his team and the wrath from on high, insisting that the responsibility was his alone. His authority was quiet and absolute. The sub-editor's room, through which all copy passes, is the hub of the office and for much of the time works under heavy pressure. The idea fostered by American films that in moments of crisis a newspaper office is a shouting Bedlam is far from the truth. Quietness and concentration and prompt execution of orders are essential to orderly production of the paper. With Bernard Twinn in the chair, the discipline was perfect and the busiest room in the office was a haven of peace. Irreverent juniors used to call Twinn's sub-editor's room 'the Dame School'. His successor in London, W. H. Piggott, on the other hand, had a touch of brilliance. It was a rare experience to see him, tense and alert, fall on a prolix Blue Book like a bird of prey, tear the heart out of it against the clock, and transform it into a smooth-reading, lucid column with every point marshalled in due order and proper prominence.

Technical developments in transmission have transferred nearly all sub-editing from London to Birmingham. Agency services nowadays are channelled through direct to head office, much material is transmitted by telephone and the wired picture service calls for a different set of skills. The London Office to-day is primarily a news-gathering organisation, staffed by reporters and specialist writers and men experienced in the selection and technical assessment of pictures. A distinct department is that of the City Editor, who is responsible for the financial and commercial columns. Functions previously combined in the London Correspondent, with his assistants, have been enlarged and

155

distributed over several specialists. The head of the office, now known as London Editor, is responsible for supervising the editorial conduct of the London Office on behalf of all the newspapers. As in many other walks of life, the balance has swung towards administration and organisation. Thanks to modern developments in communications the work of the London Office is closely integrated with head office, both on the editorial and commercial sides. Consultations, discussions, instructions and enquiries pass to and fro at all hours day and night. Something of the old freedom and scope for initiative may have gone; but a new exactness of control and a greater efficiency have taken their place. The change, which similarly affects the branch offices in neighbouring Midlands towns, can be compared with what occurred at sea where wireless telegraphy brought warships and merchant vessels under continuous control from ashore.

14

Tariff Reform

AT THE TURN OF THE CENTURY
the *Post* was on one of those plateaux of eminence that may otherwise be defined as a flat
spot. Never was its influence more assured or
its prosperity more apparent. In the world of journalism
great changes were on the way under the impetus of
Northcliffe's genius; a new reading public had been
created by compulsory education, a public that had been
taught to read, but not to think. Established newspapers
like the *Post* were accustomed to catering for a middle
class, educated, thinking public and saw no need to make
any concessions. If anything, they closed their minds
against change and were afraid to introduce innovations
savouring of 'sensationalism'. It was an unhealthy attitude, hostile to progress, and the younger generation,
even among the born faithful, began to murmur.
Brighter spirits who wrote squibs in the local magazines
made fun of the 'dullness' of the *Post*. Like the Guards
officer of whom it was said that he was so dim that even
his brother officers noticed it, the young journalists themselves retailed flippant anecdotes about their reverend
seniors. One such told how John Feeney heard in his club
a conversation about the dullness of the *Post* and spoke
about it to the editor. The editor talked to the chief
reporter, a veteran who had been on the paper over thirty
years. They communed together on the problem of
brightening the paper and came to a momentous decision. A reliable reporter was detailed to interview an
eminent authority and write a series of articles on the
New Stone Age in the Midlands. This story is wholly
apocryphal, but it illustrates the growing disrespect for
the solid, not to say stodgy, virtues of Birmingham's leading newspaper.

That the *Post* in the early years of the century was slow to move with the times was due to several factors, but more especially to a personal tragedy on the editorial staff. The conventional statement that the death of a promising young man has been an 'irreparable loss' was never so true as in the case of the *Post* and W. B. Vince. He had joined the staff in 1887, at the age of 26, as assistant editor to Bunce and was being groomed for the succession. Three years later he died of typhoid. Even to-day on reading about him his vivid personality shines across the years and leaves an indelible impression that he would have made an ideal editor. A Birmingham man, fourth son of the famous Unitarian minister, Charles Vince, he had qualified as a solicitor at the age of 20 and had to wait a year before admission to practice. He threw himself into politics in the Reform agitation of 1884 and 1885, made a name for himself as a speaker and lecturer, and wrote copiously for the lighter periodicals. He contributed articles on cricket, his other love, to *The Birmingham Mail*, which attracted attention. Eventually, those shrewd newspaper men, Jaffray and Feeney, offered him a trial. He took to journalism immediately and in a very short time was writing leaders, handling the technical business of editing and deputising for Bunce in his absence. His writing was graceful, witty and, in controversy, deadly; his weapon the rapier, not a bludgeon. 'The phantom of genius has always been too dangerously near his elbow', a contemporary wrote. It is a notable fact that the experienced and ageing proprietors and editor saw that the *Post* would need a lively intelligence and a bright mind to direct it in future. Sudden death threw all their hopes and plans into confusion.

When people say a newspaper is 'dull' they usually mean they are not interested in the subjects the paper treats as important. It is a revelation of the speaker's blind spots, not an objective criticism of the paper. To a man not interested in mass sports and gambling, nothing

158

can be duller, in this sense, than a Saturday evening football paper. Yet it is manifestly absurd to call these papers dull, for they are obviously designed on the principle that brightness is all. Reverting to that mythical anecdote about John Feeney and the alleged dullness of the *Post* fifty years ago, it is significant that the inventors could think of no better example of a dull topic than archaeology. Time has mischievously blunted the point of the story. Another medium, radio and television, has turned archaeology into an enormously popular subject, as evidenced not only by radio programmes but by the sales of books, both learned and popular, on the discovery of the past. It has been done by clever exploitation of lively personalities and dramatic incidents. The Press has been soundly beaten in this field. The moral is that nothing is dull unless it is made so and everything can be made interesting to a mass readership when presented attractively by lively minds convinced of the possibilities and the importance of their subject. A newspaper is a reflection of the directing minds behind it. A bright, interesting paper will not emerge from minds that are inherently dull or over-tired or discouraged. And shallow minds, however alert and technically competent, will inevitably produce shallow newspapers. Such thoughts could be pursued indefinitely, but the essence is that commercial and logistic aspects of newspaper production ultimately serve one main purpose, to bring readers into touch with the minds behind the written words. On the qualities of those minds depend the character, the personality and the public appeal of the paper.

These reflections have arisen while considering the fact that the *Post* fifty and sixty years ago acquired a reputation for dullness. Did it deserve that reproach? Study of the files of the period will at least show how the notion arose. To a modern reader the papers around the turn of the century are forbidding. Appearances are terribly against them. Typographically monotonous and solid, they seem to proclaim a doctrine that it is sinful, or perhaps one should say 'sensational', to look interesting, and flippant to tempt readers to read. Study of a serious morning newspaper, one feels, was not to be regarded as an indulgence, but rather as a duty and a penance. On big occasions, such as a Town Hall meeting addressed by Joseph Chamberlain, the main news page is filled with solid columns of a verbatim report; nowadays the main news page would carry a column descriptive summary and the verbatim report would be tucked away elsewhere for those who wished to read it. At other times the main news page is occupied largely by foreign news.

Other pages disclose on careful study a logical pattern: but no attempt is made to indicate their character by variations of type or subject headlines. Nor, on the leader page, is it thought necessary to put headlines on the formidably dense masses of editorial comment. In short, one has to read into the columns to discover what they are all about. An effort is called for all the time: and the surprising thing is that the effort is so often well worth while. Having overcome one's initial reluctance to plunge into the sea of type, the experience is quite exhilarating. The quality of the general reporting is extremely good, the descriptive writing is often vivid and polished, and the leaders are generally thoughtful and always of a sound literary standard. Taught by years of austerity to be brief, a journalist to-day would criticise a lack of selectivity and 'tight subbing'; but there are always among a newspaper's readers a few who can never have enough of a subject, be it a Parliamentary debate or a police court case. These old papers set out to satisfy all tastes, not by reducing the news to the lowest common denominator of acceptability, but by giving as much as possible of everything for everybody. Their conception of 'everybody', however, was circumscribed. They were written for an educated, literate public

160

Before Corporation Street

Queen's Corner

interested in public affairs more than in frivolous personalities. A charge of dullness, therefore, may be sustained on grounds of appearance and typographical limitations and restricted popular appeal. It does not apply to anything like the same extent to the contents of the papers. That it was levelled at the *Post* was due to changing tastes among a public that was being taught to discard the need for effort in newspaper reading. It was unfortunate, perhaps, that responsible newspapers were deterred from trying to meet this changing taste by fears of being thought 'sensational'. They should have grappled with their fears sooner and risked incurring an odium that came on them just the same, and proved quite transitory, when they made such daring innovations as printing news on the front page.

The *Post* sixty years ago, and its like-minded contemporaries elsewhere, were ripe for change. There were particular reasons, as well as the general climate of newspaper opinion, why the *Post* clung to the old ways. The appointment of W. B. Vince had seemed to promise better things and his premature death must have been a deep discouragement. Nor should one ignore the fact that the directors of the paper's destiny were growing old. Jaffray retired in 1894, without leaving a son to the business. John Feeney was stricken by a disastrous, crippling malady. John Thackray Bunce was approaching seventy. There was no young blood in the higher seats of authority when the editor-apparent died. Bunce was particularly hard-hit by the loss of a deputy who seemed all set to take over the succession. An elderly man looking forward to retirement, he had already passed on much of the routine work and responsibility to his young and eager assistant. Now he had to start all over again, defer hopes of an early retirement, assume full responsibility once more and shape a newcomer to succeed him in the chair. There was no time for further experiment with untrained men. The new deputy would have to be capable of taking full control from the start, and that meant he should have had previous experience as an editor.

A man with the necessary qualifications was found in Alfred H. Poultney, then editor of the *Bristol Evening News*, who, at the age of 45, had a long experience of journalism in the provinces. His daughter, Mrs. Ethel Wilson, of Haywards Heath, Sussex, recalls childhood memories of her father as a tall, dark man with a beard, 'rather serious and immersed in his work', very studious and a great reader, who taught himself modern languages. He was a keen Churchman, serving for many years as Vicar's Warden at St. Ambrose Church, Edgbaston. It was during his time as editor of the *Post* that the new diocese of Birmingham was established. He was an active member of the Bishopric Fund and of the Cathedral Fund formed for the conversion of St. Philip's Church. Bunce will have found Poultney a congenial colleague and, after eight years' collaboration, the veteran editor handed over the reigns to his successor with an easy mind. 'The impression one gets of Mr. Poultney from his appearance,' the *Birmingham Owl* said about the time of the take-over, 'is that of an alert and vigorous man approaching middle age but retaining much of the elasticity of youth. He has a highly cultivated mind and a lofty ideal of the journalist's mission, and there need be no fear that under his regime the *Post* will deteriorate or lose any of the influence it now wields.' Events proved this to be a shrewd judgment, both of man and editor. The Bunce tradition was in safe hands. In the next few years much appreciative comment was made on the *Post's* staunch support of the Unionist Government and especially of Chamberlain's conduct of the Boer War and its aftermath in South Africa. When Chamberlain in 1903 visited South Africa, Poultney's assistant, J. V. Morton, then temporarily acting as editor of the *Mail* pending a permanent appointment, took a prominent part

162

in organising a once-famous torchlight procession to Highbury,—Birmingham's ebullient send-off to the Imperial traveller. It was around this time, too, that Chamberlain's private secretary and chief official of the Unionist party, Charles Anthony Vince, was active as a leader writer and contributor to the *Post*. Relations between the paper and the Unionist leader were never more intimate and harmonious and it was common talk that the *Post* was 'Chamberlain's organ'. Coming events cast no shadows.

At this point it is necessary to pick up the threads of national and local politics. In the summer of 1902, Lord Salisbury resigned and his nephew, Arthur Balfour, became Prime Minister. At the time of this momentous change, Joseph Chamberlain was confined to bed recovering from a cab accident. He had been taken to Charing Cross Hospital with a deep cut in his head that had penetrated to the bone and made a slight indentation of the skull. Mrs. Chamberlain was relieved to find him sitting up in bed, making light of his injuries and smoking one of his black cigars. Two days later the doctors took a more serious view of his condition and ordered the complete rest which to-day would be insisted upon from the first. The consequences of this accident to a man of sixty-six were far-reaching. A friend noted that from this time he was 'never so quick or elastic again.' Chamberlain, who had seemed to have a gift of perennial youth and energy, became an old man. Yet there was no chance of relaxation. At the height of his fame, when the country at large would have readily accepted him as Prime Minister instead of Balfour, his personal position in Birmingham was endangered by a Nonconformist revolt against the Conservative Government's Education Bill. Within weeks of his accident he 'was compelled to defend his base in Birmingham as never again in his political life', his biographer says. He quelled the revolt by a masterpiece of platform tactics, but, to quote Mr.

Julian Amery again, 'he was losing touch with the people and the roots of his power were beginning to decay.' Having surmounted this crisis in Birmingham and received enthusiastic tokens of popular support, he went on his fateful visit to South Africa.

He came back a new man, reinvigorated and inspired by the new doctrine of Tariff Reform and Imperial Preference. Six months later he resigned from the Government to be free to preach his faith, leaving his son, Austen, whom Balfour made Chancellor of the Exchequer, as token of continued amity. The position was extraordinary. The Conservative Party was divided and Balfour tried to hold it together by temporising and ambiguous concessions on 'retaliatory duties' and philosophical disquisitions on the difficulties and risks of tariff changes. Within the party Chamberlain had to face the implacable hostility of the patricians, notably the House of Cecil, to whom he was still the Radical Dissenting interloper, and the opposition of representatives of the staple exporting industries,—coal, cotton, iron and steel, shipping—that had thriven on Free Trade and could see nothing but disaster in any alternative. The Liberal Party, scattered and demoralised by internal quarrels arising from the Boer War, abruptly closed its ranks and found in the defence of Free Trade a heaven-sent substitute for a constructive policy it had failed to formulate.

We who are living in a spiritually impoverished age amidst the world-wide ruins of the Liberal Experiment can scarcely conceive the moral overtones that once attached to the economic doctrine of Free Trade. Joseph Chamberlain was one of the first to see that in the international sphere the 19th century system had broken down; that a new set of moral values was necessary in a world where other nations had resisted and rejected the Gladstonian ethic and were building up armaments and protective tariffs to challenge Britain's commercial and political supremacy. He did not put it quite like that,

164

since his clear, practical mind was not given to philosophical interpretations of history; least of all of the contemporary history in which he was immersed as an instrument of destiny. But that was the inner meaning of the Tariff Reform movement and men's minds fifty years ago were not prepared to face it. They were deeply distressed and disturbed, not by the practical details of the new tariff policy, but by the underlying, half-glimpsed implications. A splendid vision of universal peace and liberty was fading in the angry sunset of the resplendent Victorian age. Few cared to admit that any single feature of the ideal of Cobden, Bright and Gladstone had lost its vitality. Free Trade was one such feature, part of the liberal-minded Englishman's secular religion, and a tangible symbol of the whole moral creed. To a great number of good people, not necessarily politically minded, abandonment of Free Trade would look like the first step in a betrayal of mankind's highest aspirations, a reversion to a condition of war of everyone against everyone, with the life of man, in Hobbes' phrase, 'solitary, poor, nasty, brutish and short.'

Chamberlain and the young hot-gospellers of the Tariff Reform League set out to carry the Free Trade fortress by assault at the next General Election, which was due at latest in 1906. Full of drive and enthusiasm for a cause, they had little idea of the weight of active opposition they were piling up against themselves. Not for them the wise words of Milner, disclosed twenty years after by Sir Percy Fitzpatrick. 'Not one General Election will be required to convert people to this new Tariff policy—several, two or three, perhaps more. It will take years.' Actually, it took thirty years, and was then almost incidentally accepted by a people stunned by the impact of world depression and financial collapse. In 1903, however, and for the next three years, the country settled down to enjoy a gladiatorial combat such as it had not known since Gladstone and Midlothian.

Chamberlain's energy was furious as he went from one mass meeting to another in provincial cities throughout the land, stirring men's minds with his burning zeal and rousing them with passionate eloquence. In his wake, however, dogging him from town to town came the apostles of Free Trade,—Lloyd George no less eloquent, Asquith, perhaps the acutest analytical mind of his generation, and the young lions of the Conservative Free Trade Party, Lord Hugh Cecil and Winston Churchill. The platforms rang with fierce blows and rapier-like exchanges. His Imperial vision moved Chamberlain to unaccustomed flights of poetical eloquence. 'Mr. Chamberlain' retorted Churchill, 'breaks into poetry worthy of the Poet Laureate (Alfred Austin) at his best or Kipling at his worst.' Among the spectators of this tremendous battle was Beatrice Webb, friendly with politicians in all camps and committed to none. She enjoyed teasing her Conservative friends. Two months after Chamberlain had resigned and launched his campaign, she recorded in her diary one such occasion at a private gathering.

'I suggested that why Chamberlain would make headway, in spite of his bad arguments, was because he had a vision; desired to bring about a new state of affairs; and was working day and night for a cause; that no one else wished anything but a quiet life and the *status quo*.'

One can see at once how the Fabian heart warmed towards a bonny fighter out to 'bring about a new state of affairs.' In the following summer, however, her heart was touched by another emotion. 'We lunched yesterday with the Chamberlain's,' she noted, 'to introduce the Irvings. Others there were the Bonar Laws and a certain Sweet-Escott, Governor of British Honduras. I sat on one side of my old friend (Chamberlain) and we talked without constraint. He is obsessed with the fiscal question; has lost his judgment over it; refuses to think or talk of anything else. He looks desperately unhealthy, rather thin, too; a restless look in his eyes, bad colour and general aspect of "falling in". But I should imagine that there is plenty of force in the man yet; an almost mechanically savage persistence in steaming ahead.' It is an alarming picture, this, drawn out of genuine affection. Elsewhere Beatrice Webb refers to Chamberlain's 'irritability, one-sidedness, pitiful unhealthiness and egotism.' The strain of campaigning evidently was beginning to tell and Beatrice Webb was not the only observer to notice it with concern. He was approaching seventy and, as already mentioned, had suffered a severe head injury two years before in an accident. Chamberlain's constitution was so strong that he had never had to give it a thought. Apart from attacks of the gout, which he accepted with humorous resignation as something at least respectable, he was never ill. He took no exercise and it used to be said of his habit of riding everywhere in a hansom cab that he would call a cab to take him from the Colonial Office to the House of Commons. But this last campaign on two fronts was the most wearing of his long political life. It seemed as though he was driven by an inner premonition that time was running short and was impelled by a passionate conviction, even so, that 'some noble work of note may yet be done.'

It is against this background of 'the most alive, sparkling, insurgent, compulsive figure in British affairs,' to quote Winston Churchill's description, that we turn to examine where *The Birmingham Post* stood in these troubled times.

15

Change of Policy

THE *POST* HAD HAD NO HESITATION whatsoever in conforming with the Imperialism that became the dominant creed of the nation in the last two decades of the Victorian era. Chamberlain and his Unionists were not alone amongst Liberals in reacting against the demagogy of the later stages of Gladstonian Liberalism. Lord Rosebery and such rising politicians as Asquith, Haldane and Grey formed a group of Liberal Imperialists at the very head of the Liberal Party. In the country at large the intellectual movement away from Gladstone was well under way while he was still on the scene. He had lost most upper and middle class support and on the other flank the Liberal Party was losing its working class adherents to the new Labour movement. In 1903 the *Post* was an ardent supporter of the Balfour Government; but always from what would be called nowadays a left-wing Unionist position. Indeed, the *Post* continued to use the name Unionist long after the term's original meaning was lost in the Irish settlement of 1922. Its Liberalism was not only a regretful backward glance to the brave old days of the Radical 'unauthorised programme' but a positive progressive attitude and a real influence on Conservative policies.

When Chamberlain launched Tariff Reform at a Town Hall meeting in May, 1903, and returned to the attack on Birmingham later in the year, the paper accurately reflected the prevalent view of Birmingham Unionists by suspending judgment. 'As it seems to us' it wrote in a typical leader, 'the safe ground to take is that, although Free Trade was a necessity of the time and although it has unquestionably been attended by an enormous increase in national wealth and a magnificent

168

advance in social well-being, yet it does not necessarily follow that the last word on the subject was said sixty years ago. The times change and we must change with them, so far as we find the change to be to the advantage of the nation.' That was by no means a discouraging reception for the new doctrine. The subject was accepted as being open to discussion. Very soon Birmingham and its leading newspaper were faced by a serious challenge to the doctrine of free discussion.

The Town Hall was taken for a meeting on 11th November, 1903, to be addressed on behalf of the Free Trade Union by two leading Conservatives, Lord Hugh Cecil and Winston Churchill. Coming only a week after Chamberlain had had a great reception at Bingley Hall, this meeting was regarded as a provocative demonstration. Lord Hugh Cecil—'a bigot even on the fiscal question, dominated entirely by a sort of deductive philosophy from *laisser-faire* principles held as theological dogma', to quote Beatrice Webb,—was particularly obnoxious to the traditional Birmingham radicalism. He stood for the patrician, High Church element in the Conservative hierarchy that had accepted Chamberlain only on sufferance and made no secret of its dislike. Public feelings were played upon by Pearson's papers, which urged Unionists to go to the Free Trade meeting and prevent the passing of a resolution on the fiscal question. On the day before the meeting, incitement rose to a climax which the civic authorities could not ignore. A squad of sandwichmen appeared in the streets with the following poster on the boards. 'Men of Birmingham. Shall Radicals be allowed to oppose our Joe? Town Hall. Wednesday. Come in thousands 7 p.m. Chamberlain Square.' One of these posters was actually displayed on the window of *The Birmingham Mail* office,—much to the indignation of that entirely innocent paper. Popular excitement was at a height it had not reached since the notorious Lloyd George riot two years before. It was

169

beyond seeing the comic irony of the inflammatory poster's description of the scions of Hatfield and Blenheim as 'Radicals' or the impudence of this misappropriation of a term once proudly claimed by Chamberlain himself.

The authorities, recognising the well-known symptoms of an underground conspiracy to create disturbance, were determined that Birmingham should not repeat the discreditable scenes of 1901. The forces of law and order went into action all along the front, under the leadership of the Lord Mayor. On the morning of the meeting the *Post* opened fire with a massive bombardment. First came a letter from the Duke of Devonshire, leader of the Conservative Free Traders, addressed to Moore Bailey, chairman of the Birmingham Central Conservative Association. Moore Bailey had agreed to preside at the Town Hall in a personal capacity and on condition that only Unionists should be on the platform and that all the speeches should be loyal to the Prime Minister, Balfour. 'I need scarcely say,' wrote the Duke, 'that I feel a great interest in the success of the meeting over which you are going to preside as chairman. The discussion on the fiscal question, which has been invited by the Government, has disclosed great differences of opinion in the Unionist Party, and a policy has been advocated which goes far in the direction of change beyond that which has been announced as the policy of the official leader of the party. Every local Unionist must desire that full expression should be given to the conflicting opinions on both sides before the party is finally committed to either of them. The arguments on one side have been already fully stated in Birmingham, and I am sure that the city which had the honour of being represented for so many years by Mr. John Bright will desire that a fair hearing should be given to the exponents of the opinions of which he was one of the foremost champions and in the support of which, either as a Liberal, or, as in his later days, a staunch Unionist, he never varied.'

170

More directly to the point was the following letter from C. A. Vince, chief officer of Chamberlain's Liberal Unionist Association. 'In view of certain rumours of intended disturbance of the meeting to be held by the Free Trade Union in the Town Hall', Vince wrote with studied moderation, 'I am desired, on behalf of officers of this Association, to beg all Liberal Unionists who may think fit to attend the meeting to give a fair and orderly hearing to the speakers. Supporters of Tariff Reform in Birmingham will have other and more suitable opportunities of declaring their sentiments, and any discourtesy shown to our opponents would be much regretted by the leader of our party.'

'These letters' the *Post* leader-writer observed, 'should dispose in summary manner of the insane notion which somehow has got abroad in the city that the Cecil-Churchill meeting at the Town Hall to-night would be an unpardonable insult to the Unionists of Birmingham. Why any such notion should have found a moment's acceptance in the mind of any reasonable man we cannot imagine. Political life would, indeed, have become intolerable, and party politics would have become disgusting, had the theory been countenanced in any way that in a city of the size and importance of Birmingham (or, indeed, in any place, however insignificant), only those who agreed to one side of a story had a right to be heard. As elsewhere, so it evidently is in Birmingham, the fiscal controversy has given rise to deep differences of opinion, even among men who have given a life-long service to the party identified with the Government now in office.

'Until the last few days we should never have supposed that so much attention would have been given to their visit to this city and it would certainly not have occurred to us that anything at all approaching an organised attempt to disturb their meeting would have been possible. Whoever was responsible for the scandalous incitements to disorder circulated through the streets of

171

the city yesterday morning should plainly be made to understand that he has not only succeeded in discrediting himself and risking the good name of the city, but that he has brought himself perilously near the borders of the criminal law.

'If ever there was a subject which deserved to be fully discussed without a taint of partisan bias, it is the one now before the country.

'It would be an insult to Birmingham to suppose that such appeals should be made in vain in a city which boasts its faith in a free platform and a free press.'

The voice of authority spoke through every line of this *Post* leader; but the arm of authority was not taking any chances. Let Birmingham feel insulted if it wished, the Chief Constable was bound to suppose that the appeals of the Duke of Devonshire and Mr. Vince would be, if not entirely in vain, then insufficient. Besides, the boisterous rabble ready on any pretext to seek and make trouble was not the *Post's* reading public. The warning would be read and perhaps taken to heart by the unknown instigators, as, indeed, it was, since they kept out of sight and were never publicly discovered; but their dupes were another matter altogether. The police detained and questioned the sandwichmen, apparently without result.

The Chief Constable on the morning of the meeting called a conference with his four divisional superintendents to lay plans to prevent a repetition of 1901. The crowd that was expected to gather in Victoria Square at 7 o'clock must be kept away from the Town Hall. Stout timber barricades were built and upwards of 500 police were mobilised, two-thirds of them to be held in reserve in case the barricades were rushed. The Lord Mayor took station in the Council House overlooking the Square to watch the proceedings. These massive precautions proved sufficient; but only just. One point of the warnings went home. Unionist Tariff Reformers kept away from the meeting. Inside the Town Hall everything was orderly and the meeting, so the *Post* said next day, 'passed off much better than the organisers of the gathering at one time had cause to expect.'

It was otherwise in the streets outside. The *Post* carried a sparkling report of scenes and incidents,—typical of the time, the excellent descriptive story was tucked away down the page, after three and a-half solid columns of verbatim report of the platform oratory. The crowds were kept on the move behind the barriers from seven o'clock until eleven. It was a good humoured crowd, on the whole, though there was some stone-throwing, windows were broken and use was made of an ugly local weapon, a bunch of iron washers threaded on a string. Attempts were made to rush the barriers, but the timbers held. The reporter noted that the crowd took its revenge and whiled away the time by smashing all the bowler hats they could lay hands on. 'He was a lucky man who, wearing a bowler hat and mingling with the crowd, preserved it intact. The wearers of that particular form of headgear were, however, rare; the majority had had the foresight to put on close-fitting cloth caps.' Just before eleven o'clock the crowd was starting to thin out. Speakers and audience from the Town Hall had been safely dispersed without coming into collision with the demonstrators. Then the police played their trump card. A fire-engine with steamer and escape dashed through Victoria Square with all the thrill, noise and panoply that belonged to the old horse-drawn, coal-fired days. Most of the remaining crowd followed this exciting lure into Broad Street and the crisis was over. There were no arrests and no hospital casualties. The police had covered themselves with glory and the good name of Birmingham was preserved more or less intact.

Next morning the papers breathed a sigh of relief. 'Common sense and a love of fair play have prevailed', exclaimed the *Post* leader, 'and the noisy rag-tag who did their best to make the result otherwise have deserved-

173

ly failed.' It was evidently not thought an occasion for a solemn pronouncement on the fiscal arguments advanced by the speakers in the Town Hall. 'Why should Unionists quarrel among themselves rather than recognise their differences? It is too early in the day to say what the final judgment of the country will be on the subject of Tariff Reform. Mr. Balfour has gone so far as to hint that no such final pronouncement will be invited for a long time to come. What the country wants is solid fact and sound argument. This is not a matter of sentiment. For our part, we are satisfied that there is a real need for some measure of fiscal reform. The true remedy will be found by-and-by. Even in the resolution adopted last night there was a declaration in favour of "retaliatory duties in exceptional cases".' The *Post*, in fact, was taking its traditional role of peacemaker between factions within the party, looking to time and free debate to reconcile differences. It was the line of Balfour's government and the *Post* was a loyal government supporter, troubled by the spectre of dissensions that could only profit the opponents of the Conservative and Unionist alliance.

For the next two years it followed as well as it could the elusive dialectics of Balfour's tortuous mind, which seemed the only chance of holding the party together. It was an unsatisfactory position for a paper that had usually had a mind of its own and no hesitation, once it had come to a conclusion on a specific issue, in giving a firm and unambiguous lead to public opinion. Balfour had no mind of his own. He was the embodiment of Beatrice Webb's diagnosis, wishing for nothing but a quiet life and the *status quo*. He believed in no particular political doctrine, loathed all economic and social questions, was bored by the machinery of government and party politics and had an eighteenth century abhorrence of 'enthusiasm' of any description. On the fiscal issue he was afflicted with an equal distaste for the ardent Tariff Reformers and the dogmatic Free Traders. Those,

174

like the *Post*, who sought to support the Prime Minister were driven to despair by his equivocation,—or driven, as Beatrice Webb predicted, into the Tariff Reform camp because Chamberlain at least knew what he wanted and offered a positive creed. The *Post* leaders during this period are unhappy reading, reflecting only too well the perplexities of Unionists and unable to give a clearer lead than the Prime Minister himself, for fear of breaking up the party. There was a decline from the clarity and vigour with which the paper had supported the government in the time of the Boer War and the Khaki Election.

In 1905 matters were coming to a head in every direction. The Parliament elected five years earlier was coming to an end of its natural life. There would have to be a General Election within a twelve-month; indeed, some Ministers had advised Balfour in the previous autumn to take time by the forelock and go to the country while there was still a chance of returning to power. The usual reaction had set in against a government that had exhausted its mandate and was merely carrying on. By-elections had reduced the 1900 majority of 134 to a bare 68 and were still going against the government. The Liberals were making the most of the disillusioning aftermath of the Boer War, including the notorious 'Chinese slavery' affair. Labour was exploiting the failure of the government to rectify the Taff Vale judgment which had reversed the generally accepted interpretation of the law governing the immunity of trade union funds. Apart altogether from the fiscal issue, it seemed probable that a General Election would go against the nerveless Balfour Government. Still the Prime Minister hesitated and proscrastinated. The Tariff Reform campaign also was going badly and there was no possibility of converting the Conservative Party in time for it to go to the country as a united body. Another period of years would be needed for campaigning within the party and in the country. Tariff Reform became the official Conservative policy after the election, when the party, in the comparative freedom of opposition, could shape its programme without fear of embarrassing a Conservative government. But in 1905, not more than half the Conservative members were committed to Tariff Reform. In the autumn of that year the pre-election campaign started in the country.

As at all previous crises of his career, Chamberlain's first thought was for his home base in Birmingham. He could be none too sure of his hold on the electors. He had lost touch with the old Radical Nonconformist foundations and he was challenging the Liberal Free Trade faith associated with the revered name of John Bright. Moreover, the Conservative vote had become an uncertain factor, because the Tariff Reform League's campaign had developed a note of hostility towards those Conservatives, including Balfour himself, who would not toe the line. The attitude of the *Post* and its associated papers was, therefore, a matter of great concern.

At this point it is advisable to make it clear that there are no 'inside revelations' forthcoming from office records about the events leading up to the *Post's* conversion to Tariff Reform in November, 1905. The facts must be left to speak for themselves, with such comment and interpretation as seem reasonable from a study of the available material. The uneasy detachment of the *Post* has already been described. In the light of future developments in Unionist policy, it is obvious that the paper's position could not have been maintained much longer. And as an interpreter, as well as a guide, of public opinion, the paper was almost bound to come down on the side of Chamberlain and Tariff Reform. For at the General Election in January, 1906, when in the country at large the Conservatives were overwhelmingly defeated, the Birmingham fortress alone stood firm and returned a solid block of Unionist members.

176

St. Bride's Avenue, Fleet Street

Sir Alfred Robbins

Opinion within the office was as divided as it was in the community outside. The evening paper, the *Mail*, inclined strongly towards Chamberlain; though that had its embarrassments. It required some effort to maintain that all was well within the Conservative and Unionist alliance. 'The opposition is fond of inventing weird stories of quarrels and disagreements between the two heads of the Unionist party,' the *Mail* informed its readers. 'As a matter of fact the history of politics has never produced a more striking case of mutual admiration. Mr. Chamberlain has an almost extravagant regard for Mr. Balfour and those who know him understand and appreciate the sincerity with which he speaks when he says he could not force a dissolution on Mr. Balfour's Government if he would, and would not if he could. No, Mr. Chamberlain would never turn on his leader.' The *Post*, at any rate, was not obliged to preserve this fiction; it could, and did, remain silent and evade awkward questions. The editor, Poultney, was in a singularly difficult and lonely position, a Free Trader himself with at least some colleagues of a like mind, and with no one at hand in whom he could confide and upon whose mature judgments in public affairs he could draw. John Feeney was absent from the office and in his last illness. The General Manager, J. R. H. Smyth, recently become a partner, though a sound business man, is not known to have taken much interest in politics. Poultney's daughter recalls that her father went through 'a somewhat difficult and stormy few months,' during which 'outside pressure was brought to bear' to persuade him to alter his views. 'It meant either retiring or writing against his convictions, which naturally he could not do, as he knew his written word influenced a wide circle of people.'

It was a painful situation, which had arisen on several other Conservative newspapers about that time, notable on the London *Standard*, which had been an influential organ associated particularly with Lord Salisbury. There

can, of course, be no argument about the right of proprietors to decide the policy of their papers, and to
appoint an editor who can conscientiously carry out their
wishes. The only point at issue is how these rights are
exercised.

The first the public knew of these differences inside
the office was from an advertisement that appeared in
the *Daily News* on 26th October, 1905. 'E D I T O R .
Applications are invited for the Position of Editor of
The Birmingham Daily Post. Applications must state and
give full particulars of present and previous newspaper
employment. Address, in confidence, to Mr. J. R. H.
Smyth, *Daily Post*, Birmingham.'

Two days later, on Saturday, 28th October, 1905, the
following announcement, circulated through the Press
Association, was published in most newspapers; but
not in *The Birmingham Post*:

'*The Birmingham Daily Post*, which has hitherto supported the official Government policy on the fiscal
question as laid down in the Sheffield programme, will
for the future give an unqualified support to Mr.
Chamberlain and the Tariff Reform League. As a
consequence of this change, Mr. A. H. Poultney will
from this week cease to be Editor of that paper.'

The announcement caused a stir in newspaper and
political circles and some rather wild speculations. The
Parliamentary Lobby, always a hotbed of spicy gossip,
had a wonderful tale of Chamberlain having delivered
an ultimatum to the proprietors, with a threat to start
another paper in Birmingham unless the *Post* promptly
lined up with Tariff Reform. Liberal Free Trade papers
made the most of the incident as another example of the
ruthless social and political autocracy of Chamberlain
in Birmingham. Much of this was mere party politics,
but it contained one germ of sincerity in the universal
expressions of feelings of respect and sympathy for
Poultney. 'The sympathy with Mr. Poultney is deep and

178

sincere', wrote a newspaper in his native West Country, 'and already a proposal has been made that there should be presented to him a national testimonial expressive of the admiration of Free Traders of all shades of opinion for his endeavours to arrest the progress of the reactionary policy formulated by Mr. Chamberlain.' The silence in Birmingham was broken by the lively weekly, the *Birmingham Owl*, which compared the change of policy with what had occurred twenty years before over Home Rule and slyly speculated on the possibility of another baronetcy coming the way of the *Post*. 'It would be a perfectly legitimate reward for a change of front which all those who know Mr. John Feeney will believe to have been the result of a sincere and honourable change of view. But what about poor Mr. Poultney, who could not reconcile it with his conscience to change his in order to retain his position? His solace must be found in the approval and respect with which journalists throughout the country have read of his unselfish and high-minded action.'

The *Daily News* concluded its editorial comment also on a personal note. 'Mr. Poultney, who retires from the editorial Chair, adds one more to the list of prominent journalists who in recent years have sacrificed position to conviction. In few other professions are such sacrifices demanded or so cheerfully made.' This last reflection, well-meant as it may have been, was singularly inappropriate. The modest, studious and retiring man in his sixtieth year, who had quietly and unostentatiously identified himself for nearly twenty years with Birmingham and the *Post*, could not make the sacrifice as 'cheerfully' as many younger men had done. 'It absolutely broke him up', his daughter says. On All Saints' Day, 1st November, he took early Communion at St. Ambrose for the last time. Soon afterwards he had a stroke and died in January, 1906.

Meanwhile, the editorial conduct of the *Post* was

undertaken by the Assistant Editor, J. V. Morton. On Friday, 3rd November, Chamberlain addressed another great Town Hall meeting and next morning readers of the *Post* received their first intimation of the paper's change of policy from its own columns. Not until the last paragraph of a 1,300-word leader was the paper's new alignment made plain. Chamberlain had quoted Balfour's most recent pronouncement on the fiscal issue: 'Fiscal reform stands in the forefront of our constructive policy, and of all the branches of fiscal reform that connected with bringing us closer to the colonies is the most important part of our policy.' Chamberlain responded to this gesture. 'I accept the policy of the Prime Minister in the words in which he himself stated it,' said the leader of Tariff Reform, 'and I am prepared to give it every support in my power.' On this formula the breach within the party was healed for the duration of the election. The *Post* leader-writer seized the opening. 'This at once brings us into line with Mr. Chamberlain,' he wrote, 'and we upon our part are prepared to give him our cordial support.' The inner meaning of the episode was summed up in a final sentence. 'Locally, at least, we have the satisfaction of knowing that when the General Election comes, be it soon or late, there will be arrayed on Mr. Chamberlain's side a cheerful, confident, united and resolute party.'

The domestic affairs of the *Post*, however, were neither cheerful nor confident. That advertisement for an Editor betokened confusion and a strange lack of foresight. The resignation of an editor had been forced without having a successor in mind; but it was also a plain intimation to the staff that the management was not disposed to make an appointment from their ranks. The reason for this reluctance is hard to discern at this distance of time. During his three months as Acting Editor, J. V. Morton seems to have produced eminently satisfactory papers and to have conducted the election campaign with vigour and success. Balfour resigned in December and his successor, the Liberal Sir Henry Campbell-Bannerman, dissolved Parliament and went to the country, with results that have passed into history. But Birmingham remained a shining exception in the Liberal landslide and the *Post* played its part in keeping Chamberlain's home base safe for Unionism. Nothing seems to have come from the advertisement, which is not surprising. Newspapers of standing do not need to advertise for editors, and any that do are unlikely to receive suitable applications. Meanwhile, in mid-December, John Feeney died at Torquay and the ownership of the papers fell into the hands of trustees. The cumbrous legal machinery of a trust, particularly in its early days, is not well adapted to management of an enterprise that often requires swift decisions and delicate personal relations.

There was much speculation in public about the next Editor of the *Post*. Chamberlain's chief political organiser, C. A. Vince, who had been associated with the paper as leader-writer and contributor, was mentioned as a likely candidate. In February, 1906, however, the management appointed a new Editor from within the office, after all. G. W. Hubbard, who had been Editor of the *Mail* for three years, was transferred to the *Post*, and the Acting Editor, J. V. Morton, became Editor of the *Mail*. In appointing Hubbard the management builded better than they knew. Looking back, it seems an obvious choice, for he was a journalist of wide experience and, since taking over the *Mail*, he had made himself *persona grata* with the Chamberlain camp at Highbury. His appointment was a success from the first day. He made some readjustments among the staff that smoothed out difficulties left by the change of policy and soon had a compact and competent team of leader-writers and editorial assistants.

But there was an unhappy sequel elsewhere. Within a year the Editor of the *Mail*, J. V. Morton, resigned to become Editor-in-Chief of the *Birmingham Gazette and Despatch*, taking with him other members of the staff, including the Chief Reporter, Arthur Mann. Mr. Mann went on to a distinguished career as an editor, first of the *Evening Standard* and then of the *Yorkshire Post*.

It remains to be added, to complete this sequence of events, that in July, 1906, Joseph Chamberlain had a stroke that removed him from active public life.

16

The New Century

FIFTY YEARS AGO *THE BIRMINGHAM Post* was made into a Twentieth Century newspaper; and the man who did it was George William Hubbard, editor from 1906 until he retired in 1933. Before describing his achievement, however, it is right and proper to deal with the new proprietorial and managerial organisation that followed on John Feeney's death and was, of course, ultimately responsible for creating the conditions and fostering the progressive ideals of what a provincial morning paper should be in that age. Under the terms of Feeney's Will, the properties were left in trust for seven years and his nephew, Charles Hyde, was given a right of purchase at the end of that period. It was, no doubt, a prudent arrangement, but in the nature of things the intervening period before Charles Hyde assumed full control was something of an interregnum. The business side of the undertaking was administered ably and conscientiously by the trustees, one of whom was the General Manager, J. R. H. Smyth, recently made a partner. He was the active and visible symbol of proprietorship in the office; but under him was an heir-apparent to whom the future belonged, and upon whom were fixed the liveliest hopes and expectations of the younger generation.

At this time, 1906, Charles Hyde was only thirty, with nine years' experience behind him, and Hubbard was thirty-six. Between them they provided the transfusion of young blood that was needed to revivify the paper and they were eager to get on with the job. It says much for the tact and goodwill of all concerned that they were able to do as much as they did under the circumstances. Charles Hyde was an attractive young man, a cheerful, friendly and candid character, well equipped to rouse

183

enthusiasm and to command the loyalty of all those under him. His keen sense of humour and high spirits were something that had been lacking in the office for many years. He had, as events were to prove, a high sense of responsibility as a newspaper proprietor,—a responsibility first of all to his staff, then to the paper and to the public—but he did not parade it and was never solemn about it. Late in life, in one of his very rare moods of confession, he told a gathering of his staff, held to celebrate twenty-five years' of sole proprietorship, something of his aims and achievements.

'It is nice to have money,' he said, 'and this is what I have done with it; looked after my staff; improved the business, the buildings and accommodation; kept race horses; interested myself in archaeology; and, above all, I have travelled.'

He remained, incidentally, a bachelor all his life and he said he had found happiness in giving away 'quite a lot' of his money. His many gifts, often impulsive and always generous, went to a great variety of good causes but more especially to those concerned with the welfare of young people. Birmingham University is deeply indebted to his memory.

His interest in archaeology was an unexpected trait in a surprisingly complex character. Owning race horses and following racing with ardent interest seemed to go oddly with financing excavations at the Roman site of Uriconium, in the Balkans and the Middle East. Moreover, he was not satisfied merely with providing money for such work, but took a lively personal interest in excavations and was a frequent visitor to Uriconium. Once two very junior members of the staff who visited that lonely and intensely dramatic site were surprised to see their proprietor chatting to the diggers and shyly tried to efface themselves. They were seen and recognised, however, and Sir Charles, as he then was, constituted himself as their guide and showed them over the site with real

184

enthusiasm. Moreover, they received thereafter copies of the periodical progress reports on the excavations and on the infrequent occasions when they met the proprietor about the office he would exchange a few words about Uriconium and archaeology. For he had the invaluable gift of remembering names and a man's interests and circumstances, which made him a rare host at staff parties. Every man was made to feel a personal guest and an individual. A pensioner recalls that Charles Hyde always made a point of speaking to every man in the Composing Room and seemed to know each man's habits, hobbies and interests. 'Sir Charles knew I was a flute player', Mr. Fuller says, 'and always asked me "how the flute was going." '

Sometimes it could be disconcerting, for the proprietor was always well posted in office gossip and had a mischievous sense of humour. He 'looked after his staff' in innumerable ways and was rewarded with a personal loyalty and a genuine liking that amounted to affection.

This, however, is an anticipation. In 1906 the proprietor-designate was far from being a rich man. His uncle had brought him up in the business the hard way and for the first nine years Charles Hyde was an impecunious clerk in the office, with no great expectations. 'If I had been born with a silver spoon in my mouth,' he said, 'I should have pawned it.' For a number of years his wages were £120 a year and when he got an increase to £13 6s. 8d. a month he thought it wealth. In the early days when he lived in apartments in Edgbaston he was, on his own admission, always hard up. To save the railway fare he used to cycle to his home at Worcester on Saturday afternoon and return Sunday night. 'Believe it or not' he would add with a touch of pride, 'it was very seldom that I dismounted either way.' Nobody was more surprised than Charles Hyde himself when he found that he had been left the option to purchase his uncle's business and properties. His surprise was not widely

185

shared by the office colleagues who knew him best. Their reaction was one of thankfulness, tempered by impatience. The disclosure of the Will made little difference to his way of life. Hard up as he was, he resolved never to take one penny out of the business until he had paid off the last farthing of the purchase money. He kept to the letter of this self-denying ordinance until at last, in 1913, he came into his own. His older partner, J. R. H. Smyth, was offered and accepted the opportunity to retire on generous terms; and at the age of 37, after sixteen years' experience of hard work and growing responsibility, Charles Hyde became sole proprietor. Even at that time, he was one of the few independent, individual proprietors of a great morning newspaper; in his later years he was the only one.

In January, 1913, the prospects were all set fair for a big forward movement. The proprietor, at the summit of vigorous manhood, was eager to accept the vast and highly responsible trust committed to his hands. In Hubbard he had an editor of the *Post* who shared his ideals and aspirations and who had built up an editorial staff unsurpassed in individual talent and welded into as fine a team as the *Post*, or any other great provincial newspaper, could boast. On the managerial side, however, the proprietor saw that he would need someone to assist him, particularly in financial and administrative matters. Fortunately, the man was at hand in the person of Mr. B. J. T. Ford, member of a firm of chartered accountants, who had been auditor and financial adviser first to John Feeney and subsequently to the Trustees. Colonel Sir Bertram Ford, as he became known to Birmingham later on, is a recent memory and more will be said of him in due course. Here it is sufficient to note that Charles Hyde appointed him general manager as one of his first acts and that the two men ran the papers together for nearly thirty years. When they took over after the interregnum of trustee management the business was in much need of extensive re-quipment and reorganisation. Charles Hyde was not anxious to make drastic changes all at once. The first year was a time of preparation for a general forward move and of planning for future developments. The paper progressed quietly and steadily under the stimulus of hope. The proprietor had much to occupy his mind in adjusting himself to his new position and responsibilities and in planning the necessary moves which would have to be made if steady and definite progress and a wider outlook were to be achieved. It was, perhaps, fortunate that this year was spent on careful thought and planning, because it is a matter of history that the following year brought an upheaval that confronted every man and woman and every business in the country with problems that could neither be foreseen nor dealt with otherwise than on a hand-to-mouth basis and by improvisation. The outbreak of the First World War threw everything into the melting-pot and was the first of the shattering events to spoil the bright prospects and to make Charles Hyde's proprietor-ship a time of troubles.

At the outbreak of war he was deprived of his right-hand man, the recently appointed general manager, who was a Territorial Captain in the Royal Field Artillery. A large number of other employees were mobilised or joined up in the first weeks and throughout four years the staff was progressively depleted by the demands of the Armed Services. Those who joined the Forces were relieved of financial anxieties by the very generous provisions made for their families by the proprietor, who considered each case on its merits and supplemented a man's Service pay by whatever was needed to enable his dependants to carry on their normal standard of living. Short of staff, short of materials and faced with sharply rising costs the production and distribution of the *Post* were alike seriously affected and the conduct of the business called for constant attention and quick improvisation. The point need not be laboured. Twenty years later another war brought much greater problems, dislocations and frustrations; and the proprietor and others in responsible positions who were called on to cope with them were twenty years older. In the first war, in the early days of his proprietorship, Charles Hyde may have been alone and certainly he was overworked, but he was full of energy and optimism. He faced his difficulties with marked courage, skill and enterprise. His long and arduous training stood him and the paper in good stead. Throughout the war the *Post* carried a daily military commentary contributed by Edgar Wallace, a capable journalist who later acquired world-wide fame as novelist and playwright. The paper also sent a senior member of the staff on a tour of the Western Front. His articles on Midland Regiments in France were republished as a pamphlet which was widely circulated and much appreciated by the public. At the end of the war the prestige and popularity of the papers were higher than they had ever been.

Not content with managing the business virtually single-handed, he threw himself enthusiastically into public service. He had had some experience in his young days during the Boer War, when he acted as joint honorary secretary of the Reservists' Fund and took an active part in an agitation against the methods of administration of the Royal Patriotic Fund which resulted in the appointment of a Royal Commission. In this First World War, when he was debarred from active service on medical grounds, he devoted himself to services on behalf of men in the Fighting Forces. He was chairman of the Queen's Hospital and was associated with the civic fund for the equipment of the Birmingham City Battalions. He continued after the war as chairman of the War Pensions Hospital Committee and on the signing of the armistice in 1918 he gave a thank-offering of £5,000 to the Lord Mayor for the benefit of disabled ex-service-men. In addition to running his own business, he did an important service for newspapers in general by organising salvage. A department was set up for the systematic collection of waste paper all over the district, to be sorted, baled up and sent to the paper mills for re-pulping and re-use as newsprint. This pioneer effort in self-help bore fruit in the Second World War, when salvage of waste paper was still more urgent. It also had consequences in the peace time economy of the newspapers, for it led to a beginning of storage of newsprint on a substantial scale and to the adoption of motor vans for collection and delivery, which grew into the large fleet of vehicles that now plays a vital part in the distribution of the papers.

On the return of men from the war, a large programme of reconstruction and replacement was taken in hand. There were not only the arrears of maintenance left by the war to be overtaken, but the plans for modernisation that had been shelved in 1914 to be revised, brought up to date and carried through in the teeth of rising prices and continuing shortages. On the mechanical side, five new Hoe presses and some linotype machines of the latest pattern were ordered; and all the old equipment needed overhaul and rehabilitation. Now, more than ever, the management had reason to bless the foresight of John Feeney in having bought the old Post Office on the other side of Cannon Street, with its tunnel under the street. This tunnel had been meant originally to connect the Post Office with New Street Station, but it was never completed. How far it went is a matter of speculation, as no plans have been preserved; but when the lower end of Cannon Street was being resurfaced about five years ago, a heavy road roller sank into a cavern under the road way which may have been a relic of the old, unfinished and forgotten Post Office tunnel. Office speleologists have not been tempted to explore the mystery. It is enough that the short section across the street, brightly lit and thoroughly secure, links the two machine rooms into a practical working unit. The growing needs of the papers steadily extruded tenants to whom offices had been let and the internal arrangements were completely altered, a process which is still going on to-day.

The work of material reconstruction was imaginatively paralleled by Sir Charles Hyde (he was made a baronet in 1922) when he turned to his first concern, the welfare of the staff. He instructed the General Manager to work out a scheme for pensions for the literary and commercial staffs, subsequently adapted and extended for all employees. Such provisions are a commonplace to-day, but in 1921 the *Birmingham Post and Mail* Staff Endowment Scheme, arranged in conjunction with an insurance company, was a striking innovation, especially in the newspaper world where fluidity of staffs had been almost a matter of principle. This contributory pensions scheme, proudly described in a book written by the General Manager entitled *Steps Towards Industrial Peace*, made a profound impression in its day, inside and outside the office. To the literary staff particularly it seemed to proclaim that journalism no longer was a precarious profession and that in one newspaper office, at least, loyal service and continuity of employment were required and rewarded. In recent years the original scheme has been merged into, and is gradually being replaced by, a modern pensions scheme geared to inflation. Those who benefit from it, however, may care to honour the memory of a newspaper proprietor who blazed the trail and a general manager who worked out a feasible scheme in negotiation with an insurance company and the Inland Revenue thirty years ago.

Another decision in 1921 that caused some stir in the newspaper world was a reduction in the selling price of the *Post* from the war-time twopence to a penny. There are two broad categories of morning newspapers, the

190

penny mass-circulation popular dailies and the so-called 'class' papers produced for a limited public of educated professional, business and industrial men who want their special interests, such as finance and commerce, adequately dealt with and the general news and comment treated soberly and intelligently. These 'class' papers, of which the *Post* has always been a leading representative in the Midlands, do not look for large circulations or to unlimited expansion. Their appeal to advertisers is that they are read, and read carefully, by, in the main, people with money to spend on quality goods and services for themselves and who in their work can influence large-scale public and private expenditure. A 'class' paper is an expensive paper to produce in relation to likely profits and circulation is not its primary objective nor the only criterion of success. The reduction in price in 1921 did produce a sharp rise in the *Post's* circulation,—from around 30,000 copies daily to over 40,000,—but it was still a small total compared with the million circulation penny dailies. Charles Hyde's motive was 'to give Birmingham a twopenny paper for a penny'; and to be different from all other newspaper proprietors.

This action brings into prominence perhaps the strongest trait in his character,—a fierce individualism that made him intolerant of any intervention or restriction on his absolute freedom to manage his own business in his own way. He was not incapable of co-operation when convinced of its national necessity, as in the wartime salvage drives; but he would have nothing to do with national or collective agreements that limited his discretion to do as he thought right with his own property or that came between him and his staff. He refused to belong to the Newspaper Society, the organisation representing provincial newspaper proprietors, or to join the Audit Bureau of Circulation that publishes certified figures of the net circulations of newspapers for the information of advertisers. He regarded circulation

191

figures as a confidential business matter and anyway as a misleading yardstick of the value of a newspaper as an advertising medium. If advertisers felt they were not getting value for their money by taking space in his newspapers, they had their remedy. They need not advertise. To demand publication of circulation figures was an impertinence. His attitude to advertisers was justified by results. They continued to buy space in his papers with gratifying regularity. As to national agreements negotiated between the Newspaper Society and the trade unions in the industry, he readily preserved his independence in the only possible way,—by paying higher wages than the national scales. By way of contrast, he was a keen supporter of the Press Association, the co-operative organisation for collecting and distributing news to the provincial newspapers, taking a full share in its work along with his fellow-proprietors and on occasions holding office on its board.

His antipathy towards the popular Press and its controllers was intense and outspoken. At a dinner held to celebrate his baronetcy in 1922, he sounded a challenge that was heard time and again in speech and action throughout his life. He did not like to strike a discordant note, he said, but he could not help alluding to 'the insane insurance schemes of the London papers, who seem to glory in the daily casualty list of their subscribers, and also to the senile football coupons issued by weekly papers. It all started with the absurd "net sales" campaign, which has become merely a competition for waste paper.' Several years later, when the first Lord Rothermere proposed to start a chain of evening papers in the provinces and advanced on Birmingham as one of his objectives, Charles Hyde welcomed the prospect of a fight on his own ground. A lively poster campaign was waged around a city centre site acquired by the invaders for building offices for the proposed *Birmingham Evening World*. It came to Charles Hyde's ears that Lord Rother-

W. B. Vince

A. H. Poultney

mere had been advised that the established Birmingham papers were merely an old family property and would fall into his hands like a ripe plum. 'Tell Lord Rothermere,' he replied, 'that far from being a decayed old family property, the papers are owned by a young bachelor who will fight him till his blood's white if he comes to Birmingham.' The threatened invasion came to nothing, for the national campaign was lost on other fronts, among them Bristol, where leading citizens got together and founded a new Bristol-owned paper to compete with a syndicated Rothermere paper. They received substantial support from the independent proprietor of *The Birmingham Post*, who sent them a printing press in their hour of greatest need.

This fighting independence was tremendously heartening and inspiring to the staff, who were proud to work for such a man: but it carried within it the seeds of a nemesis that all too often lies in wait for those who swim against the tide. For the current of national affairs and of social development was set irrevocably towards collectivism. Capital in industry was organising in larger units and responding to the national organisation of Labour with joint negotiating machinery. Under pressure from Governments, between the wars, the railways, the coal industry and other vital services tended towards amalgamation; and in the private sector the trend was towards integration, co-operation and centralisation. The newspaper industry, as the Press had come to call itself, was no more immune from the spirit of the times than any other body in the community. The days of unlimited individualism were passing away. Those who fail to realise the strength and direction of a secular movement in human affairs are likely to suffer a more lasting injury than others who are opposed to it just the same, but recognise the face of the enemy and the limitations of resistance. Charles Hyde was in the former category and the first shock to his self-sufficiency was the General Strike, when

193

his employees, along with trade unionists in newspapers throughout the country, came out in support of the strikers.

They did so reluctantly in most cases, for they had no quarrel with their employer and had serious misgivings at jeopardising the excellent conditions of employment in the office and the cordial relations always subsisting between management and men. But the call of trade union loyalty and working class solidarity came first; and they hoped Charles Hyde would understand. In this they were disappointed. He never could understand how men who were like a family to him could put any loyalty before their duty to the paper, the public and himself. When it was all over and the strikers asked to be taken back, they were treated justly and without a trace of vindictiveness; but the mischief was done once for all in the proprietor's heart and mind.

The period of the General Strike was an exhilarating experience for those untroubled by divided loyalties. Prodigies of improvisation were performed by journalists, clerks, heads of departments and volunteers from outside working strange machines and doing manual jobs quite outside their normal experience. Major Ford, as he was still in 1926, was in his element presiding over a pseudo-military operation; organising security guards over the office with its valuable machinery and equipment and for protection of the loyal members of the staff, many of whom slept on the premises until the strike collapsed; directing the activities of unskilled, inexperienced and alarmingly enthusiastic labour; arranging the commissariat to keep this band fed and nourished by day and night. First of all a typed sheet giving the barest summary of the news was all that could be managed in an emergency that, in the prevailing state of mind, could not have been foreseen. Within a few days, however, the linotype machines were working spasmodically, the great printing presses began to turn over again and *The*

194

The Birmingham Post

Thursday
May 6.
1926.

STRIKE BULLETIN.

One Penny.

Do not pay more.

1.

Notice to the Printing Trade: Official.

When the present general strike is ended His Majesty's Government will take effectual measures to prevent the victimisation by trades unions of any man who remains at work, or who may return to work, and no settlement will be agreed to by His Majesty's Government which does not provide for this for a lasting period and for its enforcement if necessary by penalties. No man who does his duty loyally to the country in the present crisis will be left unprotected by the State for subsequent reprisals.

Position in Birmingham. Position shows little change; food transport arrangements were satisfactory. An official notice stated - "Attention has been directed to overcharges made for certain articles, particularly of food and fuel. It is hoped this will cease immediately, otherwise it will be necessary to take action to prevent it."

There was a slight improvement in local train services, and it is hoped to increase them to-day.

Enrolment of volunteers proceeded steadily, but more are required for maintenance of essential services.

The Military Tattoo at King's Heath was abandoned last night owing to weather, but remaining performances will take place, weather permitting.

The Prime Minister's Message: The Prime Minister in message to "British Gazette" says constitutional Government is being attacked. He enjoins on all good citizens to bear with fortitude and patience, hardships they have been suddenly confronted with and stand before the Government who are doing their best to preserve liberties and privileges of people. "The laws of England are the people's birthright", says Mr. Baldwin. "You have made Parliament their guardian. The general strike is a challenge to Parliament and is the road to anarchy and ruin."

Government Emergency Regulations: Commons yesterday discussed Emergency Powers Regulations already issued. The Home Secretary said they would only remain in force a month. Services already declared vital included electricity supply, and continuance of railway services. The Country should not be scared by rumours. If any real difficulty occurred he would inform the House at once.

Minister: Firm Declarations: In Commons yesterday, Mr. Baldwin said no Government in any circumstances could ever yield to a general strike. The moment it was called off unconditionally Government were prepared to resume negotiations.

Lord Birkenhead (Secretary for India) stated in Lords that whatever the lengths to which this quarrel might be carried, it would be ended only with recognition of fact that there was one Government and one Government only in this country.

Among daily newspapers now being published are "Yorkshire Post", "Yorkshire Evening Post", "Leeds Mercury", "Bristol Times and Mirror", "Western Mail" (Cardiff), "Dundee Advertiser", "Scotsman", "Manchester Guardian" and "Despatch" (joint) "Newcastle Chronicle", "Sheffield Telegraph", "Sheffield Independent".

We are informed that all the local stock sales will be held as usual.

S P O R T I N G.

The Chester Cup was won by Hidennis (11/2), with Vermilion Pencil (4/1) second, and Ixia (10/1) third. Ten ran. No racing to-day, and none until further notice.

Worcestershire 115 (4 wkts.) v. Lancashire. Yorkshire 176 v. Cambridge University. Surrey v. Glamorgan and Essex v. Australians, no play. Oxford University v. Middlesex, abandoned.

Possible Developments: A news agency states important developments towards peace may take place to-day following conversations between Labour leaders last night.

Printed and published by Sir Charles Hyde, Bart., 6, Cannon Street, Birmingham, at the request of the Government for public information. Any profit will be given to the Birmingham Hospitals.

General Strike Bulletin

Birmingham Post, a recognisable but woefully attenuated sheet of two pages, once more appeared on the streets. It was snapped up eagerly by a news-hungry public, its circulation soaring for a few days by the hundreds of thousands, far beyond anything reached before or since by the *Post*. In 1926, broadcasting in this country was only three years old. It may be said to have found its feet as a medium of mass communication in the year of the General Strike, when the Press for the first time in its history was prevented from fulfilling its function in society; with consequences that are still far from being exhausted.

On the 24th of September, 1938, a few days before Neville Chamberlain flew to Munich, Charles Hyde, addressing members of his staff at the dinner to commemorate the Silver Jubilee of his sole proprietorship, made a speech already quoted from in another context. Seen in retrospect, it was a valedictory speech, for he never met a private gathering of the staff again, and in the nature of an epitaph on the grave of the old Feeney family proprietorship. Nobody present realised all this at the time; but everyone, when he sat down, was conscious of a brooding sense of coming changes in an unpredictable future, a feeling in tune with the grim news from Europe of a gathering of the war clouds. After giving his lighthearted reminiscences in his most engaging style, Charles Hyde became unusually grave. 'I have talked about the past,' he said, 'and you *must* excuse me if I tell you that I have not, and never will, recover from the darkest hour in my life,—the General Strike. It was a knock-out blow. I have never taken the same interest in my business since.' Those who had worked closely with him both before and after 1926 knew this was only too true. From 1926 to 1939 the papers flourished and the proprietor had shown from time to time his old high spirits and good companionship. But the drive and enterprise seemed to have seeped out of him. Increasingly, he

196

found it easier to say 'No' to any suggestions for change or innovation. His loathing for the popular newspapers blinded him to the progressive changes that were coming over the 'class' newspapers, such as the *Times* which he admired as it stood at the beginning of the century; though the *Times* always was, and still is, a pioneer in such things as typography, printing machinery and photographic reproduction, to mention only features of a newspaper that are apparent to everyone. His editors were saddened and discouraged by a sense of stagnation creeping over the business.

'And now about the future,' he continued in serious vein. 'There is nobody to carry on the family tradition. As long as I have health and the support of my staff I will remain as sole proprietor of this great newspaper business. When I go, others will follow me and I trust there will be as few changes as possible in the staff. After over forty years of busines and other responsibilities I am very tired, but it gives me peace and contentment to know that I have good friends as heads of my business and a good staff. So closes another chapter in our history. Our work still continues and day after day, night after night, the editorial, composing, printing and publishing people will produce newspapers which are good to read and which I am proud to own. Thank you, and God bless you.'

Within twelve months the world plunged into a war that Charles Hyde did not live to see through to victory. He died suddenly in November, 1942, at the Moat, Berkswell, deeply despondent over the low level to which his newspapers had been reduced, particularly the *Post*, by a rationing of newsprint based on selling price. He who had gloried in giving Birmingham a twopenny paper for a penny, by the tragic irony of circumstances lived to see it classed with the popular penny papers he abhorred by an inflexible decree of government.

17

George William Hubbard

IT WAS SAID IN THE LAST CHAPTER
that Hubbard made the *Post* what it was, a twentieth
century newspaper, during his long editorship, from
1906 to 1933. Though it is not always possible to
decide who was the dominating personality in earlier
periods of the paper's history, we are now dealing with a
time well within living memory; and there is no question
in the minds of those who worked under Hubbard that
his was the mind that was stamped on the paper in every
column. The proprietor did not greatly concern himself
with editorial detail. He was satisfied with a paper he
could be proud of and he trusted and supported his editor
inside and outside the office. The General Manager was
even more detached from the editorial control. Respec-
tive spheres of responsibility were clearly defined by
working experience.

Charles Hyde's interventions in editorial matters were
so rare, so far as the staff knew, that one occasion became
almost a legend. He came into the office one morning
and startled everybody by proclaiming that the *Post* must
have a crossword puzzle. For some years the most dignified newspapers had carried crosswords; but the feature
had originated in the popular press in the shape of competitions and therefore was tainted in Charles Hyde's
eyes. His abrupt conversion was the work of a celebrated
Anglo-Catholic parson who was staying as a guest at the
Moat. At breakfast the visitor had brushed aside the *Post*
and asked for a leading London paper because he always
started his day by doing its crossword. His host was
scornful of a man of intelligence wasting his brains on a
puzzle, but he was impressed with the parson's arguments. He realised at last that the crossword had grown
out of its disreputable infancy and become a regular

pastime of educated newspaper readers. So the *Post* must have one, and, of course, it had to be a good one.

Hubbard was the dominating personality on the paper; but few people outside would have thought so and quite a number of his staff were at a loss to define the nature of his influence. He was a withdrawn, reserved, shy man who seemed to cultivate a pose of insignificance. In the office, where, incidentally, he always wore his hat, he would hasten along the corridors with his eyes on the ground and be embarrassed by a civil 'Good evening, Sir' from a reporter. Many men outside the circle of assistant editors wondered if he recognised them or knew they were on his staff. They would have been surprised to learn how much he did know about them, for appearances were very misleading. One day a former member of the staff visiting Birmingham met Hubbard in New Street, walking along absently, his beard buried in his chest. 'Good afternoon, Mr. Hubbard', said the visitor, 'I don't expect you remember me?' 'Indeed, I do, Mr. — ' replied his former editor, 'I recognised your boots',—this with a faint smile. It was perfectly true. Hubbard was extremely observant of detail and especially of dress. He expected his reporters to behave and dress as gentlemen and any laxity in either would bring a reproof 'through the usual channels'. In the town at large he was scarcely known and at public functions, which he attended as seldom as possible, he was apt to be overlooked in favour of the Chief Reporter, whose business it is to be known to everyone. Leading men, however, especially politicians, cultivated the editor of the *Post*, appreciated his reticence and confided in him freely.

If his guidance of the paper was unobtrusive and impersonal, it was all-pervasive, an aloof presence in every man's mind and at all times. 'We expect good work from the men we engage', he told a young, newly-appointed sub-editor, 'and we do not tell them they have come up to expectations. Only when they fail us have we anything

199

to say.' Men could work for years on the paper and never hear a word from the editor or exchange more than the bare civilities with him. That was fully understood and, if not always appreciated, it was extraordinarily effective. Each editor exercises his authority in accordance with his temperament. Hubbard was set apart from his colleagues and subordinates by an inborn reserve and their attitude to him was one of awe rather than affection. It was powerfully reinforced by the journalists' recognition that he was a very fine editor and by the knowledge that he would, and often did, support his staff through thick and thin against unjust criticism or peevish complaint from any quarter. These qualities earned him loyal and painstaking service and made up for a lack of warmth. The 'band of brothers' relationship is not necessarily the best and an editor needs to hold aloof to perform his office as arbiter between the many conflicting interests on a newspaper. Writers, even journalists, are apt to be touchy and to take to heart the drastic treatment of their 'copy' often necessitated by exigencies of time and space on a newspaper. A glut of news, a spate of advertising, a hundred and one accidents and emergencies may relegate a most carefully-written 'story' to an obscure corner of an inside page; when the writer feels, possibly with justice, that in other circumstances it was fit to lead a main page. The better and more conscientous a writer is, the harder he may find it to accept the fact that his finished article is only the raw material of those who put the paper together. Some may seek to compensate for other shortcomings by a display of temperament. That never worked with the aloof Hubbard, who had been a suffering reporter in his time and had come to understand the other woes of the sub-editors. Nobody felt much inclination to appeal unto Caesar in these affairs, because Caesar probably knew all about it already and, if not himself responsible for the decision, would have seen and approved of the arrangements. To question anything in the paper would have been to query the editor's authority; and this was no empty formality.

As an illustration of the meticulous care with which Hubbard studied every feature of production, nothing could be more convincing than the experience of a young sub-editor of those days. He had been unexpectedly promoted to the top of the table, which meant that he was deputy to the Chief Sub-Editor. After a fortnight's grooming under close supervision he was left in control while his Chief had a week-end's rest. And what a week-end for any new man to be given the responsibility of producing a paper with such a reputation as *The Birmingham Post*! When he got to his desk on the Sunday evening he was greeted by the news that Britain's airship, the R.101, had been destroyed by explosion over Beauvais, with the loss of 48 lives. Among the victims was Lord Thomson, the Air Minister of that day.

From the many thousands of words which poured into the office through the evening and night a complete page of the *Post* was built up, and the acting Chief, going over it very studiously, convinced himself that he had not fallen down on his job. Journalistically he was probably justified, but Hubbard was more than a journalist. Next night, he called the young man to his room. 'Ah, Mr. ——'? he began, 'you were in charge last night', and, spreading a copy of the paper on his desk, he continued: 'Let me point out for your future guidance, that here you have a rule (marking the end of one section of the story) followed by a brevier space, while there you have a similar rule followed by a minion space'. The difference is one-seventy-second of an inch, so slight that it is doubtful if one reader in ten thousand would have spotted it, yet: 'That will not do for *The Birmingham Post*. You must keep the spacing uniform throughout.' No word of encouragement; not even a sympathetic reference to exceptionally trying circumstances of this first night without the guiding hand of an experienced Chief.

But that young sub-editor was not crestfallen. When he had been engaged by Mr. Hubbard he had been given to understand that he must not expect pats on the back, but would soon know when his efforts did not please. And since the only criticism of a heavy night's work was on the typographical side rather than the journalistic, it was taken as advice rather than complaint.

The full quality of Hubbard's editorship was shown, apart from the columns of the paper itself, by the brilliance of his appointments. He built up and maintained a first-class staff of reporters and sub-editors, those anonymous newspaper men honoured in their generation by the best judges, their colleagues in journalism, but virtually unknown to the outer world or to posterity. Hubbard was well-nigh infallible in his judgment of men and the best examples, because known to wider circles even than readers of the *Post*, are to be found among the specialists,—the literary editors and the dramatic and music critics. When he took over, the day of the cultivated amateur part-time critic was passing, if only because the demands of a newspaper on its critics' time and attention had grown so greatly. The paper had been well served in the past by men like Alfred Feeny, the paper's commercial editor, and Stephen Stratton, organist and music teacher, in the field of music. Theatrical criticism had passed through several competent and enthusiastic hands, from Sam: Timmins, the Birmingham 'toy' maker, to Edgar Pemberton (the pike fisherman of 'Our Shakespeare Club'), who was otherwise head of an old-established firm of brass-founders. The literary columns had been in the care of Barron Brightwell, a former editor of the *Weekly Post*, in his old age; a delightful character and a charming writer of nature notes, his business capacity was not all it should have been for this responsible position on the daily. Book reviews in those days were regarded as providential 'fill-up' material, to be used as and when the overseer in the Composing

202

Room suddenly had extra space to be filled at short notice. A drawerful of book copy, the latest reviews on top, was drawn on as required. Older reviews accumulated at the bottom, until an extra heavy call for copy delved deep into the pile and next morning the *Post* was found reviewing some books that had gone out of print and others that had run into several editions.

By Hubbard's day it was essential that the literary features of the paper should be treated more seriously; for nothing makes the standing of a newspaper so apparent as its attitude towards literature. A literary editor is responsible for the choice of books to be reviewed; for sending them with instructions to the appropriate specialists among the team of contributors he has built up; for preparing their copy for the press and for making-up the feature. He arranges, too, for literary articles to go on his page and advises the editor when he has an important book demanding notice elsewhere in the paper on day of publication and calling perhaps for comment in the leader columns. The literary editor is also often an assistant editor and leader writer. Hubbard's first appointment to this post was L. P. Hadley, a memorable and much-respected character who soon passed on to become a leader writer, deputy assistant editor and finally, in 1944, in the last year of his life, editor.

L.P.H., as he was generally known to his colleagues, was a man of striking presence and astonishing taciturnity. Like Conrad's Captain MacWhirr of the *Nan-Shan*, he never spoke unless he had something to say and, even then, with a stark economy of utterance that gave little encouragement to conversation. Those who came to know him realised that this formidable reserve concealed the kindliest heart, a keen, far-ranging intellect and adamant principles. But it was disconcerting and, by strangers, apt to be misunderstood. One day by the riverside two fellow-members of the Midland Flyfishers, who were finding things quiet, strolled along the bank and came upon Hadley fishing a pool with the dry fly and with a brace of nice trout beside him. They admired his catch and passed the usual commonplaces of fishermen. 'Did you take them from this pool?' one asked, by way of making conversation. 'No, I took them elsewhere', he replied; and the two fishermen, knowing him well, passed on with covert smiles and a good Hadley story to retail. The point was that Hadley was not only a clever and successful fisherman, but most generous with his knowledge to others and would never for a moment dream of hiding a secret from fellow-sportsmen or administering a snub to anyone. But a new member might well have been excused for misunderstanding.

Hadley was one of those valuable recruits to journalism who come from another professional sphere. He trained for the law and he belonged to a family of doctors. He embodied in his make-up the steady, unwavering point of view of the great mass of educated professional opinion, immune from the enthusiasms and passing vagaries of emotional politics. There was no better interpreter of the best mind of that important section of the community, a mind that makes up for a measure of inflexibility by a rigid code of conduct and high standards of taste in literature and the arts. As a leader-writer Hadley developed a graceful style of the greatest lucidity and a light wit that was most surprising. He was never better than when dissecting a major legal judgment or happier than in lightly demolishing a flamboyant political pronouncement. For thirty-eight years he served the *Post* with his rare talents and upright character; and even then he could surprise colleagues with an unsuspected side of his nature. A minor incident will suffice. During the air raids in 1940 and 1941, when everyone was sheltering in the office basement, a few privileged colleagues were let into the secret of a hidden hobby. Thereafter, they would often persuade him to tell a story with a piece of string. It is, one believes, an Esquimo pastime, a

204

curious relic of man's earliest ventures in the art of story-telling, illustrated with astonishing clarity in patterns of string constantly changing and developing in clever fingers. Hadley had studied this strange craft for years with the aid of scores of books from the Birmingham Library, Margaret Street, of which he was President and a keen committee man. That it should come in useful to entertain and distract a company of adult men in an air raid shelter was the oddest sequel. But, as someone said, it took the blitz to reveal Hadley's hidden talent as a story-teller.

Hubbard's most famous appointment, made soon after he became editor, was that of the distinguished music critic, Ernest Newman. Newman had made a name for himself as a writer on music while still a business man in Liverpool and was the author of two books, 'Gluck and the Opera' and 'A Study of Wagner', before he was invited by Granville Bantock to join the Midland Institute School of Music in 1903. Two years later he became music critic of the *Manchester Guardian* and in 1906 he received a 'tempting offer' to come back to Birmingham as music critic of the *Post*. It was not too difficult to tempt able and ambitious men away from the *Manchester Guardian* in the days of C. P. Scott, for, as a celebrated veteran of that time has recorded, 'he seemed to think we had no private lives and all had private incomes.' Newman came to the *Post* with the burning zeal of a crusader and the acid pen of a master controversialist who had crossed swords with the re-doubtable George Bernard Shaw and not been worsted. His impact on Birmingham is preserved for posterity by Francis Brett Young, whose novels of Birmingham and the West Midlands are delightful in themselves and a brilliant contribution to social history. In 'Portrait of Clare', the music-loving lawyer, Ernest Wilburn, is urging the heroine to make the best of life in Birmingham. 'You have to live your own life, make your own

205

interests, find your own friends; and if you can't do that in a city with three-quarter of a million inhabitants there must be something wrong with you'. With this piece of salutary advice, he goes on to speak of an interest they had in common.

'It seems that we are going to get some good orchestral music at last. Oldham, the critic of the "Mail", is responsible for it. It's not that North Bromwich is musical; but Oldham has been pushing Leeds and Manchester down their throats, and North Bromwich people can't bear to think that anyone else is ahead of God's Own City. So they're buying a new orchestra, just as they'd buy a new sewage-farm or fire-brigade or a new Velasquez, to show others what their money can do. And humble people like myself and Oldham get the benefit of their stupid competitiveness, so we must not complain, even if they, poor souls, are bored. Sir Joseph and Lady Astill will go to every concert. Sir Joseph will make a speech and talk about "'Aydn".'

A sharp passage, that might have been written by the fictional Oldham; or the real Newman. For Hubbard allowed his specialist writers a wide latitude of comment and vigour of expression. His courage in this respect was quite extraordinary for a man who, one would say, preferred a quiet life, and many were the battles he fought on their behalf with outraged citizens wounded in their pride. 'Some say this town has no intelligence', Newman wrote of a poorly-attended concert, aided financially and artistically by Sir Thomas Beecham, 'others deny its possession of morals; and certainly it cannot boast of much in the way of beauty. After last night, one is inclined to say that it has no manners,—which is the most damning indictment of the town.'

Some allowance should be made for the grinding monotony of a critic's life when night after night he has to attend commonplace concerts and turn out notices that conceal his boredom and make entertaining reading.

During the fortnight of promenade concerts Newman used to refresh himself by slipping away from the Town Hall and going down to the Hippodrome to see the last turn or two of the second house before going to the office to write his concert notice. 'You know, Sandford', he said to a reporter he met in the passage, 'I do envy those music-hall fellows. There they are, playing the same old tricks to a new audience every evening, and I have to find new tricks for the same audience every morning.' The temptation to shock that same audience with an outrageous trick could be well-nigh irresistible ; and Newman did not always put up a strong fight.

After the First World War, Ernest Newman carried his broadsword to London and was succeeded on the *Post* by A. J. Sheldon, who also came from Manchester. He entered on the thankless task of following a resounding genius with modest confidence and gradually worked his way into a position of authority with the Birmingham music-loving public. He did not try to adopt the swash-buckling style of his predecessor and his concert notices and weekly articles were marked by an innate chivalry and kindliness. This did not stop him from delivering telling thrusts when necessary; but his intention always was to be helpful and constructive. He measured up to the most exacting test that can be applied to any specialist writer, in that he was read with pleasure and enjoyment by those who were not greatly interested in music.

Occasionally he exercised a *Post* critic's licence to stray beyond the formal boundaries of his subject, as in his comment on the newly-decorated Town Hall of which the City Fathers of that time were unduly proud. 'Early Metro-Goldwyn-Mayer' he called it casually in the course of a concert notice and the gibe struck home. He entered into the musical life of Birmingham, giving a lead in the formation of the Birmingham Opera Club. His premature death in 1931 was felt as a sharp loss to the city.

The next music critic, Mr. Eric Blom, who is still

207

happily at work in London, was another inspired Hubbard appointment. Birmingham University appropriately conferred on Mr. Blom an Honorary Degree after his *magnum opus*, the editing of the fifth edition of *Grove's Dictionary of Music*, which he undertook on leaving Birmingham in 1946. For Mr. Blom is essentially a scholar of music and a man of letters. As a critic his weapon is the rapier rather than the broadsword and he wields it with the button on the foil,—to tickle rather than to wound. There is no need to enlarge on his delightful polished style, for his books, including a collection of his weekly articles under the title *A Musical Postbag*, are current literature. While in Birmingham, he carried on the tradition of a licensed commentator and many people will still remember and treasure one celebrated remark. An artistic evening in Birmingham, he sadly reflected, starts in an aura of high tea and ends in going to bed too early because there is nothing else to do. His newspaper colleagues particularly recollect with professional appreciation a naughty digression in a weekly article on the subject of technical terms in musical writing.

'On the other hand, jargon as such is as tiresome in musical writing as in any other; it is as well to use current words whenever they express the writer's thoughts with precision. One has no patience with the avoidance of useful words of common parlance merely for the sake of impressiveness, nor with such pompous clichés as journalism of the baser sort insists on substituting for plain English on various more or less solemn occasions. If such journalism is to be believed, it is quite an unknown occurrence, for instance, for a queen ever to buy anything; she always purchases. Thus the verb "to purchase" has become a technical term connected with the simple act of shopping when performed by royalty, just as in music *pizzicato* is believed to be the polite expression for the plucking of strings. A queen, I take it, would never in any circumstances buy a plucked fowl; she can just

Sir Charles Hyde, Bart.

G. W. Hubbard

The Birmingham Post.

General Strike, 1926

King George V Supplement, 1936

possibly be imagined to purchase a chicken *pizzicato*.'

How his editor must have chuckled over this elegant thrust!

It fell to Hubbard to appoint only two dramatic critics, F. A. Besant Rice and R. Crompton Rhodes. In the hey-day of the popular theatre before the cinema and television had lured away the mass audience, the term 'dramatic critic' covered a wide range. At one extreme were the intellectuals who talked about 'theatre', without the definite article; deplored its imminent death, at least on the English stage; or, in their more cheerful moments, awaited a coming 'dawn' that was breaking over Russia, Scandinavia, Germany and anywhere else beyond the British Isles. At the other limit was the 'Old Laddie and Astrakhan' type of theatre gossip writer, who was apt to get involved in back-stage feuds and intrigues and to let his paper in for a lot of trouble. The critic of a provincial paper like the *Post* needs to have his feet firmly planted on the ground and his eyes lifted to the hills,—to be able to appreciate and assess the entertainment value of popular shows, from music-hall to touring companies with musical comedies and farces, and at the same time to be ready to apply standards of metropolitan and continental dramatic art to the rare visitors that deserve the compliment and, where such exists, to the local repertory theatre with artistic aspirations.

Besant Rice, who served the paper from 1906 to 1913, was a thorough-going man of the theatre, who had been secretary to Sir Arthur Pinero and had had considerable experience as a producer. He doubled the parts of dramatic critic and literary editor (he was son of the Victorian novelist, Walter Besant), and, to judge by his forthright notices and occasional articles, he was a man of confident opinions and essentially practical ideals. His sympathy with the intellectuals was tempered by a firm insistence on the fact that the first duty of the theatre was to provide entertainment for a public that

209

was paying to be entertained. That sentimental abstraction 'the people' which, so it was assumed by the idealists, 'needs must love the highest when they see it', found no place in his philosophy. Yet he left the *Post* in 1913 to become the first producer of modern plays for the Birmingham Repertory Theatre, which under Sir Barry Jackson had evolved from the Pilgrim Players, whose performances he had watched and criticised from a professional standpoint. Reminiscences of the early days of the Repertory Theatre preserve a sharp picture of Besant Rice, a figure like an Englishman's idea of a Frenchman, —tight-waisted coat, yellow gloves, waxed moustache,— always smoking particularly pungent cheroots, and given to displays of temperament.

His successor as dramatic critic, R. Crompton Rhodes, was a very different type, a product of King Edward's School and Birmingham University, a student of the drama and an enthusiastic amateur actor, with an inherited taste for literature, history and archaeology. He was temperamentally an enthusiast in everything that took his interest, a delightful companion with a flashing sense of humour and a zest for life in all its aspects. He carried a brilliant scholarship lightly. His books on 'The Stagery of Shakespeare' and the First Folio broke new ground; and his biography of Sheridan and his editing of the three volumes of Sheridan's plays and poems are authoritative standard works. Outside the world of the theatre, he was a local historian of high repute and promise and at the time of his premature death in 1935 he was engaged on a projected centenary history of Birmingham commissioned by the Corporation. He put his historical learning and knowledge of stagecraft into the preparation of several historical pageants in the Midlands. He was a stickler for accuracy over details of heraldry and would wage cheerful controversy with other experts in this esoteric field of scholarship. His many-sided interests and polished literary style raised the standard of the *Post's* dramatic criticism and theatre articles to a level that commanded national respect. His weekly articles were often perfect little essays, sometimes only loosely attached to the subject of the stage and always read with relish by many people who were not theatre-goers. For his sense of history told him that the art of drama was not confined to performances on the modern proscenium stage and included every medium from its religious origins in ancient Greece to its latest manifestations in the cinema. He was not one of those theatre critics who affect to despise 'the pictures' and was one of the first of his kind to take the popular art seriously and to apply to it the critical apparatus of a scholar. The cinema was welcome to him as a new adventure in the world of drama, enlarging his sympathies and giving scope for a very pretty wit.

Hurrying from the theatre to write his notice one bitterly cold night, without an overcoat, as was his eager, happy-go-lucky manner, he caught a cold which developed into pneumonia and, like Garrick's, Crompton Rhodes' death 'eclipsed the gaiety of nations and impoverished the public stock of harmless pleasure.'

The appointment of a successor falls outside Hubbard's editorship, but it is convenient at this point to follow through the narrative of the *Post's* dramatic criticism to the present day. T. C. Kemp, who is still a living memory on the paper and in the community he served so well for twenty years, came into journalism comparatively late in life. He had been an occasional contributor to the paper, but his background of school teaching and librarianship, his innate modesty and diffidence and his studious, literary approach might not have seemed the best preparation for the haste and pressure and quick judgments of newspaper life. However, Record's insight in selecting him was abundantly proved in course of time. Kemp started quietly, making no attempt to emulate his ebullient predecessor, and soon adapted himself to newspaper conditions. His profound knowledge of literature and his abiding enthusiasm for the drama carried him on to a stage of authority as a critic that was recognised in the Critic's Circle. His love of the theatre and devotion to its well-being made him an influential figure, particularly in the affairs of the Birmingham Repertory Theatre. He was also a founder and past-chairman of the Crescent Theatre, a sponsor of the Open Air Theatre and a past-President of the Shakespeare Club at Stratford. His advice, encouragement and practical knowledge were always at the disposal of any sincere enterprise concerned with the drama, professional or amateur. He was a good lecturer and broadcaster and never spared himself in the cause of the theatre. To him the cinema was a great potential art form and his film notices were among his finest work. He fought steadfastly a losing battle against tasteless commercialism on stage or screen and never ceased to uphold the ideals of artistic and intellectual integrity that inspired his own work.

Tom Kemp, as he was known to his colleagues, was a most lovable man. They watched with growing respect the transformation of an essentially bookish man into a graceful, witty and lucid stylist. He was always constructive in his criticism, severe when standards were debased but infinitely kind wherever he could discern honesty of purpose and sincere artistic aspirations. At the same time, he was not solemn and could administer a reproof with pleasant irony or spice indignation with wit. In conversation he was a charming companion who could have been a devastating controversialist but for a kindly modesty that inhibited him from dealing the death-blow. One came away from a lively, even flippant, conversation with Tom Kemp feeling all the better for it, with much to think about and a restored faith in humanity and ideals. In short, he was a good man.

To return to Hubbard, the theme of this chapter, which has sought to show something of the influence that radiated from his withdrawn presence. On two occasions, and two only, in his long editorship, he spoke in explicit terms of the ideals and aspirations that guided his conduct, of the *Post*. The first occasion was at a staff dinner to celebrate the Jubilee of the *Post* in 1907, not long after he had become editor. Looking back on the half-century, he ascribed the position won by the paper to the fact that 'it had never swerved in its efforts to give the public that which was clean, that which was reliable and, above all things, that which was honest in the way of news and of opinion'. They had, he said, a glorious tradition; but they could not live on tradition alone. 'He that lives in the past might almost as well be dead'. The young editor turned to the future. 'We have to see that the paper maintains its influence, its fairness, its accuracy, its authority; and that there is no falling off in the literary tone of the production'. He returned more than once to 'literary tone', a quality that is something more than literary style, for it includes subject matter, mode of treatment, quality of thinking and standards of ethics. The paper aspired to exercise an influence with intelligent and intellectual people, which 'nowadays includes a large proportion of the working classes, who have had nearly forty years of sound education and have, especially in Birmingham, made good use of their opportunities'. Reading these forward-looking sentiments fifty years afterwards, they breathe a spirit of youthful optimism. It was perhaps expecting too much to hope that the first generation of elementary schoolchildren should want to read a newspaper written for public school and university men and women. Yet that is the aspiration of all who conduct the better-class newspapers,—that public education eventually will raise standards of discrimination to higher levels. There are some signs to-day that newspapers that have maintained quality are beginning to come into their own; but the process is taking much longer than the pioneers of public education expected.

213

Hubbard's second recitation of an editor's creed came twenty-six years later when he acknowledged the staffs' presentation on his retirement. He had always held, he said, 'that a respectable newspaper, like a respectable man, should never cease to strive to act as a gentleman. It should never depart from the truth; should never deliberately tell only a part of the truth, so as to trick people into believing a lie without openly telling one; should never descend to the level of its least intelligent readers; should never in its leader columns, by "special pleading" or the suppression of disagreeable facts, forget that its true function was to contribute to the formation of a sane and thoughtful public opinion, rather than to impose upon the public an opinion based either on prejudice or on distortion of the premises on which the opinion was to be reached'.

He believed that the *Post* had throughout been an honest newspaper, had always been clean, and had always depended solely in its appeal to the public upon the news value of its contents. 'We have never descended to "stunts". We have never attempted to swell circulation by appeals to the cupidity of our readers, by the promotion of competitions or the presentation of gifts. Thank goodness we have always been able to hold our heads high as journalists, conscious of at least honest effort to live up to our ideal.'

18

Policy Making

FROM THE BEGINNINGS OF JOURNAL-
ism most newspapers have had and have used
political influence: at the worst, pressing a party
view; at the best, forwarding a particular philosophy. Certainly, the *Post* is no exception. In the hundred
years of its existence, it has, time and again, played a
part in forming public opinion and so in influencing
public affairs—local and national. It seems worth while
then, to discuss just when and where and how the *Post*
has discharged this function—generally regarded, till
the last decade or two, as a newspaper's most important
function.

Approach may conveniently be along two separate
lines—consideration given, first, to the effect on the
reader; secondly, to the internal mechanism by which
that effect is produced. First, then, for the effect. Speaking broadly, the *Post* has sought not so much to give direct
guidance to its readers on this or that specific issue;
rather, it has tried to foster in its readers a particular
political philosophy, so that each individual issue, as it
arose, produced from the reader the response the *Post*
hoped.

The creation of this sort of *rapport* between a newspaper and its readers, certainly the most effective way of
acquiring political influence, is not an easy thing. It takes
years, generations perhaps, and there are certain essential
pre-conditions. The first, of course, is that readers believe
in a newspaper's sincerity; the other, closely allied, is
that readers appreciate its consistency. Belief in a newspaper's sincerity comes when readers recognise that, on
any and every subject, its presentation of news is un-
biassed; that, on any and every subject, the conclusions
reached from the news are logical and honest. One ten-

215

dentious headline, one specious but fallacious leading article and the whole structure of reader confidence is undermined. Faith in a newspaper's consistency is a plant even harder to grow. It demands, in effect, that readers shall be satisfied that all the many and varied political and social and economic problems, local and national and international, arising in the interpretation of news, are seen from the same spiritual point of view, approached with the same political philosophy as background.

Consistency in the rigid, narrow sense, is impossible for a great newspaper as it is for a great statesman. Peel, Chamberlain, Churchill—they have changed their views, sometimes more than once. Twice at least—over Irish Home Rule and over Free Trade—the *Post* has changed its views on subjects of first-rate importance. That, doing this, it has yet maintained its influence is the strongest evidence that its readers have believed in both its sincerity and in the essential consistency of its philosophy.

So much for the newspaper as political force making its impact on public opinion. How, though, has this effect been produced? What of the mechanism? Behind everything, throughout the *Post's* long history, has always been the Editor. But in changing times and conditions editors of differing character have worked in different ways. John Thackray Bunce, by repute the *Post's* most influential editor, living in a relatively small Birmingham, where every citizen of importance knew every other, exerted an influence almost wholly direct and personal. With very little concern about the appearance and make-up of the paper, he was able to write almost all the leading articles of any importance—and was never averse from owning their authorship. Because his personal influence was something worth having, statesmen cultivated him, often opened their minds to him—most important of them all, Joseph Chamberlain. That was, in part, because Chamberlain always needed, as he always had, Bunce's support

216

in local affairs—in the sweeping away of the old, ugly undignified Birmingham the industrial revolution had produced and the building of a new forward-looking Birmingham, for generations the envy of other English provincial cities. It was in part, though, because Bunce was a notable judge of the public mind and of the trend of electoral opinion in a day when both the House of Commons and the City Council counted for far more than to-day. It seems certain that the influence of the *Post* in Bunce's day was largely the influence of an individual personality and that it was greater than ever before or since. In local affairs it played a major part in the reform movement, so bitterly resisted and so stoutly pressed. Not the least significant of its services, however, came towards the end of Bunce's reign. When controversy was raging in the late nineties over the future development of Mason College the decisive influence of the *Post* was cast for what Joseph Chamberlain, its most powerful advocate called 'a complete and integral University', as opposed to a University College in a loose Midland federation. To Bunce, only less than to Chamberlain, is due the fact that Birmingham was the first provincial university. In national affairs the *Post* had much to do with the success of that Liberal Unionist movement which, starting as an opposition to Gladstonian Irish policy, brought into the Conservative Party a notable stream of Liberal, even of Radical, ideas. Long after Bunce had passed away, even after the Home Rule controversy had ceased to be acute, the Unionism of Joseph Chamberlain's city was essentially Liberal. That is why Birmingham resisted so long the assault of Labour.

G. W. Hubbard, who ranks only second to Bunce in the list of influential *Post* editors, was wholly different in character and methods. Outside the office, as in it, he was a shy, reserved man, preferring the fact of power to its display. His personal contacts were fewer and less readily seen. To the majority even of responsible citizens

217

he was not even a name.

Two of Hubbard's qualities, in particular, were quite invaluable to the *Post* in its relations with the world outside. He was wont to say to his leader-writers that 'an editor has no politics'. By that he meant, he would explain, that every issue must be considered, without prejudice, in the light of what seemed to the editor to be the national interest, not that of either party. In the event, no doubt, Hubbard being the man he was, the result of his consideration was usually support for a Liberal Unionist—not always a Conservative—policy. But the way his conclusions were reached made for a moderate and fair-minded statement of his case, a statement that carried to his readers conviction, if not always that he was right, invariably that he was honest. Hence the *Post's* influence in local as well as international affairs.

There was one other notable effect of this quality. Asking and getting from his leader-writers this sort of approach to every problem, he was able to use effectively the pens of vigorous writers whose own political leanings were very different.

Hubbard's other quality enabled him to make the most and best of his political contacts. He never broke a confidence; but he never fell into the commonest of the traps set for journalists by politicians, allowing himself to be told 'in confidence' something he already knew or surmised. One illustration may serve. Hubbard came back from London, a day or two before the Locarno plan became public. He went to his foreign affairs leader- writer. 'I want you', he said, 'on this particular piece of news, to write generally on ways and means of bringing France and Germany closer together. I'm giving no "guidance" because I've just been talking to Austen Chamberlain.' Party leaders knew him as a man of superlatively sound judgment—whose advice, given only when asked, was always sensible and often invaluable. Just a chosen few found in him, too, a man of inflexible principle.

218

Inside the office, Hubbard's methods were his own. It has been said already that he was the complete journalist, concerned to turn out a paper whose every line showed quality. That in itself made it impossible for him to write very much, nor in fact did he write very often or conspicuously well. More surprising still, he rarely offered much direction to the succession of able leader-writers he appointed—the elder Whates, Sutherland, L. P. Hadley, T. W. Hutton and the rest. He expected them to know, and in fact they did know, the 'line' the *Post* must presumably take on any given subject.

Not less important, with an instinct that was almost genius, he knew each man's particular interests, his particular prejudices and preferences. Normally, all he had to do was to ask for a leader on a particular topic, adding what was ordinarily a purely formal question: 'Any difficulty?' On rare occasions, if some modification of editorial policy were afoot, the 'regular' would be asked: 'Would you rather not take the "leader"to-night?' Hubbard never wanted a man to write from a brief he did not honestly accept. One recalls a leader-writer, who had been 'taking' the miners' strike which overlapped the General Strike of 1926, being thus excused. One recalls, too, what happened when the Irish Treaty (1921) was being negotiated. Unionist as he and the *Post* were, Hubbard believed the settlement inevitable and intended to say so. He came to a leader-writer not normally concerned with Irish affairs and asked him point-blank his personal view. It coincided with Hubbard's own. 'Good', he said, 'Take the leader to-night, please. Mr. —— feels he would prefer not to write.' The same thing happened more than once over India, when the Indian expert—and he really was an expert—was felt to be a trifle too liberal in his attitude to Reform.

To turn over the files of those days and consider the many problems a newspaper editor had to face is to wonder more and more at the way Hubbard, with so little overt control of his colleagues, kept *Post* policy on an even keel. His reign divides itself naturally into three periods—the pre-war years, with Irish Home Rule, the Lloyd-George Budget, the Parliament Bill; the years between 1914 and 1919 with, quite apart from the need to explain and analyse war-news, the complications occasioned by such political storms as the break-up of the first Coalition, the conflict between soldiers and politicians, and the gradual splitting of the Liberal Party into two bitterly hostile factions; and, finally, the after-war years, with greater importance attaching to foreign affairs and, at home, social and economic elements more and more influencing the political strife between Conservatives and Unionists on the one side and, on the other, not the Liberal but the Labour Party.

German reparations, Britain's war debt, unemployment and industrial strife; the League of Nations, its hopes and its failures; disarmament and German rearmament; the gradual return, willy-nilly, to power politics— these things made the third period of Hubbard's reign by far the most difficult. Three or four General Elections, a General Strike, the break-up of the Lloyd-George coalition—these were mere symptoms, from an editor's point of view, of a general malaise at home. Abroad, the movement towards a more liberal régime in India, the failure of all efforts, general or sectional, to secure adequate limitation of armaments, the increasing evidence of the failure of the League of Nations, the pressure of events towards a renewed and revived policy of Imperial Preference, which some elements in the Conservative Party had been disposed to abandon and, simultaneously, the changing pattern of the British Empire—these things demanded, in journalists as in politicians, open and flexible minds.

Happily for the *Post*, Hubbard's temperament and technique, the spirit he had encouraged in his leader-writers, were admirably suited to this changed and

220

changing period. It is probably true to say that the *Post's* prestige and influence at this period, not only at home but in foreign capitals, stood as high as at any time in its history. Hubbard had given Sir Charles Hyde what Sir Charles wanted—a quality paper, quality in every line of it, with an influence wholly incommensurate with its relatively small circulation.

One must note here a single episode—as important as it was isolated—that was an exception to two general rules—that Sir Charles Hyde never interfered with the conduct of the *Post*; and that Hubbard never loosed the reins, however lightly he might seem to hold them. The *Post*, it has been said, had come out firmly and decisively for the Irish settlement and stood by it consistently despite its failure to bring the peace that had been hoped. The Treaty was in 1921. In the following year, very largely because of the Irish Treaty, a powerful element in the Conservative Party demanded—and finally secured—the break-up of the Lloyd-George Coalition. What, in the days when the fate of the Coalition was in the balance, was to be the attitude of the *Post*? That was decided—a thing wholly alien to *Post* tradition and probably unique in *Post* history—by what might be called a political council of war. Hubbard, by an accident of illness, was absent. Present were Sir Charles Hyde himself, Sir Alfred Robbins (London Correspondent) and the chief assistant editor, L. P. Hadley. No record of the proceedings seems to have survived, nor is there still alive any of those present. The decision, however, was to acquiesce in the break-up of the Coalition and, in so doing, to part company for a time with the Conservatives who had elected to stand by Lloyd-George —two of whom, Austen Chamberlain and Sir Robert Horne, were close personal friends of Hubbard.

Hubbard, of course, followed the decision loyally, even though he had appeared at one time to be sympathetic with the idea—to-day, indeed, it sounds a fantastic idea

—of the Coalition, in due season, becoming a Middle Party. He never had the almost pathological dislike of Lloyd-George which some Unionists felt; his Liberal Unionist background, moreover, made him less averse than some to certain liberal ideas which Conservatives disliked; and perhaps he feared what then seemed a remote possibility, the effects of a head-on clash between the Conservative and Labour Parties with an electorate increasingly turning Leftwards. The episode is mentioned as the sole occasion, in a long reign, when for a moment Hubbard did not, at any rate did not manifestly, decide the *Post's* policy on a major political issue.

He remained in office another ten years or so—long enough to see many of the peace and disarmament hopes of 1920-21 disappointed; long enough, however, to see Austen Chamberlain acclaimed as author of Locarno, seemingly a great move the same way. He saw, too, the General Strike and the gradual deterioration of Britain's industrial position which brought about the financial crisis of 1930; but he saw also another son of Joseph Chamberlain securing, at Ottawa, much for which Joseph Chamberlain had striven at the beginning of the century.

Through it all, Hubbard was never known to be worried or perturbed; and most certainly never lost the confidence of his colleagues on the editorial side. That confidence was based mainly perhaps on recognition, first, of the breadth and depth of a political knowledge he never paraded; second, on an appreciation of the common-sense he brought to bear on every problem—as cooling to rash enthusiasm as it was damping to excited irritation. With those who knew him best—and it took years to know him—there was added a real affection. It has been said that, for most of the staff, Hubbard was a reserved, aloof presence. In the front of the office that was not quite true: Hubbard was human. Here, too, whatever may have been true elsewhere, he would occasionally offer praise, though he preferred to do it indirectly—by quoting some word of congratulation he had heard or passing over some laudatory letter, merely adding: 'I quite agree'. In the last resort, all over the office, his power rested on one thing; that he always knew what he was doing and—more surprising and more important—what other people were doing. Nor did that apply only to the office side of things. More than once, colleagues were astonished at his knowledge of their affairs. Invariably, too, he used his immense personal influence with Sir Charles Hyde not only to protect members of his staff who were in error, which after all is an editor's duty, but also to help members of his staff who were in trouble. His retirement through ill-health in 1933 came as shock, since for much of his time as editor he had been a sick man and yet carried on. It came also, to his immediate colleagues, as a personal sorrow.

To most members of the *Post* staff, at any rate in Birmingham, it was something of a surprise when E. W. Record was appointed to succeed Hubbard. Much as his work in the London Office was admired, impressive as was his personality to those who had met him, his Birmingham colleagues had always thought of him as a dyed-in-the-wool Londoner, with his ear very much to the Whitehall and Westminster ground—a man pre-destined to be a second Sir Alfred Robbins, as influential as the Editor but in a different way. L. P. Hadley, on the other hand had seemed cast for the part of Hubbard's successor. His long years of service, more than thirty, on the editorial side; his knowledge of Birmingham affairs and Birmingham people; his always competent and not infrequently brilliant leaders; the many and sometimes protracted periods when he had taken Hubbard's place with conspicuous success and to Sir Charles Hyde's expressed satisfaction—all these factors must surely have been taken into account before the appointment was made. None the less, it was Record who was appointed—to his own intense surprise, as he himself in after years admitted. Nor, one can seen now, was the appointment mistaken. Record's editorship, through the years that saw the Abdication, the developments that led to the second World War, the early part of the War itself, did much to enhance, nothing to diminish, the *Post's* reputation as a great newspaper.

It may be, too, that Sir Charles Hyde felt the paper needed a man who had mixed freely and would continue to mix freely with his fellow men. Record had a sound knowledge, from his early years, of the Midlands. He was an extraordinarily good mixer, making himself both liked and admired almost on first acquaintance. Quite unlike Hubbard, he rather enjoyed the limelight. It was not many weeks before he had won the affection of his colleagues in the office; not much longer before he was more generally known in Birmingham than ever Hubbard had been. His ideals for the paper, of course, were those of Hubbard—else Sir Charles Hyde would not have appointed him. His outlook and methods, on the other hand, were wholly his own.

Fundamentally, Record was a reporter—and a very good reporter at that, as his high reputation earlier, on the *Manchester Guardian*, had shown. His knowledge of the sub-editor's trade, in general or in detail, was limited; his outlook on public affairs rather that of the political columnist than of the writer of editorials. He was more interested in personalities than in principles and his fund of recollections shed light on people rather than on affairs.

And, by a curious coincidence, the event with which Record's editorship will be longest associated—the circumstances leading to the Abdication of King Edward VIII—demanded precisely the qualities he had in fullest measure. The story is worth telling in some detail. It was in 1935, when Record was well settled in the saddle, that

Sir Austen Chamberlain

E. W. Record

L. P. Hadley

T. W. Hutton

The Lord Iliffe, G.B.E.

rumours began to link the name of His Majesty with that of Mrs. Simpson. The more circumstantial rumours were American and Dominion. In England, even in most of London, there was no circulation of these rumours; the Press twenty-five years ago was not that of to-day.

On December 1, the Bishop of Bradford, for reasons even now obscure, speaking to his Diocesan Conference about the Coronation, made a reference to the matter clear enough to those who knew, quite obscure to those who did not. The news came into the office fairly late in the evening. Shortly after, the Editor of the *Yorkshire Post* came on the telephone. His problem was not whether or not to publish Dr. Blunt's address, including the significant phrase: 'His Majesty will need God's grace if he is to do his duty faithfully . . . We hope he is aware of the need; some of us wish that he gave more positive signs of his awareness'. The question was rather whether to elucidate for his readers what to most of them must be utterly obscure. Elucidation meant, in effect, letting out of the bag a cat that, so far as the Press of Britain was concerned, had been most conscientiously imprisoned. The *Yorkshire Post* was not, it would seem, prepared to act alone. Record's line was that he would comment, discreetly, if the *Manchester Guardian* would come into line. After telephoning and cross-telephoning, so it was decided. These three great provincial papers broke the news. The leader, written by L. P. Hadley, after noting that the Bishop of Bradford had addressed to His Majesty 'words of reproof such as nobody has thought fit to address to a King of England for many a long day', went on to point out that this mere fact was evidence that 'rumour and highly sensational tale-telling as to one particular phase of His Majesty's life is not without its basis of solid truth'. Most important, it laid down that 'the private and public life of the King Emperor are inseparable.'

It was not much, perhaps, but it was enough. Record

225

can claim as great credit as any man for courageous and decisive action. The problem presented was one particularly suited to his special gifts. Its solution depended on the reporter's assessment of how soon the secret would be no longer a secret—and the reporter's desire to be first with the news; on a fairly close understanding of personalities, inside and outside newspaper offices; on a weighing up, perhaps instinctive rather than reasoned, of public reaction to a great shock; on an understanding that the public's reaction would depend largely on the way this sensational news was presented.

This was, clearly, no normal editor's problem. The case was one for quick decision; the responsibility was not to be shared with any of Record's colleagues, even by way of consultation.

Normally, his method was wholly different. Perhaps because he lacked Hubbard's solid political background, he liked to hear what his leader-writers had to say on any given subject before the paper's 'line' was decided. He initiated, soon after he became Editor, a leader-writer's conference to which his colleagues came with suggestions for subjects and their treatment. Since at least two leader-writers held strongly political views, especially on foreign affairs, not wholly compatible, the conference sometimes might degenerate into a heated debate. Record's interest in and knowledge of personalities occasionally tended, too, to side-track the proceedings. On the whole, though, this quite different method had much the same result as Hubbard's. A line, usually the right line, was found and followed consistently—perhaps partly because Hubbard had long ago established for his leader-writers a general attitude to affairs which persisted after he had gone. It is relevant, though, to quote one disgruntled member of the conference, who much preferred the Hubbard technique. 'The man', he murmured as the conference ended one evening, 'is an eavesdropper, not an editor.' Certainly it is true that, on some

226

intricate issues of international affairs, and concerned mainly with Italy and Germany, those responsible for writing leaders would, on occasion, have appreciated the quiet but firm influence of Hubbard. Over Abyssinia 'sanctions' were first supported and then their abandonment approved, at least implicitly. Nor would Hubbard's *Post* have been quite so enthusiastic over Munich as was Record's. To say that is not to criticise Record: he erred in common with the editor of the greatest of all English newspapers. It is, rather, to pay a final tribute to Hubbard: he would have been less strongly influenced than Record by the personalities of Stanley Baldwin and Neville Chamberlain.

One quality of Record's, however was greatly appreciated. He liked his leader-writers to meet and get at first hand their impressions of people who counted; and he used his personal contacts and his influence generously to provide opportunities. In one respect, though, he was less careful than Hubbard. Hubbard read, thoughtfully and critically, every line of leader 'copy' before it went to the composing room; Record did not. Since a mere turn of phrase, a slight difference in balance, may alter the effect of a 'leader', the conscientious writer, anxious to produce exactly what had been decided, found writing a leader rather more difficult under Record; he had to guard more closely against his own sub-conscious bias. One of them put it that writing leaders nowadays was 'rather like driving a car without brakes'.

For all that, Record's method had one good effect. It brought new life and vigour to a team of writers whose long service might soon have made them a little mechanical and wooden. It tended, too, to widen the range of subjects deemed suitable for editorial comment. On the personal side he was well-loved in Birmingham as he had been in London. His sudden illness and his death were mourned no less than had been Hubbard's retirement.

19

Landfall and Departure

WITH THE COMING OF THE blitz the office arrangements were put to the test and came through with honours. The usual physical precautions had been taken to safeguard machinery and staff against bombing; the fleet of vans and cars was dispersed to some extent; emergency lines of communication were provided to give alternative channels for receiving agency and other news; and the local newspaper offices prepared schemes for mutual assistance in bringing out their own and each other's papers in case of trouble. Nobody, of course, knew what to expect in the way of hazard and dislocation but the trial was faced with determination to keep the presses turning and bring out the paper next morning. In the event *The Birmingham Post* and its associates got off lightly and never once was production and distribution totally disorganised. The most serious damage was the destruction of the garage and the greater part of the vehicles. Two men were killed in this raid, the only men to lose their lives while on duty. The head office took its share of incendiaries, including one that came down a ventilating shaft and penetrated to the Foundry Melting Room in the basement. They were all dealt with promptly and effectively by the staff. Away from the office, 868 tons of newsprint at Curzon Street railway depot went up in flames. Thereafter, stocks of newsprint were dispersed in five open-air depots under tarpaulins and no more was lost by enemy action. Everybody had his 'bomb story', some of them tragic enough, and the nightly ordeal of bringing out the paper under bombardment was no light experience. Innumerable acts of quiet courage and devotion to duty passed unobserved or into oblivion. Their memorial is that the paper always came out. Men of the night staff in particular, afflicted as they were by anxieties for what might be happening to their families and homes, deserve to be remembered. They were sustained by that 'steady fidelity to what is nearest to hand and heart in the short moment of each human effort' which Conrad found to be the only needed saving grace for the great mass of mankind.

One incident of the blitz remained firmly graven on the minds of all who worked through those nightmare months in the office. This was the example set by the General Manager, Colonel Sir Bertram Ford. Night after night he came down to the office to supervise affairs, sharing the risks and by his presence encouraging and heartening those who had to be there. It gave them an altogether new insight into his character and a feeling of respect and gratitude for a man of genuine courage and sense of duty. In fact, one had to revise one's ideas quite a lot and to reflect once again on the complexity and unexpected depths of resource in human nature. For one had to realise that this soldier *manqué*, whose fondness for uniforms and peace time martial display had been a subject of jest, really did have the greatest of military virtues, moral and physical courage. Fate had cheated him of his dearest ambition in the First World War, when as a Territorial officer he had taken his battery to France, only to be invalided home before going into action and relegated to home service for the rest of the war. His time came in 1940, when he was over seventy, and the proof of character was all the more convincing since the occasion was civilian and unspectacular.

That he would have made an efficient regimental officer was never in doubt. He demonstrated his abilities constantly by his manner and conduct in ordinary business about the office. There is perhaps no more civilian-minded occupation than journalism and no class of men less amenable than journalists to regimental discipline. Their professional outlook and general habits must

229

always have afflicted the tidy mind of the General Manager. He endured much, too, from the mocking humour of his proprietor, Charles Hyde, who seldom missed a chance at a staff social occasion to allude mischievously to uniforms and decorations. They were always good for a laugh. On the day after a great ceremonial parade in the city where the Colonel had commanded in his glory, Charles Hyde came briskly into the General Manager's office, 'Morning, Ford,' he exclaimed before the assembled company, 'How did the Boy Scouts go yesterday?''

Interviews with the General Manager were apt to start stiffly and, on his part, explosively; but when a man knew his own mind and was confident that he was right, the interview would develop reasonably and end amicably. For at heart Ford was open to conviction, even to a conviction that some hasty decision of his had been mistaken, and in personal affairs he was fundamentally just and always strictly honourable. He was quite incapable of a mean or dishonest action, his prejudices dissolved at a call to humanity and he would go to any amount of trouble to help a man in difficulties. His close associations with the hospital services and the medical profession enabled him time and again to put a man in the way of the best advice and treatment for an obscure condition, and few things gave him greater satisfaction than to learn that his layman's diagnosis had been confirmed by the appropriate specialist. Of no man was an old saying truer,—his bark was worse than his bite.

On Charles Hyde's death in November, 1942, the future of the papers became a matter of acute concern and apprehension, not only to the staff but in the city at large. So far as was known, he had made no plans for the succession, such as his uncle John Feeney, also a childless man, had begun to make before the turn of the century. There was no heir-apparent in the business, and no young man in the managerial department to carry on the

230

traditions of the Feeney family. When his Will was published, appearances were not falsified. The properties were left to be sold and the proceeds divided equally between Birmingham University, the Queen Elizabeth Hospital, Dr. Barnardo's Homes and the King George the Fifth Fund for Youth Welfare. The Executors were the Midland Bank Trustee Co., Mr. Noel G. Hyde, a solicitor member of the family in Worcester, and Sir Bertram Ford. At the request of his co-Executors, the General Manager assumed control of the papers and announced that they would be carried on as heretofore, until they were dealt with under the terms of the Will. There were safeguards in the Will for the Staff Pension Funds and an express wish that when the papers were sold their tone and character should be maintained on the same lines. How far the testator's wishes could be carried out rested entirely with the Executors' interpretation of their legal and moral duties. The plain fact was that this immensely valuable newspaper property was thrown on a virtually open market. The anxiety inside and outside the office was concentrated on a fear lest the papers should fall, directly or indirectly, under the control of one of the national newspaper combines. The Birmingham public had a right to feel concern about newspapers that had grown up in the community and in a sense belonged to it as a part of its life. There was no lack of readiness in the community to assume a measure of responsibility for assuring that the newspapers should continue to serve the community as an integral part of its life. Many enquirers from outside also sought to ascertain the financial position of the papers and several tentative offers were made from various directions.

The heavy burden of negotiation and decision rested on the shoulders of Sir Bertram. There was never any doubt in anyone's mind about his deep regard for the welfare of the papers which he had served in various capacities since the days of John Feeney. But he was an

231

old man to undertake such responsibilities in addition to the day-to-day management in sole control of the business, with all the worries of war-time shortages of staff and equipment. It was an added blow when a few months after Charles Hyde's death, the Editor of the *Post*, E. W. Record, suddenly died and his place was taken by the deputy editor, L. P. Hadley, whose health also was precarious. The year 1943 was an unhappy period for everyone. It was, therefore, with enormous relief that the staff learned that the whole undertaking had been purchased by Lord Iliffe. The new proprietor was known by repute to everyone as a vastly experienced and successful newspaper proprietor, who had disposed of all his newspaper interests,—except an old family property, the *Coventry Evening Telegraph*—before the outbreak of war. He was a Midlands man, variously known and respected as, on the one hand, former head of the great Iliffe house of trade and technical periodicals and, on the other, as a Warwickshire County tennis player and a pioneer motorist. He had sat in Parliament for the then Tamworth Division of Warwickshire from 1923 to 1929 and his constituency included Sutton Coldfield, Castle Bromwich and Solihull. During the war he devoted his abounding energies and business abilities to chairmanship of the Duke of Gloucester's Red Cross and St. John Fund which collected over fifty-seven million pounds. More precisely to the point, as seen by the staff, he was known to Fleet Street as a model employer who commanded the loyalty and respect of all who had the privilege of working for him.

The terms of the purchase required the purchasing company to enter into a Deed of Trust to give effect to the desire expressed by Sir Charles Hyde in his will that the papers should be carried on as hitherto and adopt the same policy. Under the Deed the company covenanted with the trustees that:

(a) Until 1965 no person shall acquire any share giving

control except with the approval of the trustees;

(*b*) the company shall not alienate the goodwill of the newspapers without the consent of the trustees;

(*c*) the company shall carry on the newspapers substantially on the same lines and with substantially the same policies as pursued by Sir Charles Hyde and in particular:

(i) provide a full and impartial news service with only such comment as is fair and free from bias,

(ii) preserve the independent and local character of the newspapers and their freedom from control by any political party or trade association or any London newspapers or any combine or syndicate of newspapers.

The trustees are the Lord Lieutenant of Warwickshire, the Principal and Vice-Chancellor of Birmingham University, ex-officio, and Lord Iliffe.

Certain important implications were involved in Lord Iliffe's acquisition of the newspaper. The first and most vital was that the papers were confirmed in their most precious tradition, independence, — independence of ownership free from association with any of the newspaper combines and independence of political control. Next came the promise of stability. The ownership was vested in a public company,—The Birmingham Post and Mail Ltd.—with Lord Iliffe as chairman and the Ordinary shares held by himself and members of his family. At a later date, when circumstances became propitious, a block of Ordinary shares was offered for public subscription, with special facilities to the staff to subscribe, and the papers thereby acquired the added stability of a tangible public holding. From the start, Lord Iliffe's elder son, the Hon. E. Langton Iliffe, who at that time was serving in the Royal Air Force, was a director and subsequently identified himself with the control and management. The last general implication was that, under this experienced and efficient management, *The*

233

Birmingham Post and its associated newspapers would be brought back into the main stream of up-to-date, progressive newspaper proprietorship. The great changes that would be necessary after the war, all the re-equipment and re-development that would need to be undertaken to make up leeway and lay foundations for the future, would be in the highly capable hands of knowledgeable newspaper men with wide business experience. The prospects could not have been more encouraging and they put new heart into a disheartened and sadly depleted staff.

Newsprint rationing condemned the *Post* to ten years' suspended animation; and when the paper was given a still-rationed blood transfusion of extra newsprint in 1950, it returned to expanding life in a vastly changed world. Conditions had so altered that nothing less than a virtually new paper was required to meet the new and harsh climate of the post-war decade. As already explained, rationing was based on selling price, with the result that the *Post* was treated as a penny newspaper and reduced to that smaller category. In a typical week in the summer of 1939 the *Post* printed 16 pages daily, with a 20-page paper on Saturday. A year later the size had fallen to 6 pages daily, and by April, 1941, to 4 pages, with a 6-page paper on a Saturday about twice a month. There it remained until 1946, when occasionally as many as three 6-page papers were issued in a week. By 1950 the papers had crept up to 6 and 9 pages on alternate days and in September, 1953, a memorable Saturday paper actually attained 12 pages. This revival, however, was spasmodic, unpredictable and subject to abrupt setbacks, for newsprint bore the brunt of the recurrent dollar crises and once at least contracts for overseas supplies had to be cancelled. The early increases in newsprint were largely devoted to increasing, not the size of the paper, but the number of papers printed; for circulation had been 'pegged' during the war and there was a considerable unsatisfied demand from a larger and redistributed public. Increases in circulation, however, did nothing to ease editorial problems. In addition, savings in newsprint took other forms, such as a reduction in the size of the pages, narrower columns and compressed typography, all of which changed the face of the paper and added to the difficulties.

These frustrating years were a wretched time for those who had known the old paper and had taken pride in its standards. Cherished ideals and traditional features went by the board. It is impossible to preserve the character of a quality newspaper in one-quarter or less of the space. Four pages, two of them advertisement pages, and the most tremendous news of the century demanding admission,—it was enough to break the hearts of conscientious journalists. Early on, however, the editor took an important decision that did as much as anything to preserve a fine thread of continuity. This was to retain the literary and artistic features, even though in little more than token form, and to give all possible scope to the editorial leading articles. The paper could have been filled over and over again with sheer, hard news and would have been, no doubt, scarcely less acceptable to the majority of readers. But the things that make a newspaper different from all other newspapers, that give it, in fact, its individuality and flavour, are the original articles and the attention devoted to minority interests of cultural significance. Throughout the severest years of restriction the *Post* strove to uphold its character as a newspaper for educated, thoughtful readers, to assert its claim to be a quality paper in spite of a rationing system that would thrust it into a lower category. That was the contribution to the future made by the Old Guard of *Post* journalists.

One by one the links with the past were broken during and immediately after the war. The change in proprietorship from the Feeney family ownership to the present limited liability company under the chairmanship of

Lord Iliffe who with his family continues to own a majority of the Ordinary shares; the deaths in quick succession of two editors; the retirement of older members of the staff, including several veterans who had remained beyond the normal retiring age to see the paper through the war years; the dispersal of younger men from all departments into the Armed Forces and to war work in more vital industries; these were the more obvious breaches in continuity. What they involved is most readily illustrated by the situation on the editorial staff of the *Post* when Mr. T. W. Hutton became editor in 1945. Apart from himself, the only senior members of the staff still occupying their pre-war positions were the Deputy Editor and Literary Editor, Mr. C. V. Hancock, and the Chief Sub-Editor, Bernard Twinn. A virtually new staff had to be built up, not from the bottom, but from the top. His most urgent preoccupation was to create a new team of assistant editors, to bring in new men from outside, to imbue them with the *Post* tradition and to train them as journalists. It was urgent because everyone fully expected that expansion to pre-war dimensions would come about immediately the war was over and the new management would be eager to initiate policies of development on an enterprising scale. It may seem an unsympathetic thing to say that perhaps it was for the best in the long run that these post-war expectations were disappointed. Another five years of rationing, with all its bitter discouragements and frustrations, were to pass before the *Post* obtained even a little room for manoeuvre. Yet the interval gave time for new men to find their feet, to get to know each other, to absorb what they could from the past and to plan for the future.

One major development was carried through by Mr. Hutton, the change on 23rd September, 1946, to front page news. People outside a newspaper office can have little idea of the immense complication of an operation such as this, turning a newspaper literally inside-out,

236

and yet preserving its essential character. It has often been done, of course, both before and since; and sometimes with the deliberate intention of making a paper look entirely new. It is much more difficult to make such a drastic transformation and to persuade readers at the same time that their familiar newspaper is not altered in tone and status. Some readers, indeed, will never be so persuaded. The change on the *Post*, however, was most skilfully accomplished and is by this time forgotten except by that section of older readers to whom any change in things familiar is apt to be distasteful.

Sir Bertram had discharged his trust with honour and satisfaction and, with a load off his mind, he seemed to acquire a renewal of youthful vigour in his seventy-fifth year. On the formation of the new company he became Managing Director and for the next three years he appeared to enjoy a second spring. When he retired as Managing Director in January, 1947,—he retained a seat on the board until his death in 1955—there was about the farewell a warmth of feeling, amounting one might say to affection, from older members of the staff that would scarcely have been forthcoming at an earlier period. The Editor of *The Birmingham Post*, Mr. T. W. Hutton, who had known and worked with him for nearly 34 years, put these feelings into felicitous words. They felt, Mr. Hutton said, they were losing not only a leader, but a friend. The qualities that had made Sir Bertram a man they were loath to lose were his sense of honour, his personal courage and, greatest of all, his loyalty, first to one proprietor, then when there was no proprietor and lastly to the new regime. His loyalty to the papers was shown in his efforts to increase their prestige and influence and reputation for honesty and dignity; and he also realised he must be loyal to his colleagues.

That the occasion marked the passing of the old regime and the inauguration of a new era was further exemplified by Lord Iliffe's tribute to the retiring Managing

237

Director. 'Having regard to the wishes expressed by the late Sir Charles Hyde in regard to the sale,' Lord Iliffe said, 'the negotiations undertaken by Sir Bertram and the executors were very difficult and complicated, but they were conducted with the highest impartiality. Sir Bertram carried them through in a way of which Sir Charles Hyde would have approved, and the papers remain, under the terms of a trust deed, not only local in character, but free from control by any political party or trade association or by any group of newspapers.

'I felt, indeed, proud when, with my son, I was able to purchase the undertaking from the executors. I can fully understand the pride which Sir Bertram has always had in these newspapers and it is my hope that they will remain with my family for very many years—I nearly said generations—and that they will serve the best interests of Birmingham and the Midlands, which Sir Bertram can claim they have done under his able direction. It must be a source of satisfaction to Sir Bertram to realise that the papers, at the time of his retirement, have never been in better shape. The influence and reputation of the *Post* have never been greater than to-day, and it is interesting to know that its present sale is higher than at any time during the ninety years of its life.'

Sir Bertram was succeeded as Managing Director by Mr. E. M. Clayson, the present holder of the post. Mr. Clayson is so well known in the business and commercial community that it is unnecessary to enumerate the many public and semi-public offices he has filled since his appointment as Managing Director in 1947. Like several other newcomers to the papers mentioned in this narrative, he has identified himself whole-heartedly with the life of the city.

Ten years later, at the 13th annual general meeting of The Birmingham Post & Mail Ltd., on the eve of the *Post's* centenary year, the Chairman made another significant statement of policy. In the intervening decade

238

a tendency had developed for some provincial morning newspapers to approximate more to national newspapers and to seek circulation outside their own areas, at the expense, inevitably, of their regional character. Lord Iliffe made it clear that the proprietors of *The Birmingham Post* had no intentions of transforming it into a national newspaper.

'The position of our newspapers remains, I am glad to say, satisfactory. I would, however, like to say a few words about *The Birmingham Post*, as it is well that everyone should realise clearly what is our policy in regard to that newspaper.

'We do not think we should be serving this large, important financial and manufacturing area in the very heart of England in the best way if we endeavoured to make *The Birmingham Post* into a national newspaper. We believe the best way we can serve the Midlands is to produce a paper which every person of authority and influence in the area wishes to read; which means that we must deal with local news to an extent which would be inappropriate in a national newspaper, and at the same time cover all national and international news so that our readers are well informed upon both national and local topics.

'We believe our policy is gradually bearing fruit, as there is a growing appreciation throughout the country of the importance of Birmingham and the Midlands as one of our greatest industrial areas, and, moreover, advertisers are increasingly aware that by means of *The Birmingham Post* they can reach, in their own homes, the very men they desire to attract as investors in industry, real estate or other property.

'I feel that our aim should be not to publish a national newspaper, but rather to ensure that our readership is based on the educated, thinking section of the community living in this great industrial centre.'

Plus ca change, plus c'est la meme chose. Compare this

239

declaration of policy in November, 1956, with the leading article in the first issue of *The Birmingham Daily Post* on the 4th December, 1857. The similarity, indeed the identity, of purpose is most striking. The paper enters its second hundred years with the same firm determination to remain a local, regional newspaper devoted primarily to the interests of the industrial and agricultural Midlands and appealing to the same 'educated, thinking section of the community.'

In this same year, 1956, *The Birmingham Post* absorbed its old rival, *The Birmingham Gazette*. This was no occasion for jubilation. As Lord Iliffe said at the Annual General Meeting, ' It is always very sad to see a long-established paper lose its separate identity.' The *Gazette*, which has been mentioned before in this history, was the daily lineal descendant of *Aris's Birmingham Gazette* which was founded in 1741 by Thomas Aris, a London man who in that year moved his printing and publishing business to Birmingham. Its fascinating history, interwoven with the story of Birmingham's emergence into the Industrial Revolution, is a proper subject for separate treatment. Here it is only possible to give the briefest summary. The weekly *Aris's Birmingham Gazette* was transformed into a daily newspaper in 1862, four years after the foundation of the *Post*, and remained until the turn of the century the vigorous Conservative rival of the Radical *Post*. In the first decade of the twentieth century it passed through various vicissitudes. First Northcliffe bought it from its Conservative proprietors, but his mind was fixed on other battles and in 1904 he sold the *Gazette* to Arthur Pearson, who amalgamated it with his *Midland Express* as the *Birmingham Gazette and Express*. But, as the Westminster Press Provincial Newspapers handbook puts it, Pearson's venture 'never came within measurable distance of success.' An extensive reorganisation in 1907, involving, as already mentioned, the recruitment of several senior journalists from the *Post's* associated evening paper,

240

Colonel Sir Bertram J. T. Ford

W. V. Reynolds,
B. Litt., M.A.

E. M. Clayson

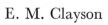

The Birmingham Mail, improved the paper considerably; but financial troubles continued and in 1912 Pearson applied to the High Court for the appointment of a receiver and manager in a debenture holder's action. The *Gazette* and its associated papers, plant, goodwill and copyright were sold at auction for £16,250.

The purchasers were Charles Starmer and Mr. J. B. Morrell, and in due course the *Gazette* became a member of the Westminster Press syndicate of Liberal newspapers. The paper thus secured a new lease of life between the wars under vigorous management and capable editorial direction. Throughout its life as a daily paper the *Gazette* had always represented in Birmingham the minority political interest, first Conservative in the Radical era and subsequently Liberal for the past forty years. Under that handicap it has fought back against the dominant party and, journalistically speaking, it has commanded the respect of its rival. It has been a lively, well edited and enterprising paper, with a broader popular appeal than the *Post*. That it has been unable to weather the economic storm is a reminder of the severity of the conditions, not a reflection on its merits as a newspaper. The amalgamation of the *Post* and the *Gazette* and the acquisition of control over the *Gazette's* associated papers, should achieve some substantial economies, as, for instance in distribution costs and the avoidance of wasteful expenditure on competitive activities.

Meanwhile, the technical editorial problems of combining two newspapers with different traditions, different styles and diverse appeals have been successfully surmounted under the supervision of the present Editor, Mr. W. Vaughan Reynolds, the same policy as to the kind of reader sought and the circulation area to be covered applying to the combined paper as it did to the *Post* alone. Experience so far is that the merging of these two morning newspapers will prove even more advantageous to readers and to the Company than the management

241

dared to hope; the circulation today over 85,000 is far higher than it has been at any time in the long history of the *Post* and the advertising value of the paper is widely recognised and appreciated.

Following the merger, two Directors of The Birmingham Gazette and Despatch Ltd. joined the Board of The Birmingham Post & Mail Ltd. The Staff of the *Gazette* have found employment on the combined newspaper, apart from some older men who have been given an opportunity to anticipate retirement on pension. This amalgamation, coming in the last year of the *Post's* first century, sets the seal on the closing of an era. Sir Bertram Ford's death in 1955 severed the last link with the Feeney family. Mr. T. W. Hutton had retired in 1950 from the editorial chair of *The Birmingham Post*, and was succeeded by the present editor, whom he had appointed as a leader-writer in 1945. Now the paper itself has acquired an addition to its title and has taken a new departure for a voyage into its second century.

This is a history, not a chronicle. More fortunate than most histories of a living, thriving concern, it can appropriately end at a clear landfall and the setting of a new course into the future.

Appendix

A Faith for the Future

by

W. Vaughan Reynolds,
B.Litt., M.A.

Editor of *The Birmingham Post*

THE BIRMINGHAM POST HAS A hundred years of achievement to its credit. Its centenary is, very properly, a time for looking back, for recalling successes, for measuring failures in the perspective of time. Looking back, however, is a luxury a newspaper can rarely afford, to be indulged in only on high days and holidays. Its business is with the present. Its yesterdays seem an age away. There is nothing so dead as an issue which has lived its day. While it records and reflects the affairs of the present, a newspaper must be forward-looking. If it is a live paper, that is because it is perpetually self renewing, changing with current demands while preserving standards of abiding value, and anticipating the needs and moods of to-morrow.

Adaptability and resilience are particularly essential qualities in a newspaper at the present time. The conditions in which the newspaper industry operates have been changing for some years and are likely to continue to change; it is possible, indeed probable, that the Press may be called upon to meet new challenges which will develop with alarming suddenness. It will succeed only if it is organised to assess, evaluate and supply the changing demands of a changing public.

243

It is not the business of this appendix to discuss the economic facts of life as they affect the newspaper industry. The enormous costs of newspaper production to-day and the rise of new competition for advertisement revenue have had consequences obvious to any interested observer, and many of the weaker units have suffered. A number of newspapers have gone down before the storm. It may be necessary for the industry to be organised in larger groups with fewer units. All who value the freedom of the Press must regret the disappearance of individual journals which added essential variety to the newspapers of this country.

On the other hand, it must be stressed that the ultimate guarantee of Press freedom lies in the fact that the newspaper industry is a commercial enterprise. Newspapers must stand on their own feet; such is the price of the freedom which they so constantly assert, a freedom which would at once be compromised by the acceptance of subsidy or subvention from the State. Those who conduct newspapers must accept and do accept the harsh truth that the public owes no journal a living, however admirable may be its content, standards and conduct. It must earn that living for itself.

It must earn that living in the face of competition not only within the newspaper industry, but also from new media of information, enlightenment and entertainment. We live in a rapidly changing age. In the first half of the twentieth century means of mass communication have been transformed. Events of which the newspaper readers of the first twenty years of the century could learn only through the columns of their chosen daily are now projected visually into the homes of millions by television. What developments the remaining years of this century will see none can tell, but they are likely to be spectacular in both senses of the word. The prospect is one of continued challenge.

Newspapers, however, have so far had remarkable

success in meeting the challenge the century has offered. This has been due in part to their possession of the qualities of adaptability and resilience referred to above as now more than ever essential. Not all newspapers have commanded these qualities; but they have been developed and maintained remarkably by those which have survived the strains and stresses of modern competition.

Compare to-day's issue of a successful newspaper with a typical number not fifty, but only twenty-five years ago. Even the 'populars' of those days seem staid, indeed ponderous, compared with the vivid, easy-to-read, well-illustrated and attractively produced newspapers of to-day. The far-reaching changes in newspaper production have been due in part to the different reading habits nowadays obtaining, in part to the expansion and changing character of the newspaper reading public. On the whole, journalism is a more highly skilled, and more exacting profession nowadays than a quarter of a century ago. There is less leisure for reading newspapers than there was. In days when life is lived at an ever-increasing tempo, readers demand matter easily assimilated and digested. This means that writing must be tighter and more economical; sub-editing must be more skilled, highlighting the essential facts of a story; pictures must be arresting, truly illustrative rather than decorative; and the art of display extends to every page.

The other major factor which has enabled newspapers to meet the challenge offered by competing media of information is the endearing habit of the public—which, fortunately, appears also to be enduring—of wanting to read about what it has already heard or already seen. Nowadays, a Coronation, or a Royal marriage, a Cup Final or a Test Match is seen or heard by a vast audience in millions. Yet those millions still turn to newspapers for the printed record of such events. Indeed, seeing and hearing in some measure stimulate the desire to read. Add to this the fact that newspapers ordinarily contain a great number of stories other media for various reasons cannot cover, and one has the explanation of why newspapers remain, and seem likely to remain, the great and favoured means of informing the public of the myriad transactions of the world in which it lives.

How, in this strenuous and exciting age of challenge and competition, do the provincial newspapers stand? A lamentable feature of the twentieth century, and particularly of the last few years, has been the high mortality rate among newspapers in the provinces and especially among the mornings. None can view the passing of so many once prosperous and eminently valuable journals without sorrow and without consciousness of the serious loss which their passing means to our national life. London is no more Britain than Paris is France, and local and regional communities are the poorer for not having a newspaper of their own. Journalism, too, suffers a grievous loss with each succeeding collapse of local enterprise.

The inexorable economic fact, however, remains: that the public owes no newspaper a living. Nevertheless, the operation of this law to the extinction of so many papers outside London does not mean that the day of the provincials is drawing towards evening. One might as well assert that because some national papers have died, and others are having grievous difficulty in surviving, the shadows are lengthening for Fleet Street too.

The future of the provincial mornings lies in their being provincial in the fullest sense of the word. That does not mean that they can afford not to be complete newspapers; for in a high proportion of the homes they enter they are the only paper taken. They must aim at giving the most complete service of news in their power to provide. This means international, national, financial, sporting, regional and local news, in addition to the special articles and features which give a paper its distinctive character.

246

Yet the prime aim must be to supply readers in the provincial's circulation areas with a service they need and can obtain nowhere else—the fullest possible coverage of regional and local news, information which affects their daily lives and which they cannot afford to do without.

This does not mean that provincial papers must 'go parish pump'. It does mean providing a balanced, factual news service, giving readers, in just perspective, the information they must have to be fully aware of what is truly significant in the life of their locality and the region of which it is part; the information which is the raw material of intelligent judgment.

The provincial paper mirrors the life of a community. It is not a distorting mirror—unless it is allowed to become locally partisan. It is a mirror which enables a region to see itself not only by direct reflection, but also in relation to the wider life of the nation, even of the world. In reporting some policy decision taken at international or national level, the provincial paper serves its readers by indicating the way in which that decision will affect their fortunes, the prospects and prosperity of their locality. Conversely, it may record some local development and show how the consequences may be of national significance. The provincial paper's essential appeal is to local and regional consciousness.

It is vitally important that this appeal should be sustained. In these days of centralised authority there is a tendency for people to think nationally, to regard a mysterious body of administrators in Whitehall (collectively referred to as 'they') as the arbiters of their destiny. It is one of the principal functions of provincial newspapers to remind their readers that local authorities still exert wide powers, and control extensive and essential services whereby their lives are daily influenced—and to remind them that they are the ultimate masters of the local authorities in question. In other words, these news-

247

papers are organs of the local and regional democracy whose vigour is essential to the survival of the national democracy itself.

Similarly the cultural life of the nation draws its strength and nourishment from the culture of the regions and local communities. It is for the provincial newspaper, through its music, art and drama critics to record and guide this varied cultural enterprise, to relate it to the artistic life of the nation as a whole. And what is true of cultural interests is also true of the religious, commercial, industrial, educational and sporting activities which distinguish the life of a flourishing community.

Provincial newspapers are edited, written and produced by men living as citizens of the communities they serve. It is for them, by the accuracy, objectivity and reliability of their reporting, by the quality of their writing, by the soundness of their judgment and by the integrity of their policy to earn and keep the respect of their readers. A provincial newspaper, in a very special sense, speaks to and for its readers. It can, and ought to, become the voice, as well as the recorder, of its region.

It can never do this unless it attunes itself to the real needs of its readership. A newspaper is a living thing—as long as it remains sensitive to the changing demands of developing communities. It cannot stand still and live. Among its readers there will always be some, conservatively-minded, who complain that it is 'no longer what it was.' It is no longer what it was because by remaining static it must die.

Accuracy, balance, fairness: these are the cardinal virtues. There is no reason, however, for these to be coupled with pomposity, dullness and gloom. Indeed, to survive, a newspaper must be lively, attractive and readable, always clear sighted and courageous and occasionally daring, which is rather a different thing. If in *serving* their readers provincial papers avoid being tempted away from their established standards to become pale

imitations of papers fulfilling an entirely different function, they will continue to command respect and support: and while they deserve respect and earn support,
their future, even though it must have its share of difficulties, will be one of unfolding opportunity.

Index

251

252

Salisbury, Robert Cecil, Marquis of, 27 et seq., 125, 163
Saturday Evening Post, 44, 47-48
Scholefield, W., 14
Schnadhorst, F., 121
Scott, C. P., 152
Sheldon, A. J., 207
Showell's Dictionary, 4
Smyth, J. R. H., 97, 177, 183, 186
Stamp Duty, 9
Stratton, Stephen S., 112, 202
Sturge, Joseph, 32-33

Tangye, Richard, 77
Times, The, 12, 20, 197
Timmins, Sam, 106, 108 et seq., 202
Town Crier, 4, 41
Traill, Dr., 122
Trevelyan, G. M., 10, 68, 122, 131
Trust Deed, 232-233
Twinn, Bernard, 154-155

University of Birmingham, 95, 183, 217
Uriconium, 184

Vince, Charles, 73
Vince, Charles Anthony, 163, 171, 181
Vince, W. B., 158
'Vote as you are Told', 104

Wakefield, Dr. Russell, 151
Walter Press, 50-51
Warren, Thomas, 12
Webb, Beatrice, 118, 166-167
Whally, 86
Whates, Harry Richard, 147 et seq.
Wickwar, W. H., 132
Wilson, Wright, 5
'Woodman Era', 71
Wright, Thomas Barber, 77

THIS VOLUME COMMEMORATING THE Centenary Year of *The Birmingham Post* has been produced at the Journal Printing Office in Cannon Passage, a department of The Birmingham Post & Mail Ltd.

Type used for the text is 12-point Baskerville, a faithful recutting of that used by John Baskerville in 1757 for his first book, 'Virgil'.

The Initials are Eric Gill's Perpetua.

Set and cast on 'Monotype' machines and printed on Spicer's Penrose Text Paper, with illustrations on Matt Art Paper.

Henry Mills Limited, of Birmingham, have done the binding.

Consultant Typographer
Leonard Jay

1957